MOTHER / FOUNDER

MOTHER / FOUNDER

68 WOMEN ON THE TRIALS AND TRIUMPHS
OF STARTING A BUSINESS AND RAISING A FAMILY

AMANDA JANE JONES & JENNIFER FERNANDEZ

PHOTOGRAPHS BY MOMOKO FRITZ

ARTISAN | NEW YORK

———————————————

Library of Congress Cataloging-in-Publication
Data is on file.

ISBN 978-1-64829-345-0

———————————————

Design by Amanda Jane Jones

Artisan books may be purchased in bulk for
business, educational, or promotional use. For
information, please contact your local bookseller
or the Hachette Book Group Special Markets
Department at special.markets@hbgusa.com.

The publisher is not responsible for websites (or
their content) that are not owned by the publisher.

The Hachette Speakers Bureau provides a wide
range of authors for speaking events. To find
out more, go to hachettespeakersbureau.com or
email HachetteSpeakers@hbgusa.com.

Published by Artisan,
an imprint of Workman Publishing,
a division of Hachette Book Group, Inc.
1290 Avenue of the Americas
New York, NY 10104
artisanbooks.com

The Artisan name and logo are registered
trademarks of Hachette Book Group, Inc.

Printed in China on responsibly sourced paper
First printing, September 2024

10 9 8 7 6 5 4 3 2 1

FOR OUR CHILDREN
AND THE FUTURES THEY CREATE FOR THEMSELVES

contents

introduction

Luck. Divine intervention. Fate. Whatever you call it, Amanda and I were on the receiving end of it in November 2021. I had been commissioned by the home design website Domino to write a feature on Amanda's renovated mid-century modern home in Provo, Utah. I already knew who she was—one of the founding editors of *Kinfolk* magazine and a self-employed graphic and product designer, artist, author, and influencer who uses her forces for so much good—but for all intents and purposes, this was an assignment like any other. That is, until we had our phone interview.

We both work from home, and we were still in the Covid-19 pandemic lockdown, so our kids were literally all up in our businesses. My younger daughter, Maren, was whining to be carried, as one-year-olds do, then crying intermittently throughout our call. Amanda says her three kids were making noise of their own, but I don't recall hearing them. What we both agree on is that in that moment, there was an understanding that these kinds of interruptions were just the cost of doing business when you're a mom. Neither of us perceived them as professional faux pas or sources of embarrassment; we didn't silently judge each other or grit our teeth to get through the call. And we immediately established a friendly rapport that we both had been missing in a lot of our corporate work interactions. I remember ending the call and thinking, *Wow, there still are some genuinely nice people out there!*

I wrote the story and things went on as usual. But then out of the blue a few months later, Amanda wrote me with an exciting proposition: She had an idea for a book about mother entrepreneurs and small-business owners and was looking for a collaborator. I was all in from the get-go and eager to hear more. I'll let Amanda take it from here. . . .

Back in February 2021, I settled down one night to watch *LuLaRich*, a docuseries about a multi-level marketing scheme that recruited hundreds of women—many of them mothers—to sell defective leggings under the banner of work-from-home empowerment. I cringed behind my bedcovers through the first episode, relating deeply to those women who so desperately sought a way to support themselves and their families while also being an active presence in their children's lives. I won't spoil the ending for anyone, but I can tell you it's not a happy one.

It's also nothing new. That these enterprises exist isn't the tragedy; it's that women continue to sign themselves up for this sort of exploitation again and again because they feel it's their sole alternative to the kind of inflexible corporate work that has come to define American career culture—the only way to work and still see their kids. As a mother of three who has been self-employed for twelve years, I can tell you from experience that it's not.

As more and more women are reevaluating their career choices and seeking jobs that offer more money, more flexibility, and greater opportunities to be with their families, the logical answer for some has been entrepreneurship. But this way of life—this level of autonomy—is foreign to so many. I started dreaming up this book to help any woman who wanted to find the kind of work-life balance I enjoy yet didn't know where to begin. But, of course, what works for me might not work for you!

There are roughly eighty-five million mothers in the United States, each with a unique set of circumstances and goals, so of course there isn't one proven path to entrepreneurial success. By collecting the stories of more than sixty female entrepreneurs, we hope to have created in *Mother / Founder* an empowering resource for anyone needing inspiration as they forge a new path or career for themselves, whether they want to work from home five hours a week for some extra income or dream of owning their own Fortune 500 company.

The list of women featured here is broad but by no means comprehensive. Working moms are *busy*, and some of those we approached simply couldn't find time in their schedules to participate. But those who did donate their time to this project are some of the most inspiring we've ever met. We hope you feel seen by their stories and find advice that sparks your imagination, suits your family's needs, *and* helps you take ownership of your dreams.

———

To quote the great Brené Brown, "It is a terrible myth to believe that once we have children, our journey ends and theirs begins. For many of us, the most interesting and productive times in our lives come after we have children." In fact, the two of us found that our ability to be productive and problem solve in our work increased exponentially after having children. We wanted to spend more time with them *and* do great work (and make good money), so we were smarter and wiser with our time. This is why we feel so deeply passionate about this book and its message. We want to empower mothers—to support them and raise them up—because we know they are already equipped with many of the tools necessary for success. We want to reassure them that loving their children doesn't have to mean sacrificing their professional identities if they don't want to—and that finding meaning in work doesn't have to mean sacrificing their relationships with their children. For whoever needs to hear it, we want to scream from the rooftops, "There is room for you."

the plant-based mom

There was a surreal moment during Roma Desai Patel's tenure in the marketing department at Coca-Cola when she was charged with helping to create lasting relationships with the next generation of junk-food consumers while growing one of its members in her belly. The idea didn't sit well with her.

"Professionally, I didn't want to work with a company that was pushing the bad-for-you snacks, and then personally I was really curious about nutrition," says Roma, who was diagnosed with hypothyroidism during her first pregnancy. She tried every protein powder in the health-food aisle but nothing was satisfying. "They were too chalky or tasted terrible," she says. So after her maternity leave, she decided not to go back to her job, instead chasing the idea of developing a health-food product that she could be proud of.

"For me, it was never about working for myself versus a corporation," says Roma of the launch of Tejari, a line of plant-based, nutrient-dense protein blends to boost the health content of everyday foods. "It was more about working for a purpose, challenging the norm, and creating a healthier future for my children and generations to come."

It was also about creating a sustainable work-life balance that allowed her to spend more time with her sons, Tej and Ari, for

"Work makes me who I am, and it makes me a better mother."

whom Tejari is named. "Leaving my stable, full-time career was a huge leap, but a better work-life integration has allowed me to focus on myself and my family without being stretched so thin all of the time," she says. That doesn't mean starting the company didn't take focus, especially in the beginning.

Roma invested $30,000 of her personal funds, setting up the business while working with food scientists and nutritionists for more than two years before landing on a signature blend and securing an organic certification and FDA approval. To cut costs, she leaned on her marketing background and handled the branding, outreach, and packaging on her own. "Frankly, I was doing everything, so I was saving a lot of money," she says. "In the earlier days, our basement was Tejari." And though she has always had support from her parents (who live a few hours away), a babysitter whom her boys love, and a husband who helps divide and conquer on the home front, Roma says her days were filled with a lot of juggling and figuring out how to push forward. "It's sometimes glossed over how challenging and hard and isolating being a founder is. You see the success stories of what they have now, but it's not easy, and a big part is that you're still trying to manage life while creating a business."

Roma tells a story from early in her company's timeline, when she was still working part-time as a consultant while nurturing the idea of Tejari and raising her kids. "I had a business trip five weeks after I went back from maternity leave, and I was still breastfeeding. I had to ship milk back via a cooler, and my nanny didn't receive the package, and at that point my son had never had formula. It was such a stressful time for

health-food
purveyor /
mother
of two

me and taught me that if I'm not ready to travel and if I'm taking on too much, then I need to deprioritize certain things at work."

Though Roma now outsources many tasks to contractors—she works with a content writer for social media, a creative designer, and someone to oversee brand partnerships—she still handles a lot of organizational tasks herself, and often includes her children after their 3:00 p.m. school pickup. "They sometimes come to the UPS Store with me and we do a little packaging station," she says. "One will get a note card, the other will get a recipe card, and they have fun with it. But I do try to have boundaries. I try to carve out specific times where it would be a fun activity for them, rather than a chore. "

Giving the boys a glimpse of the inner workings of her company helps them feel invested in its success but also allows Roma to teach them about the value of her ambitions. "When I was doing a lot of demos at Whole Foods Market on the weekends, I'd have my husband bring them so they would understand why I wasn't home. We're really trying to get them involved. Just the other week, I took them to the warehouse, and they were like, 'Wow!' They know all of the effort that goes into that."

For Roma, work has always been a family affair. She says much of her drive came from watching her parents go from being employees at convenience stores to owning more than twenty-five of their own. Eventually, their empire grew to include dry cleaners and real estate. "My parents had a way of finding and developing employees and making them feel part of something bigger," Roma says. "They came to the United States with less than $50 in their pockets and worked endlessly to raise my brother and me. They're the hardest-working entrepreneurs, and it drives me every single day to make them and my sons proud."

"Being an entrepreneur can be very difficult and isolating at times, but I always know I can turn to my friends, family, team, and advisory board when I need help."

Advice from Roma Desai Patel

START RECRUITING ADVISORS. "Setting up an advisory board was the best legal expense I budgeted for early on. I had no experience with a formal advisory board, so I hired a lawyer to tweak a friend's contract for me. Every advisor has different terms and deliverables, but I structured it so they would get shares of the company with vesting opportunities. And I was very clear that I wasn't going to go to them for an hour a week; you want to be mindful of their time, too. Having a trustworthy resource who is invested in you is one of the best aspects of being a founder. The board was such a big component of the business's growth and figuring out how to handle situations. During wins and losses, they're the first people I call, and I gain so much insight, feedback, and direction when I consult with them."

MAKE CONNECTIONS. "I've never been afraid of reaching out: cold emailing, sending LinkedIn messages, DMs. When I was working on the corporate side, if there was a vice president of brand marketing who I wanted to learn from, I would email them and say, 'Can we get coffee together?' I took that confidence and applied it to my own business. People would be like, 'Yeah, I'm happy to get on a call with you for thirty minutes,' and from there it was constant follow-up until we began a friendship, and then they started to become an advisor."

BUILD HEALTHY HABITS. "I started to build a habit of daily walks. I walk 3 to 5 miles (5 to 8 km) a day in the morning and strength-train five times a week. I think it helps me start the day in a more peaceful way so I'm not going through the laundry list of things to do. I have six or seven other founders that are some of my best friends; once a week, I get on a call or text them or we get together and talk things through. It's wonderful having founder friends because they're going through it, too."

TRAVEL WISELY. "When I travel, I usually take the first flight out and the last flight in. I try not to spend more than two nights away at a time and heavily rely on my husband or mom for support back home. I'm very open with my children about traveling—I let them know ahead of time and talk to them about it. I usually leave notes for when they come home from school, along with Legos or something else as a treat. After learning the hard way, I now avoid FaceTiming or calling them too much, since it disrupts the flow of the evening and makes them sad. It's much harder on me, but it's for the best."

the bestseller

A funny thing happens when Emma Straub walks down the street in her Cobble Hill, Brooklyn, neighborhood. "I'll run into people—friends, neighbors, strangers—and they'll point to me and say to their small child, 'Do you know who that is? She owns the bookstore!' It's wonderful," says the bestselling author, who despite a very successful novel-writing career has become something of a local celebrity after opening Books Are Magic with her husband, Mike, in 2017. (She opened a second location nearby in Brooklyn Heights in 2022.)

Yet it took a lot of hard work to make it so. Emma had just had her second child when she and Mike, a graphic designer by trade, learned that the beloved thirty-five-year-old bookstore where she had worked in her twenties, and which anchored her Cobble Hill community, was closing, so they scrambled to find a new location to open a bookstore of their own. "All of our friends said, 'Don't do it.' Except Ann Patchett," she says of her fellow author–bookstore owner friend. "Ann Patchett said, 'Do it.'" She laughs. "We just had fallen in love with the idea and could not be dissuaded. It's like having children in that no one could have talked me out of it. We thought, *If this can just pay for itself, that would be great.*"

The learning curve was steep, but Emma and Mike braced themselves with research,

digging in online and talking with as many booksellers as they could find. (As a writer, Emma knew quite a few.) They salvaged thirty 8-foot (2.4 m) bookshelves from the now defunct shop and stored them in their garage while waiting for their lease to start. And they leaned into their relationship with a contractor friend and the experience they had gained manning the merchandise booth while on tour with their friends, the indie rock band the Magnetic Fields. "We didn't know what we were doing, but there were some things that we did know," she says. "We knew how to design things and how to sell them. We knew how to make the space look good. And we knew a million authors and had them coming in from day one, which continues to be a huge part of our success."

Everything else they had to learn along the way, including what it meant to be managers and how to create a supportive environment for their now twenty-four employees. "I love hanging out with people who are twenty years younger than me," she says of the team that works at her shops. "It's actually going to prolong my life. It's certainly made me smarter. It's an incredible gift to know how much I've learned from our booksellers about existing in the world."

That the wife-and-husband duo has done this while raising their two sons and finding time for Emma to continue writing is a testament to their ability to delegate and communicate as much as their flexible schedules and the store's close proximity to their home. They also put in equal time with their boys. "In the beginning, we were basically always playing hot potato with the babies, and it was great," says Emma, who started using a babysitter for her seven- and

> "My older child is very proud of me, and my younger child is very embarrassed by me."

bookstore
owner /
mother
of two

BOOKS ARE

"The thing that I've come to accept is that change is a constant."

nine-year-olds only a couple of years ago; she also gets help from her mother, who lives nearby, when she's traveling on book tours or working events at the store. "Then, as now, I understood that I had certain windows of time in any given day, and in the windows that belonged to me, I had to work," she says. "We ran on fumes for the first two years, but I wouldn't do it differently because I was and remain pretty obsessed with my children. If they're home, I can't stay away."

For that reason, Mike manages Books Are Magic full-time, but Emma is a constant presence. "All kudos to my husband, whereas I come in like Amelia Bedelia or a fairy godmother, depending on your perspective," she says. "I'm like an enthusiasm hurricane, leaving chaos somewhat in my wake. But also joy." Likewise, the shop looms large in Emma's brain even when she's not there. "When you're operating a small business, you're not working full-time hours—you're working *way* more than that. There's always something to think about or figure out."

But despite the increase in mental gymnastics, the bookstores sustain and fulfill Emma in ways she never could have anticipated. "At this point, they feel inextricable from my career as a writer," she says. "On the one hand, it's been horrible for my career because I have so much less time to write. But my relationship to other writers is so different than it would have been otherwise. I get to catch up with Jennifer Egan for a half hour while she signs some books, and that wouldn't happen if I didn't own a bookstore. At heart I'm a fan, and I get to be that every day."

Advice from Emma Straub

ADJUST YOUR WORK EXPECTATIONS. "When you have a very small child, your day is broken up into distinct segments: eating, sleeping, pooping, reading this book, playing this game. Your loop starts so small and then changes over and over again. From when my kids were born, it was about identifying the windows of time that were mine and using them. When I was younger, I'd write twenty-five pages a week. Now, the idea of writing twenty-five pages a week is a fantasy. But if I can write ten pages, I write ten pages. And that's okay."

DON'T FEEL GUILTY—ABOUT ANYTHING. "I know that I'm extremely present and extremely loving. I have no time or desire to indulge in feeling guilty about being away. I just took it off of my plate. And that's true for everything. My children's food intake is my biggest failure as a mother because they don't eat. They might have a chicken nugget and a strawberry for dinner, and that's it. But the truth is my kids are safe, they're healthy, they are fine. They have a lot of years in their life to try sushi. Some people have really strict rules about screen time. We have rules and we have limits, but my kids watch *The Simpsons*—and they've learned a lot! I enjoy watching movies, and my kids enjoy them, and it's something that we can do together. It's all fine."

DON'T WORRY ABOUT MISSING OUT. "There are opportunities that I've had to turn down because I was nine months pregnant or just had a baby. Many things in life are not truly once-in-a-lifetime; I've been offered them again. Some are, but so is having a baby."

"I just believed I was going to be a writer. I just believed it was going to happen even though people kept telling me it wasn't."

NEED TO
READ?
→
OPEN
EVERY DAY

the private-practice mom

Every once in a while there's a moment of levity in Chamin Ajjan's therapy sessions, in the form of an unexpected visitor: her six-year-old son, Kingston. "If my kids may be at home or they have a sick day, I give my clients the option to reschedule; if they don't want to reschedule, they know that Kingston might come in, even though he knows not to," says the New Jersey–based psychotherapist, who conducts telehealth appointments from her house, while her staff clinicians see patients out of her practice's office in Brooklyn. "They all know him because he often *does* come in, and they say hi and get to see him briefly, but that's something that's agreed upon."

Chamin says that therapists are often expected to be blank slates, but being seen for who she is is important to her, whether in her sessions or on her Instagram account, where she frequently posts images of her children and their adventures together. "I made the choice to be my full authentic self, and that's worked for me," she says. "It doesn't work for everybody." Hence the Kingston cameos, which are welcome though not always encouraged. "I have an open-door policy—I don't want my kids to feel like they can't access me—but we talk about the difference between needing me and not needing me.

> "There's something so rewarding about having a business that is yours, that you create from the ground up."

And then Kingston will knock and say, 'I need you,' and ask for a Popsicle."

Much of the reason Chamin established her private practice in 2011, before she left her full-time job at the nation's third-largest labor union, was to lay the foundation for a more flexible schedule whenever she decided to have children. Today, that foresight is paying off. She's proud to say she's never missed the childhood rites of passage—the baseball games or dance recitals and the like. "I could cancel and reschedule sessions if I needed to. If something's important I'm there, and even if it's not important I'm mostly there."

Chamin was intentional about being available by choice—not by necessity. "From the very beginning, I made sure he knew how to do her hair," she says of her husband, a musician who sold gym memberships to pay the bills during the day while she was at home with their daughter, Brooklyn, and took on many of the child-rearing tasks at night so that Chamin could offer evening sessions to clients. "I work when he's not working, and he works when I'm not working. I made sure we were sharing the tasks so he knew how to do everything that I could do, and the transition was pretty seamless." (He now works in music education.)

But as flexible and accommodating as she's made her schedule, Chamin acknowledges that sacrifices are still part of the deal. "There are conferences that I miss out on all the time," she says, "opportunities for retreats and things that I'm not willing to do at this stage. But it excites me that that's something that's on the horizon. It shows me how much more potential is out there for growth. As my daughter got a little older, I started playing around with that, but then I had Kingston so

therapist /
mother
of two

I had to reset. As he grows, I'll do the same to figure out what the boundaries are and what makes sense."

For now, that means getting back to date nights—even if they're date *days* spent running errands or grabbing lunch with her husband while fifteen-year-old Brooklyn bonds with Kingston at home for an hour or two. It's all part of her evolving relationship with motherhood. "Change is uncomfortable, even if it's a wonderful change," she admits. "But we can be successful putting ourselves in these uncomfortable spaces, and it's such a rewarding experience to do that and grow."

Advice from Chamin Ajjan

CONSULT AN EXPERT. "There is no business psychotherapy practice class that you take in graduate school, and people hold that information very close to them. I didn't have a mentor or anybody to turn to, so I just went to my CPA, who had worked with other people who had private practices, and asked him what I needed to do to incorporate my business. He helped me decide the structure for taxation, made sure I knew how to file everything. I really just relied on him initially, which was pretty naive, but it all worked out."

HAVE A DAILY MINDFULNESS PRACTICE. "I can sometimes catastrophize about a situation, but being mindful allows me to stop, get out of my head, and tune in to what's happening in my body. Washing the dishes or taking a shower can be extremely mindful experiences because I'm listening to the sounds of the water or the clanking of the dishes; I'll shift my focus to the smell of the dish soap or the temperature of the water or how the sponge feels in my hand. When a thought pops in, I'm able to recognize it and then refocus on what it is I'm doing, and that eventually allows me to do the same when I'm not intending to be mindful. It allows me to have those thoughts and not hold on to them for so long, to not let my thoughts lead me into being reactive. I'm able to think about that thought more critically."

STAY OPEN TO CHANGING YOUR MIND. "I thought I was going to be a stay-at-home mom—I wanted to be the Black *I Love Lucy*—but I probably would have been miserable. There was obviously a piece of me that I needed to express or do something with even if I couldn't verbalize it at the time, but I don't know that I would have known that I needed it had I not been a mother."

Dream Big

When I speak to young mothers about running my own business, one of the questions I'm asked most is, "Where do I even begin?"

I always start with a goal list. Setting personal goals has been key to my professional success. Something I had to wrap my head around early on was that no one was going to make my career but me. In design school, I wasn't the frontrunner. In fact, I was one of two students left out of the internship program, which was an important step to employment in the design field. So I made my own way and ended up in New York. In my early years, I wasted time feeling jealous and wishing I was doing what others were, but eventually I learned to say to myself, "That's amazing. Good for them!" and then ask, "What is my plan to get there, too?"

To start your own goal list, think through the questions below. Don't be overwhelmed—just begin by tackling one thing, and then move on to the next.

1. *What do you want your life to look like?* Be very specific. What *exactly* do you want to be doing day-to-day—regardless of what your spouse, society, or parents think you should be doing?

2. *What would you like your work-life balance to look like?* Do you want a side hustle while your kids are in school? Or do you dream of owning a business with a twenty-member team?

3. *How much money do you have set aside to start a business?* It's important to know whether you have enough to support your family while you get the business up and running and/or enough to put start-up capital into your business. Will you need to keep working and build your business on the side during free time?

4. *Will you need additional childcare?* If so, what will it cost? If you can't afford it, what are some alternative solutions or ways you can raise funds to make it a possibility? Can family help? Are there local programs your kids can attend?

5. *How much do you need to live each month, and how much can you spare for business start-up capital?* List your costs: childcare, supplies, studio space. But think carefully through that last point. For my first five years, a desk next to my bed was my office. Amanda Stewart (page 130)

ran Mochi Kids out of her basement for three years. You don't need everything at once.

6. *What are your strengths?* What things do you think you'll be able to handle for your business, and what will you need to hire out? For example, I work with an accountant and web developer, and some days I think I need a personal assistant. I also occasionally hire people to help me pack and ship.

7. *Does your dream job require a degree, or do you need any special training?* Do you need to take any classes before you begin? How much will these cost? List your options and research scholarships and grant programs that offer parental support (see page 233 for a few recommendations for entrepreneurs in the arts).

8. *Do you have the resources to set up your business as an entity?* It's better for your taxes if you do. I filed as a sole proprietor for five years before switching to an LLC. Talk to an accountant, who can help you find the right options for your specific company.

After the basics, it's time to write out the fun stuff. Don't feel intimidated by dreaming big. I find it empowering and exciting! The fun stuff might be financial goals, people or brands you'd like to work with, or career milestones you're aiming for. I'm a huge believer in manifesting and putting your hopes and dreams out into the universe. For example, over the past decade, a few of my big goals have been to write a children's book, create a mural, make an art exhibit, and meet my favorite artist (Maira Kalman, page 38!).

Place your goal list somewhere that's easily accessible—not in some notebook you're going to forget about. I keep mine on a screen I look at every time I open my computer. This way, when I have a lag in my client work or I'm waiting for feedback on a project, I'm reminded to switch over to one of my personal goals. When I put my ideas and dreams into the universe *and* put in the work, I'm happy (but also a little shocked) to report that all of these goals have become real-life opportunities.

As you move forward with your goals, big or small, write about your experience. Keep a work journal with all your accomplishments and ideas. When you're feeling low, you can look back to see how far you've come. And remember: baby steps! Success doesn't come overnight.

the O.G. blogger

When Joy Cho's design studio was operating at its peak size, the founder of eponymous lifestyle brand Oh Joy! found that she had inadvertently fallen into an all-too-familiar trope of motherhood—only it wasn't her children she was losing herself to, it was her seven-person staff.

"I was working all day, going home and having my family time, and then working again after the kids would go to sleep. I was also working every day from evening until bedtime. I did that for years," Joy says. "I loved the growth, but I was having to constantly hustle to continue getting more and more jobs to pay for it. It was a lot of pressure on me, and I realized I was working so hard to make my employees' lives the best they could be, but I wasn't doing the same thing for myself."

She faced a difficult but necessary decision: take on an investor, hire another high-level person to help her grow, or scale back. Ultimately, she chose to downsize. "The thing is that I don't regret having grown my team to that size because I loved it. There was so much magic happening," she says of the more than forty-five licensing partnerships with brands like Target, Band-Aid, and Petco that her small but mighty team helped her bring to the market over the last eighteen years. "But I overextended myself, I burned myself out, and I was not happy. If I am not happy running my business, then something's not right."

Joy had started doing freelance graphic design in 2005, temporarily, while she was between jobs after a move back home to Philadelphia. With her future husband in surgical residency, it was up to her to support her small family, finding clients on Craigslist and honing her aesthetic point of view with a somewhat unknown hobby: blogging. But Joy soon realized that her blog was an important marketing tool for her business. As more and more people began to read and share her colorful content, it brought her worldwide recognition and opportunities for collaborations with big-name brands, expanding her once-temporary business into a very permanent, successful one.

"It was exciting to be in control of the work I did," she says. "There's so much flexibility in being self-employed, but there's also so much that goes into it. You're working beyond typical hours. You have to really love it to be spending that much time making it happen."

That wasn't a problem when she didn't have children. It was a little harder seven years into the business, when she welcomed her first daughter. "At the time, I had given myself some cushion with my clients to transition from a short maternity leave to part-time work, then to full-time work," she says. "But it was still hard because sometimes you get more pockets of work and sometimes you get fewer." Steady childcare helped, but by the time Joy had her second daughter, the struggles were exponential. "Not only was I trying to figure out how to be present for two kids, but my business had also grown. I had a few employees and an outside office that I was paying rent on. While I had help both at

> "You can evolve, and if something doesn't work, there's always another way to go."

designer /
mother
of two

home and at work, I was so much busier and had more people relying on me, so it was a lot harder for me to take time away, to ease back and dedicate uninterrupted time with my baby. There are a lot of things I would redo, but at the time I did the best I could to be available for everybody."

Now, Joy is back to working on her own, maintaining her blog, writing books, launching products through licensing, and coaching fellow entrepreneurs from an office next to her home. Her weeks once again resemble those from when she first started her company, only now her busy days spent at the computer while the girls are at school end with silly family dinners and quiet evenings. Most important, she's happy. "The interesting thing about self-employment is that you can revise the way you work whenever you want," she says. Would she ever scale up her business again once her girls are older? "I could," she says, "but I don't think I will. Scaling back has allowed me to not say yes to every job. I can be more choosy about the work that I do because I don't have to support the same number of people."

These days, she makes sure she has dedicated time to be with her family, but her work is a constant. "I joke that I want to retire, but I don't really. I love working," she says. "I admire women who can be stay-at-home moms, but the balance of work life and home life is good for me. Sometimes I'm doing terribly at both things, but my work helps me grow in ways that make me a better parent for my children."

It also gives her daughters a unique perspective on how they can take charge of their futures. "The cool thing about the way my kids have grown up is that most of my friends are business owners," says Joy. "My girls know these other successful women in their lives, who have these amazing companies or retail stores that we shop at, or are on covers of magazines and receiving awards. It's really empowering to see that."

> "I offer paid time off to my employees, but when you're the boss, you don't have that perk. Money still has to come in."

Advice from Joy Cho

BANISH SELF-DOUBT. "When I first started my business, all I had was self-doubt. I had ended my last job making what I thought was a decent salary in my early twenties. I didn't know if I could do that on my own. At the time, my brother-in-law was staying with us, and he went to the same college and had the same major as I did, so he knew the industry. Something he said that still sticks with me is 'Who says you can't?' He was calling me out on my self-doubt and reminding me that it was only me who was telling myself that I couldn't do it. If you want it bad enough, you figure out how to make it happen."

BE REALISTIC ABOUT YOUR EXPENSES. "I was starting a business during the most terrible time. We were broke—I had no money saved—and my husband was in residency. It wasn't the most logical way to go. However, being a graphic designer is all about your services. You don't really need any money to start it. I already had a computer. I already had a printer from college. I just had to market my services. It took me a good six months of my workload slowly growing before I saw the potential."

SET UP A PROPER PLAN FOR YOUR MATERNITY LEAVE. "It's important that you set yourself up in advance for maternity leave and make it clear to your employees what you need to happen and what availability you have. That is what I did not do. If you make yourself available when you feel like you should be with your baby, people are going to take you up on it, and you're going to feel overwhelmed. I should have set more boundaries during that time to protect those precious early days of motherhood."

HAVE PASSIVE INCOME. "Write books, do design collaborations, sell prerecorded video classes, or have something that is available for sale while you're not working. You have to promote it, but then after that it's out there in the world continuing to sell in some capacity. It doesn't work for every industry, but if you're in a situation where there's space for passive income you should explore that."

"I never would have imagined having the job I have today. As social media evolved, I was able to use it to my advantage and see what made sense as my business grew."

the PR powerhouse

Like so many postpartum mothers, Priscilla Vega found the best ideas for decorating her newborn daughter Ina's nursery on blogs and Pinterest and Instagram. But the deeper she went down the rabbit hole, the more she realized just how digitally inept some companies were. "It was the early days of social media—people were looking for new, creative ways to reach an audience—and I just kept seeing all of the ways I could help them with a customized approach," says the communications specialist, who was then a public relations strategist for NASA. She had also been an events producer for Oracle and Cisco in her former life and missed some of the bustle and excitement of working on deadline.

It was like a lightbulb went on. Priscilla was reaching the end of her maternity leave, remote work wasn't yet a thing, and she was stressed about finding a way to be home with her daughter while scratching the creative itch that was already beginning to fester. "I'm such a busybody, and I felt like I had all of this bandwidth to do stuff at home." She also felt like she could be an advocate for mother entrepreneurs and small-business owners of color, who perhaps didn't have the support to facilitate growth in unconventional ways. "One of the great things about being your own boss is the ability to curate your client roster," she says.

So she told her managers that she wouldn't be coming back to work and started making

> ## "There is no more efficient person on the planet than a mother."

calls while Ina was sleeping. As a new mother, she reached out to women-owned brands and start-ups in the baby industry, then expanded into wellness, beauty, and fashion, putting out feelers with friends and cold-calling people whose work she admired to help with small projects at first—newsletters, social media promotion, and media pitches—then full-scale PR consulting and brand strategy. "Even while I was establishing my company, it never occurred to me that I could be an entrepreneur," she says. "It just wasn't something in my mind at that point."

One client turned into sixteen and, she says, "it just snowballed into 'Can you do more?'" The answer was always yes. "I'm not a no person," Priscilla says with a laugh.

That was how she found herself four years later answering emails and taking phone calls—at 5 centimeters dilated—while in labor with her son. She was writing pitches just two days later. "In a service-based industry, availability is one of your key requirements," she says. "I had built up this momentum and set the expectation that this is the pace I need to go at."

Learning to outsource work helped alleviate some of the stress and free up her schedule to accommodate more downtime. "Providing work for other women in my industry who are also hustling to provide for their clients is one of the best parts of my job," she says. While Priscilla manages the big-picture strategy and outreach for her clients, she hires contractors for event support, newsletters, copywriting, influencer outreach, and web development. "I know what I'm good at and what I'm not," she admits. But busy as she has been, she's never felt like she wasn't available to her children.

media
strategist /
mother
of two

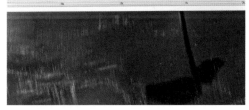

"I was there for every diaper change and meltdown and feeding," she says.

That's still true today—minus the diaper changes and meltdowns. You'll most often find Priscilla at her kitchen counter with her laptop open, ready to send and receive emails about the day's objectives. (She also works in a chic Airstream trailer that's parked in her driveway when it's not in use for family vacations.) There have most certainly been hard times and moments of stress, but that's when she reminds herself of her purpose. "I often questioned what I was doing and if I was doing it the right way, but I was blazing my own trail. I was doing it for the best reason I know: to spend more time with my children."

Advice from Priscilla Vega

LEAN INTO TECHNOLOGY. "When life got really busy, there were platforms that helped alleviate the logistical side of things. I automate invoices and use Calendly to send everyone a link to my schedule so they can book time."

TRUST PEOPLE. "My biggest pet peeve is 'ASAP.' Everyone values their time. I trust they're doing their work as efficiently as possible. 'ASAP' feels like you don't respect a person's schedule."

CHOOSE CLIENTS WISELY. "A great thing about being the boss is the ability to work with people who 'get it.' The only time I got calls at five in the morning and was expected to respond on weekends was when I had a male client. That was a teaching moment. I work with a lot of mothers, and there's an understanding that we all have lives outside of work. We're all busy at around the same times and mindful of 'offline' hours."

PRIORITIZE LIKE A MOTHER. "When my oldest was a baby, I worked until midnight and somehow felt the need to make up for hours lost throughout the day. I was still stuck on the corporate culture of putting in the hours. But I eventually learned the 'work smarter, not harder' mantra. At the end of the day, you're going to clock out. Some days it's later, other days it's earlier. You just have to identify the greatest need and allow yourself some grace. The work will always be there in the morning."

> "I have no time for impostor syndrome. By accident or by hard work you're here, so just do what you need to do."

MAIRA KALMAN

the illustrator

Before the artist and writer Maira Kalman purchased a studio on the ninth floor of the Greenwich Village building in which she and her family lived, her then seven-year-old son Alex was asked to write about his mother for a class. She remembers he penned, "My mother has brown hair and blue eyes, and when I come near her she says, 'Don't knock my chair,'" Maira recalls with a laugh. "Out of the thousands of hours of fun, that's what he came up with, so clearly I needed my own space."

With a studio of her own, Maira could focus on the art and illustration work that sustained her—and that, even as a child, she felt was her destiny. From the time that she was in her early twenties, after she pivoted from studying literature to telling a story with words and pictures, she says she knew that her work would be her life. But she was just as enamored with the idea of having a family, so she mapped out her future, almost willing it to fruition. "My work would allow me to travel. And I would have two children and a very happy home. And I did that. With all of the ups and downs, I did that. But there was no second plan. I say, not in a flippant way, that whatever you wish to have happen will happen. Maybe

"Even though children take tremendous energy and can be distracting, they were also inspiring and fulfilling in ways that I never dreamed possible."

not in the same form that you imagined it. Maybe it takes twenty years more than you thought it would. But there has to be some kind of inner drive of 'This shall be.'"

As determined as Maira was to forge her own way, dropping her portfolio off with art directors at magazines across the city and waiting for a call, she was also open to the possibility of chance. "In the best of all worlds, one thing leads to another," she says of the starts and stops that she and her husband, Tibor Kalman, experienced on their path to opening his legendary design studio M&Co, to which she contributed ideas and illustrations on a regular basis. "It was a zigzag of getting there, but it was very clear to me. We were constantly working, but it wasn't rigid. We were both very motivated, and Tibor was fantastically work-oriented, so I learned from him and with him how not to stop working."

To do that, the couple created their own schedule and organized their lives around it. When they decided to have children, they continued to find outlets for their creative urges, with Maira pivoting to writing and illustrating children's books. "It was an inspiration for work," says Maira of having children. "Of course, there's the organizing of schedules and the figuring out of who does what, but we had help. Tibor would go to work, and I would work from home or then go to the office, but my mother was here helping, and we also hired a nanny. So between this group of people there was a really wonderful congenial system, and it fit into this idea of 'I want my life to be my work.'"

At seventy-three, Maira admits that the details of the division of labor are a bit fuzzy to recall, but nothing stands out as being unfair because of the mutual respect she

artist /
mother
of two

shared with her husband. "We didn't have roles; everybody did stuff. Because he was so committed to working, he would come home and make dinner, and then he'd put the kids to bed and go back to work. Physically go to the office. I probably did more because I was home more, but I never felt it was disproportionate. The important things were shared fifty-fifty, and because we had literally a 24-7 dialogue about art and design and architecture, there was a tremendous connection between us, so all of the little things that make everybody crazy and that you have fights about, well, there they were, but they weren't that big. He respected me more than anybody, and I him."

For those reasons, she says she never had to limit her work because of her home life; both were seamlessly intertwined and held equal importance. "In the bigger picture, I got to do everything I wanted to do," she says. "I wasn't doing anything that required being taken away from home. Being an illustrator means you work very quickly on deadline. You find out what you can and can't do, and I found out I can make a deadline and not take on too much work; I can have time for my family and still have time to work with Tibor at the design studio. So I was very fortunate."

But by her account she took every opportunity to counter the couple's work-hard ethic with a play-hard mentality at home. "If I could, I would celebrate all the holidays no matter what the religion," she says. "I love the idea of play and celebration and being able to turn all the furniture upside down in the living room and a lot of literature and art and travel. That was how we raised the kids."

Maira's bohemian approach to family life endures even now. She often collaborates on art pieces and films with her son, Alex, and writes illustrated letters to her granddaughters Olive and Esme, the children of her daughter, Lulu. "That idea of play

"When I'm not working, my mood really plummets. I get incredibly cranky and lose all hope. There's a sense of humor about all of this, but it would have been a very bleak life had I not been able to do my work."

continues. I know that the atmosphere of the home and the connections we had as a family were real and true. I couldn't imagine a life without it."

It's a theme she touches on in her latest book, *Women Holding Things*, in which she examines all of the items, both literal and metaphorical, that women carry with them. "What do women hold?" she asks. "The home and the family. And the children and the food," she writes. "The friendships. The work. The work of the world. And the work of being human. The memories. And the troubles. And the sorrows and the triumphs. And the love."

Advice from Maira Kalman

CHASE THE IDEA. "The most important thing is if you have an idea, pursue it, as opposed to thinking you're not entitled to. Because you already don't have it, so the only thing that can happen is that you become a little bit fearless and go after what you want. To get a contract at a publishing house was much easier with David Byrne as the coauthor, but then after that I told my editor that I wanted to do my own book, and that grew to all of the books."

EMBRACE THE FEAR. "In some ways, I have the track record to understand that I can do what I do, but each time I come to a project, I lose all hope and I am completely despondent. And then I say, 'Okay, that must be part of the process—to make yourself vulnerable, not to be so sure of yourself, to wonder and ask questions and to be curious.' It leads you to a place that's interesting as opposed to 'Oh yeah, I know how to do this; I've done it before.' That's boring. And so I've accepted the fact that I drive myself crazy even though I wish I could say, 'Who needs it.' Doubts and worries and tears still exist. But in a funny way, the doubts make you grow because you know what failure is, you know what the inconsistency of work is."

FREE YOUR MIND. "Not having boundaries is a very particular way of looking at a career. It's really about what's interesting, and if you're curious you can do a variety of different projects. The success is when people want you to do more of yourself."

the no-microplastics mom

New moms always want what's best for their babies, but Sarah Paiji Yoo took that concept one step further: While on maternity leave with her first son, she went deep into research mode, weighing the pros and cons of everything from baby food and formula brands to the kind of water she'd be mixing into said formula. The move was well within her comfort zone. After graduating from Harvard, she had parlayed an investment-banking job at Goldman Sachs into a coveted consulting role at McKinsey & Company, so she was used to finding and analyzing information. Later, as a student at Harvard Business School, she met and learned from the female founders behind game-changing brands like Gilt Groupe, Rue La La, and Stitch Fix before she and two partners launched a successful fashion search engine start-up that was acquired three years later. In other words, she had the connections, work ethic, and real-life training to handle the grueling work hours and type A personalities that come with entrepreneurship.

But an idea wasn't entirely forthcoming, and she had her son, Noah, to take care of. "At that point, I realized that if I was going to be the primary caretaker, it was going to be really hard to have time to reflect on what was next for my career," she says. "So my husband's parents started coming in to watch Noah to allow me to create a bit of space." It was during that time—while raising her son and having the freedom to investigate options for his well-being—that the ideas began to flow and the beginnings of Blueland started to coalesce.

"I was googling if bottled water is cleaner than tap water," remembers the cofounder and CEO of the eco-friendly products company, which started with plastic-free, water-soluble hand-soap pods in refillable glass bottles and has since expanded to spray cleaners and personal care items. "That's when I learned about how pervasive microplastics are in our food. The zero-waste movement was bubbling up, and we decided to make a commitment as a family to avoid as much single-use plastic as we could. But doing that opened my eyes to how hard it is to avoid. I thought, *I can have a much greater impact outside of my family's tiny consumption if I could find a way to give people more and better choices.*"

Sarah experimented with toothpaste before landing on hand soap, enlisting a group of forty friends and family to be her test subjects. Having spent so much time bringing brands to market throughout her career, she had a blueprint for success and was able to secure investments from venture capital firms that helped get Blueland up and running. And because she and her business partner established Blueland as a direct-to-consumer company, they could point to sales of more than $200,000 as proof of concept. That put Sarah in a position to ask for even more funding during an appearance on the hit investment television show *Shark Tank*. But she realized that this time around, her days weren't all her own, and that she would have to take a more even-handed approach to hustling to get her brand into the consumer spotlight.

> "Being a mother as well as being a founder has made me a lot more open to asking for help."

eco goods purveyor / mother of two

"It was a huge adjustment but a really great one," says Sarah, who later had a second son, Colin, and hired a nanny to give her in-laws some space of their own. "Becoming a parent has forced a level of balance that I think I would have struggled to get to on my own. I was always like, 'I can do it,' no matter how big or small the task. But these days there are more constraints on my time. Now I know there are only so many hours in the day."

Setting boundaries allows Sarah to stick to a schedule that works for her family and helps create a culture of balance within her company. "I try to be off by 6:00 p.m.," she says of her daily shutdown. "It gives permission to the rest of the team if I'm actually doing it. No one messages each other after 6:00 p.m.—everything is schedule sent. The same is true for weekends. The company is quiet. Tuesdays and Wednesdays are for in-office and any in-person meetings with the team. I try to keep Mondays and Fridays lighter. But some weeks, it feels like every nook and cranny gets packed."

When that happens, she knows she can lean on her husband, a portfolio manager who loves to cook dinner for the family—then do the dishes—for support. "He recognizes that there are a lot of things he doesn't even see that I may be managing: groceries, school forms, doctor's appointments," says Sarah. "We know that a true fifty-fifty split is impossible, but we each try to put 100 percent into our family life based on where we are and what we can do." In the end, the old adage is true: Teamwork really does make the dream work.

> "It makes me a better mother to have an identity and a small world that is my own."

Advice from Sarah Paiji Yoo

LEARN FROM EARLY SETBACKS. "We explored six ideas before we landed on Blueland as it is today. As part of my zero-waste lifestyle, I was making toothpaste tablets at home. Once you mix a tablet with water, you get the same foam, and I was confident I could make it just as efficacious. I thought, *Why wouldn't everyone do this for the planet?* I got friends and family to use my toothpaste tablets and checked in on them every other day for two weeks. Over 80 percent of the people said they wouldn't do this. It was, 'I don't like chewing my toothpaste' or 'I don't like having powder in my mouth.' I realized that there are certain products that are easier for people to switch to. Anything sensory isn't going to work."

LAY THE FOUNDATION. "You should be building trust and relationships with investors *before* you pitch. It looked like I was able to raise funds very quickly for Blueland, but I'd worked hard for years to prove to these investors they could trust me."

APPEAL TO INVESTORS. "You need to provide proof that you are addressing a real problem in the market by showing early traction—revenue, user acquisition, partnerships—that demonstrates demand and potential for growth. It's also important to highlight your skills, passion, and relevant experience. Investors bet on the founders and team as much as the idea."

HOW DO YOU INCLUDE YOUR KIDS IN YOUR WORK?

"After dinner, I'll sometimes say, 'Let's draw together.' I turned one of Archie's drawings from preschool into a tiger pattern that became fabric and wallpaper for my line with Lulu and Georgia. He is *super* proud of that, so now he'll be like, 'I'm going to work on some new wallpaper.' And Clover is always designing bedding and pillows. It's so freaking cute!"

**SARAH SHERMAN SAMUEL,
INTERIOR DESIGNER (PAGE 114)**

"My nine-year-old and I went for a walk and started making up stories about who lived in all of the neighbors' houses. And then one of the stories that we were telling just kept going and going, and I thought, *Oh, this has changed from this game that we were playing into a real idea.* It's so much fun to do that together."

**EMMA STRAUB, BOOKSTORE
OWNER (PAGE 16)**

"When my kids were younger, they were on my social media, yet as my sons get older they don't want their picture taken as much. But my daughter likes it. She thinks she's one of my employees."

**AMANDA STEWART, KIDSWEAR
DESIGNER (PAGE 130)**

"I travel with my kids constantly when speaking at a conference or doing media events. A couple of years ago, I spoke at the Ernst & Young conference, and my girls sat in the front row and got to go backstage and meet Simone Biles. They loved it. I try to impress upon them that Mommy *gets* to do these cool things, not that Mommy *has* to do these things."

**SUNEERA MADHANI, FINTECH
FOUNDER (PAGE 316)**

"Our kids are very much a part of my business—by request. They love to feel included. We've always wanted them to be compensated for their contributions, so we've set up savings accounts for each of them. Their small monthly stipend goes directly into the account, which will accrue interest over time and hopefully be a good stepping stone for whatever they decide to do in life."

AMANDA JANE JONES, DESIGNER

"When my daughter has vacation from school she likes to help me. She's my best cashier because she's really good at talking to people and she educates them on how the dishes are made. She does it so naturally that I love to have her with me."

**WENDY JUAREZ, CATERER
(PAGE 102)**

You're Your Most Valued Employee

Of all the questionable advice I've been given in my lifetime, one of the worst tips came from the college professor who told us that a good student was a disheveled one. He expected us to show up to class after an all-nighter with greasy hair—the mark of success in his book. The first year, I complied, at the expense of my physical and mental health. The next year, I listened less to that professor, took care of my mind, paid more attention to my body, and had a much more productive and gratifying year. I've never done my best work when my body was in crisis.

It's easier said than done when you're a parent supporting a family (trust me, I know!), but do your best to prioritize sleep and exercise. I try to exercise first thing, even if it's just twenty minutes; otherwise, the day gets away from me, and I know all too well that it won't happen. If I can't do it in the morning, I work it into my day: I bike to school pickup or run around with the kids at the park—anything to get my blood pumping and wake up my mind.

When I take care of myself, I sleep and feel better, which means I take better care of my business and am a better member of my family. In fact, before writing this book, I'd often go for runs or walk with the Notes app open on my phone, dictating all the ideas that would come to mind. My brain is invigorated by exercise and, I'd have to say, so is my creativity.

I'm not the only one who thinks so. This book is filled with women who say their mental health and productivity take a nosedive when they don't set aside time to address their physical needs. Immigration lawyer Leonor Perretta (page 148) has adopted a strict post-work CrossFit practice to help her transition from the office bustle to more relaxing home life. Activist Adrian Lipscombe (page 164) doesn't schedule meetings before 10:30 a.m. because that would interfere with her workout schedule. And Sunday Suppers founder Karen Mordechai (page 242) says she won't start work until 11:00 a.m. because "mornings are for yoga, walking, stretching, and meditating." Find what works for you.

the expat mom

As a child growing up in Ghana, Nina Barnieh-Blair was all too familiar with the classic child-rearing maxim *It takes a village.* Like most Ghanaians of a certain age, her parents followed the post-British colonial model of emigration, pursuing education and employment in the United Kingdom, while her maternal grandmother and an army of aunties raised her back home. The environment was loving, but it never bridged the physical and emotional distance Nina felt from her mom.

"My first mother was my grandmother," says Nina, who was sent to London to visit her parents during summer holidays before permanently joining her mom and stepfather in the British countryside when she was eight. "I had missed out so much on not connecting with my mother. Not being with her definitely shaped my views on motherhood and what I wanted it to be."

So many years later, when Nina began to warm to the idea of being a mom and found herself emotionally and creatively unfulfilled by her career as a public relations consultant—a compromise she made to satisfy her parents' preference for traditional parameters of success after studying business and marketing rather than tending to her artistic tendencies—she began to fantasize about quitting her job and creating a situation that gave her the flexibility to have a career and

> ## "I always strive to be there for my family, even if it means making sacrifices in my career."

raise children on her own terms. She made a pact: "If I'm going to have a child, I need to have the time to spend with them so that they don't miss out on what I missed out on."

"In that sense, starting a company was always a question of how it would serve me once I became a mother," she says. But it was also a question of practicality. By the time she and her husband began to seriously consider parenthood, they were living in New York and painfully aware of the lack of a social safety net for American mothers.

"A lot of my friends in England had children, and they got up to a year of maternity leave," Nina rationalized. "Our family in Iceland got *years* of maternity leave. And they also have full-time childcare. The system allows them to be parents. But employers here were saying six weeks or eight weeks, and then you can use all of your vacation to extend it. I thought, *Well, that seems quite cruel.*"

Armed with the knowledge that she'd never have the time she felt necessary to devote to her family while working in a corporate setting, she threw herself into a second career as an interior designer, attending classes at Parsons School of Design, taking on house-renovation side projects for her parents and friends during consulting downtime, and eventually working and sharing resources with an architectural firm that she found through a mutual friend. When she was finally ready to become a mother and start her business as a self-employed designer, she thought she had a good balance for maximizing both bonding time and professional development. She was taking on small design projects and felt fulfilled in both arenas. But there were always sacrifices. Two

interior
designer /
mother
of two

months into her maternity leave, a project too good to pass up arrived, demanding her time and energy.

"In hindsight, I should never have taken it on," Nina says. "I was exhausted and hadn't fully recovered from childbirth, both physically and mentally. But when you're writing the checks yourself, you feel like you have to work doubly hard to make it work." The experience taught her that it's okay to say no, especially when the circumstances don't favor her relationship with her children. Concurrently, another instance strengthened her resolve to keep her family in focus.

"One day, I was sitting in the playground with my son, and it was one of those days where he was crying a lot and he wasn't sleeping, and I was just happy because we made it outside," she remembers. "You think, *Okay, we're good*. And then someone came up to me and said, 'You're so good with him. Which agency are you with?' At that point it took quite a lot for me to not cry or scream. Living in Manhattan, my children's experiences of people of color are often limited to the service industry, but as a Black mother in the city, that's not the vision I wanted my children to see. I needed to change my kids' perception of what a woman of color could be."

For Nina, being an entrepreneur gives her the chance to rewrite the narrative, even if that means trading off some professional freedom and personal luxuries. "By running my own business, I have the opportunity to provide a role model for my children, showing them that Black people, and particularly Black women, can exist anywhere and be successful. It's hard. Sometimes I would love to just sit and read a book at night instead of working. But children learn more from what they see, and I believe that the intersection of parenting and running a business can serve as an inspiring example as they grow up and find their own paths in life."

Advice from Nina Barnieh-Blair

DON'T LET GUILT TAKE OVER. "I have come to accept that whether I work or don't work, I will always feel guilty for not spending all of my time with my children. But I can only do my best. I try to remember that I have taken time out during their early stages and treasured these precious moments. And while I have increased my workload as they have grown older, they are always my priority."

RELINQUISH SOME CONTROL. "I'm learning to do more outsourcing, but it's difficult when you are really bad at delegating and feel responsible for everything in your practice. It feels like you're losing control, but the truth is that I'm able to focus on the things I'm good at when I outsource administrative work. And I have realized that things like three-dimensional renderings and some ordering processes are better done by someone else."

USE YOUR MOTHERHOOD AS A BLUEPRINT. "It's so hard to say no to work. But as the kids have gotten older I've started to think, *I've given up a lot to get to where we are*. Slowly I'm taking on more projects, and it feels really good."

the meat-market moms

To say that the situation in which Erika Nakamura and Jocelyn Guest became parents was complicated is a supreme understatement. The partners in work and life were deep into the monitoring process for becoming pregnant and had already identified a sperm donor when, just weeks before Christmas, they learned that one of their business partners at the acclaimed New York City restaurant where they ran the butchering was involved in sexual misconduct. They put in their notice.

"It's hard to make a living in food and to have children," says Erika, who has worked in butchering for the last fifteen years. She says that she never recalled thinking about what her life would look like with a child until her relationship with Jocelyn became more than a working one. That prompted an unexpected conversation. "At that point, I knew that I wanted to have children. I was in my midthirties, and the clock was ticking."

Jocelyn, though, wasn't sure if she felt the same and had what she describes as "the coldest feet." But she quickly warmed to the idea once she let go of her insecurities. "I always wanted to be a mom," she says. "Also, my mom was a stay-at-home mom who would give me homemade cookies in my lunch box. The pressure was on. I was like, 'I cannot mess this up.'" Adds Erika, "I had to make a deliberate decision for us because we're women. We're not just going to get knocked up. There was a lot of intentionality."

So the news at work in December shocked them and their families, but it wouldn't derail the plan. "Erika's mom and my mom were like, 'Y'all really think this is the right time?'" recalls Jocelyn. "It was so cinematic. But at that point, the toothpaste was out of the tube." Erika's mom bought them sperm for Christmas, and Erika was three months pregnant by the time they left the restaurant—with no other full-time job prospects lined up.

While still at the restaurant, however, they had started working on a side project, a line of sustainable and organic packaged sausages called J&E SmallGoods. After leaving the restaurant and moving upstate to be near Erika's family, they used the rest of the pregnancy to launch the brand. "We were just trying to start small and scrappy," says Jocelyn. "At the onset of that particular business, we were coming from behind a meat counter in a restaurant environment, working twelve- to seventeen-hour days and knowing how unsustainable that was already for our lifestyle," says Erika. "And now we were throwing a child into it. We were trying to set the groundwork and create a life where we could focus and work really hard but not go into a restaurant, not physically have to do the manual labor to earn our paycheck."

They reached out to customers from a previous gig and friends from the restaurant

> "Being a mother makes you more courageous *and* more conservative. You say, 'I have to provide for these children. I have to do something lucrative and wise.'" —JOCELYN GUEST

butchers /
mothers
of two

to fundraise for the project, but it turned out not to be enough. "In the bigger picture, we should have fundraised more," Erika admits, saying that things were humming along until about a year and a half into the company's life, which was, coincidentally, when Covid-19 began to spread. "It was such a bizarro time to be approaching anyone with your hand out. We had distribution, but we were supposed to have a phone call with our investors literally the week that shutdown happened. It was a really humbling, horrific experience." Adds Jocelyn, "The second phone call, which felt so hollow and stupid, was the week after George Floyd got murdered. It all felt very small in the scheme of things."

So the duo did what they do best and pivoted, this time to a small pop-up shop conceived to address the area's food-insecurity issue and help farmers sell their product at a time when no one wanted to go to a grocery store. The result was Butcher Girls, an omakase meat subscription service that absorbed their earlier business. "J&E never died," says Erika. "It disappeared into something else. We were still producing those sausages, delivering all over the five boroughs and shipping nationally."

Meanwhile, Jocelyn was now trying to get pregnant with the couple's second child through IUI and having difficulty, and Erika's parents were pitching in, watching their daughter, Nina, when she wasn't playing at a makeshift water table made from a bus tub in the rented butcher shop where Erika and Jocelyn did their business. "It all sounds so psychotic when you say it out loud," says Jocelyn. "We would drop Nina with Erika's folks on Sunday afternoon, then they would bring her over on Tuesday evening and we'd have family dinner, and then Erika and I would alternate days off."

Once the world opened up again, Butcher Girls struggled to compete. "A company that thrived off $10,000 in savings isn't ever going to be a contender against ButcherBox and

> "I just need other moms in this space, because we have to share in the tragedy and dignity and the incredible honor and integrity of it and give each other the support that we need to push each other along."
>
> —ERIKA NAKAMURA

Fortune 500 companies that do what we do at a corporate-giant level," says Erika. "And we realized we probably should have charged an annual or cyclical membership fee instead of just a starting membership fee because the growth was really front-loaded, and we started to spin our wheels a little bit." So they once again pivoted, moving back to New York City and building out the front end of their virtual butcher shop into a sandwich stand called Due Madri ("two mothers" in Italian) in the Pier 57 market.

"We knew that we wanted to make something scalable, something easy to manage," says Erika. "In the past, we'd wanted to make everything by hand, and we knew that always came with a pretty excruciating labor price tag, so we were trying to work backward to undo some of the difficulties we had." Adds Jocelyn, "Years ago, we went to this really spectacular lunch in Modena, Italy. We asked, 'Where do you make your salumi?' And they said, 'We aren't producers; we're selectors.' We took that to heart. We're not going to make a capicola or prosciutto, so let's find the most interesting thing that we can."

Today, Erika and Jocelyn say that their partnership makes life both easier and more complex. "I think because we met at work and we thrive under the gun, we really do know how to divide and conquer," says Jocelyn, who spent weeks on bed rest with preeclampsia before having an emergency C-section to deliver baby Huey nearly two months early. "But the thing that's hard about working together is that when one person is struggling at work, it's usually both of us struggling. We're on the same suck schedule." Adds Erika, "If there is a trash fire at work, we both have to tend to it." The same is true at home. "Yesterday, Huey woke up at 5:00 a.m., and I had worked a double the day before and Erika was going to work all day," says Jocelyn. "And she brought him in and was like, 'I can't deal with this right now,' and went back to bed. So I was up with Huey, and then at 8:00 a.m., Erika and Nina woke up, and I was like, 'Cool, I feel like I'm gonna die right now. Give me half an hour. I'm gonna go take a power nap.' Sometimes it's like everyone's uncomfortable at the same time, and we do a good job of really seeing when the other is struggling and being like, 'Okay, go do what you need to do.'"

They also acknowledge that life could be easier, but there would be inherent trade-offs in pursuing a more traditional path. "Every time I shut down a business, I'm like, 'This is my moment to go corporate,' and then I'll apply to a bunch of jobs and go through rounds of interviews before I don't get hired," says Erika. "Typically, it's because as a founder and serial entrepreneur, I'm too well-rounded and I have too wide of a scope of knowledge that people don't want to hire me. They're like, 'You're a red flag for a lot of different reasons.' And then I'm like, 'Whatever. I'm an entrepreneur.' It can feel so daunting, but you have to remind yourself that it's what allows you to sit in power." Adds Jocelyn, "And stay home with your kid when they're sick.'"

WHAT WE'VE LEARNED
Advice from Erika Nakamura & Jocelyn Guest

DIFFERENTIATE YOUR PRODUCT. "Kids are always going to want hot dogs, and they don't have to eat crappy, going-to-lead-to-congestive-heart-failure hot dogs," says Jocelyn. "There's a way to be gentler to our bodies and on the environment and still scratch that itch at a cookout. We have nieces and nephews who don't live in major metropolises that have beautiful bespoke butcher shops, so we thought, *Let's contribute in that way.*"

KNOW THAT IT'S NEVER GOING TO BE FIFTY-FIFTY. "When you have a child, one parent always thinks they're pulling more weight than the other," says Erika. Adds Jocelyn, "Brené Brown did this thing where she was like, 'If anyone tells you that a marriage is fifty-fifty, they're full of shit.' Someone will come home and say, 'I'm only at twenty today.' And then the other says, 'Well, I'm at ten.' And then someone has to make up the difference. Or they have to be okay that it's going to be a bit of a trash fire for a while, and they're never gonna make it to 100 percent."

THE CHORES CAN WAIT. "I am working on allowing myself to enjoy and relax," says Jocelyn. "Yesterday, I had a mountain of laundry to fold, but it was my one day with the kids, so I was just like, 'Forget the laundry.' It makes me want to jump out of my skin, but it's so important."

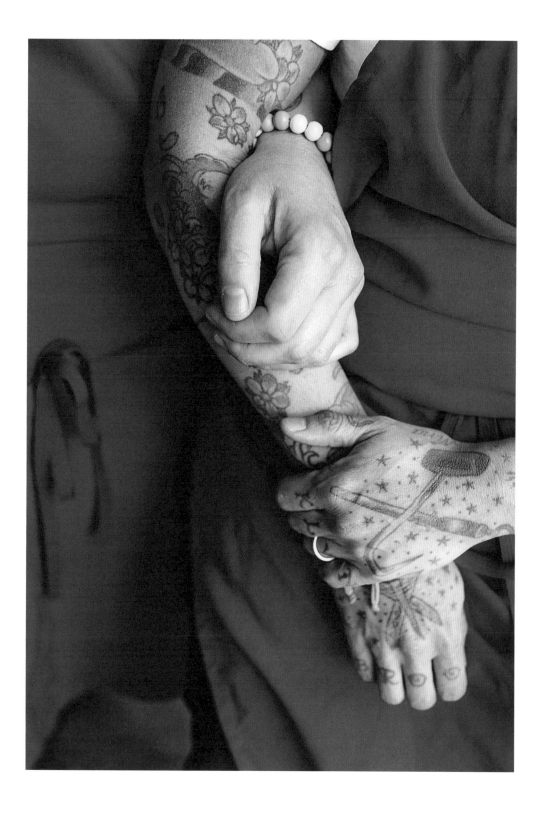

the NRA's worst nightmare

In December 2012, Shannon Watts was folding laundry at her home in Indiana when the unthinkable flashed across her television screen: Twenty children and six staff members had been gunned down at Sandy Hook School in Newtown, Connecticut. Reeling from the news and exasperated by a culture of complacency, the then stay-at-home mom did something unexpected. She took to Facebook and drafted a post that would become the mission statement of the nation's largest grassroots organization aimed at eradicating gun violence.

"It was an earthquake in my life," recalls Shannon, a former communications executive and self-described "accidental activist" who had only seventy-five Facebook friends at the time. Yet her Moms Demand Action page hit a nerve and went viral. Within a month, she was fielding calls from reporters, organizing rallies and marches across the country, and mobilizing hundreds of volunteers to lobby their local congressional leaders to enact stricter gun control laws. She had no experience in community building, volunteering, or nonprofit work, but she used skills acquired in her former career to get her organization to a place where she could recruit people to fill in the gaps in knowledge she didn't have.

"Through my communications background, I knew how to build a brand that empowered women; I knew how to tell a story and create a message," she says. "I had written speeches and knew how to pitch stories to the media. In those early days, that made us seem even more sophisticated and established than we were." In 2023, Shannon was named one of *Time* magazine's 100 Most Influential People.

"I had never imagined I'd be a public figure—it was just meant to be an online conversation," she says. But the role came naturally to her, and women from every walk of life started reaching out to help in their spare time, in any way they could. "A lot of it felt like divine intervention," she says. "Anytime there was an obstacle, we overcame it. I used to spend hours manually deleting comments from trolls on our Instagram posts, and a woman volunteered to sit there at home and delete them herself. We had women breastfeeding their babies in the halls of Congress. We had people entering data into project management software. We were all so passionate and bolstered each other through hard times, when a piece of legislation failed or there was another tragedy. Doing this work reveals the best of humanity."

But behind the scenes, it was hard to maintain her equilibrium. "I felt like I was drinking out of a fire hose," she admits. Only a few weeks earlier, she was considering dusting off her résumé and reentering the workforce after years spent raising her children at home; now, video conferences for major news networks and red-eye flights were how she started her mornings. "It was all-consuming, but I was obsessed with this issue."

> "The system is set up to keep women from wanting, achieving, and leading. Expect people to dislike it when you challenge the system."

activist /
mother
of five

The upheaval was also jarring for her husband and teenage kids. "I had only been [re]married for three years and was always very available to my family," Shannon says, "and then to have a husband who was like, 'Where'd you go?' I'd just cry in the closet because I was so overwhelmed." But like the legion of volunteers who helped grow Moms Demand Action, her family was inspired by her sense of purpose. Her ex-husband pitched in with drop-offs and pickups, family dinners, and after-school activities.

"There's a real benefit to having three parents—every woman should have two spouses," she laughs. "It became this unspoken agreement that anything I couldn't do, my husband and ex-husband would take care of. And the kids were grateful that I was focusing my attention on something other than them."

But when her daughter was diagnosed with an eating disorder, she also learned how to come up for air. "I think as women we feel diminished when we have to step back, but it's so important to have priorities and take breaks," she says, recalling that she was on the way to the airport for a fundraising event when she made the decision to go back home. "Activism is a marathon, but it's also a relay race. The work will always be there, so you have to know when to pass the baton."

It's a lesson Shannon took to heart in 2023, when she made the difficult decision to step back from her leadership role to volunteer. "Organizations have to evolve, and it's important not to let your ego become a driving force of what you do," she says. "I'm incredibly proud of all of the work we've done and am happy to make space for others to step forward while I figure out what's next for me. I spent my whole career using my skill set to be in the corporate world of capitalism, but I see the hand of the divine in doing activism. What an honor it is to do this work and make a real difference in people's lives and have that feeling of joy guide your days."

WHAT I'VE LEARNED

Advice from Shannon Watts

MAKE EVERY MINUTE COUNT. "The most valuable time with my kids was in the car during pickups and drop-offs. I knew I could always talk with them there."

START TRAINING YOUR MIND FOR BETTER THINGS. "Hope is a discipline. You always want to feel like you're winning, but it's easy to say nothing's happening, nothing's changing, when you see a tragedy. That's when you have to look for the good and find your people. For us, it's the untold number of lives saved because of policies we've advocated for together."

WORK WITH WOMEN. "When men are involved, they make the strategy and take the spotlight while the women are asked to make the snacks and set up chairs. When you're not at the table, you're on the menu. I wanted to build a badass army of women."

the mixed-media artist

Early one morning in January 2023, Los Angeles–based artist K'era Morgan and her husband got the call that would forever change their lives. "It was a regular day—my husband was at the office, I was working—and the phone rings and they say, 'Hey, we've got a little sixteen-month-old who's in need of a home—yes or no?'" recalls K'era of the day she learned that she would be a mother through California's foster-to-adopt program. "In training, we'd go through these mock scenarios to play out what the situation would be like when you'd get a call, what kind of questions to ask and what it's like, and I remember my husband saying, 'No matter what, if I get a call and there's somebody on the other end saying that there's a child who needs a home, I'm saying yes.' And that's exactly what happened. By five in the evening, he was home with us."

Though adopting a child was always part of the couple's parenthood plan—especially when their attempts at IVF had failed—nothing could have prepared them for the shock of it all. "It flipped my life around and turned it upside down and inside out," says K'era, whose sister lives nearby and helped gather essentials in the hours after the call. "In a way, it kind of felt like giving birth. We

> ## "I'm more deliberate in the choices that I make, how I move through the world, the people I work with."

were all scrambling around. I think we left a shopping cart filled with random stuff in the middle of the aisle at Target because we just did not know what we were doing."

Because both K'era and her husband are self-employed (he's a writer, director, and producer), they felt good about being able to stop working at a moment's notice and trusted their employees to pick up where they left off. But they quickly realized that they had been naive about what they could accomplish at home with a toddler on the loose. "Our schedules are flexible, so we obviously thought it would be easier," says K'era. "I remember thinking, *We can trade off: Certain hours you can have him, and then I can have him for a few hours,* but it doesn't work like that. We couldn't get anything done, and we weren't sleeping."

A nanny provided some immediate relief—and some time for K'era to get back to her studio—but new motherhood has affected her in other, less tangible ways. "The time that I have to work is limited," she says. "It's definitely changed the output of my work, and I'm trying to feel okay with that. Even the style and the feel of my work has changed. As a painter and artist, my feelings kind of flow onto the canvas. It's different but it's me."

Feeding off the fear of uncertainty and using it to propel her forward is a recurring theme in K'era's life. After attending art school and climbing the corporate ladder as a public relations executive, a move made for financial stability over passion, she went into business for herself, turning her artwork from something abstract and unrelatable to most consumers into something more approachable: a capsule collection of eight throw blankets that became the basis for her

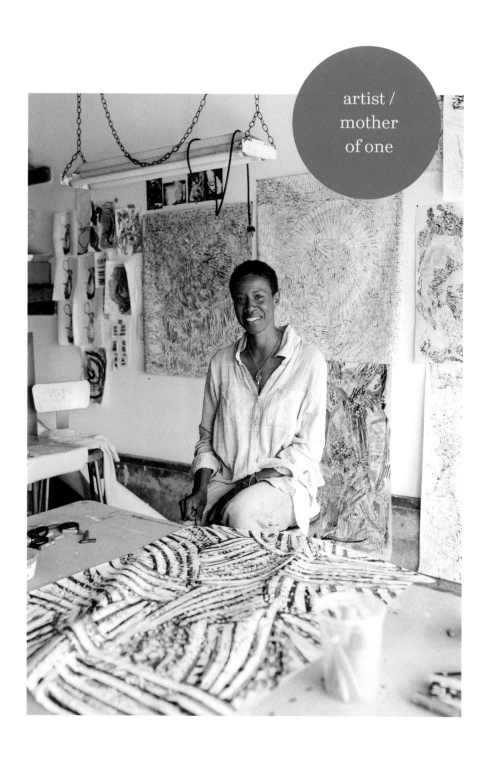

artist /
mother
of one

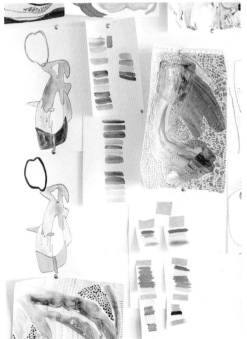

side company, K-apostrophe. Encouraged by industry friends, who generously slid her wares into larger pitches when they could, K'era contacted everyone she knew, went to some big artisan shows to get consumer feedback and her name out into the market, and had some lucky breaks with coverage in magazines like *Dwell* and *Elle Decor.*

"There were moments that were really scary, and it was so hard," she says, revealing that it was her husband's financial and emotional support that encouraged her to take K-apostrophe from a side project to a full-time endeavor. "It wasn't like there was some big pot of money we were sitting on—I started with only a few thousand dollars. I promised my husband that I wouldn't touch our savings to get started, so we had to bootstrap. But a lot of my stuff was made to order, so I wasn't spending a lot on holding inventory. Instead of getting bogged down by plans and funding, I just forged ahead on a small scale, making do with what I had."

Now K'era makes herself available for commissions and custom projects in addition to creating the textile-driven home decor products she's become known for, with a new focus on balance. "I have very clear boundaries around work and family so I haven't really had to turn down things," she says, noting that she goes to her studio when her son is in daycare. "I've been honest about what I can handle schedule-wise, and most of the time people have been extremely flexible. It's best not to force something because then you regret it."

And she's open to seeing how her needs and desires transform as she adapts to her new family situation. "Things will continue to evolve as my son evolves and our relationship grows. It's daunting, but I like this change. It's been the most challenging and heart-opening and messy and scary and exhilarating thing."

Advice from K'era Morgan

TALK TO AN EXPERT. "Based on advice from my CPA, I started my company through LegalZoom. The advice was: Keep it simple, especially in California, where taxes are high, as are the costs of living and running a business. He broke down the advantages and disadvantages as well as financial implications of sole proprietorship versus S corp versus LLC."

SEEK OUT YOUR PEERS. "At my first artisan fair, another Black business owner gave me a lot of good advice. She said that you should always walk the different shows or markets before you pay to participate. And through her, I met somebody else. For the most part, people have been very supportive."

FOCUS ON ONE THING AT A TIME. "I launched with a collection of eight blankets. As a creative, you want to experiment and explore, but my husband said, 'Get good on one thing so it's a well-oiled machine, and then expand little by little.' I realized that I needed to be able to work out all of the kinks in communication, production, and shipping before adding another product and complications to whatever I had going on."

the playwear designer

A hostess at a sushi restaurant. An analyst at an investment firm. A merchandise executive at a venture capital–backed start-up. Veronique Nguyen has taken a circuitous path to get to her current gig as founder of children's clothing brand Les Gamins, but she says each job has helped her develop the skills it takes to not only launch a business but sustain it. Yet of all the hats she's worn, it's her role as mother that continues to prove an unexpected parallel to her path toward entrepreneurial success.

"Both require lots of multitasking and patience," says the mother of three, who launched Les Gamins two weeks before her second child was born. "It might not have been the best timing, but Les Gamins feels like our family's little business because of this. The kids feel very invested in it."

Much of that is because Veronique works out of her Brooklyn home, at one point fulfilling a portion of the company's orders from her basement (she now works with a small women-owned distribution center). And her children have witnessed the company's growth from the ground up, involving themselves—to her delight—in every step of the process. "They love to pick colors and give feedback on styles—some feedback being more helpful than others," she says. "Zack asked to add pockets to our harem shorts, which was a great call. And Margaux loves to press the launch button, making the website live, and watching orders come in when we're introducing new products."

Yet Veronique accepts that not every interaction is a productive one. "I used to have my kids in all of our photo shoots, but it got way too crazy," she confesses. "They'd be making ridiculous faces, wrestling with each other, asking me to carry them the whole time. We now do all of our shoots in Los Angeles. It's way less stressful if someone else's kids aren't listening or cooperating."

On-the-job revelations like these have been commonplace as Veronique navigates her way around ownership and parenthood. "There is no magic formula for either parenting or running a business," she says. "We're all trying to do our best and figuring it out along the way." But correcting and learning from work mistakes does come a little quicker now. "I tried doing too much and offering too many products too early. Being in a creative field, it's easy to get carried away and want to develop all the amazing things you get inspired by, but it's expensive and inefficient for a small business just starting out. I quickly realized that the majority of our sales were coming from a handful of bestsellers, and it made more business sense for us to focus on growing those categories rather than constantly launching new products. But it's not always easy to remind my creative side to listen to the business side."

> "I sometimes feel like I am missing out on so many opportunities but also know I don't have the physical, mental, or financial bandwidth to do everything I'd like to do right now."

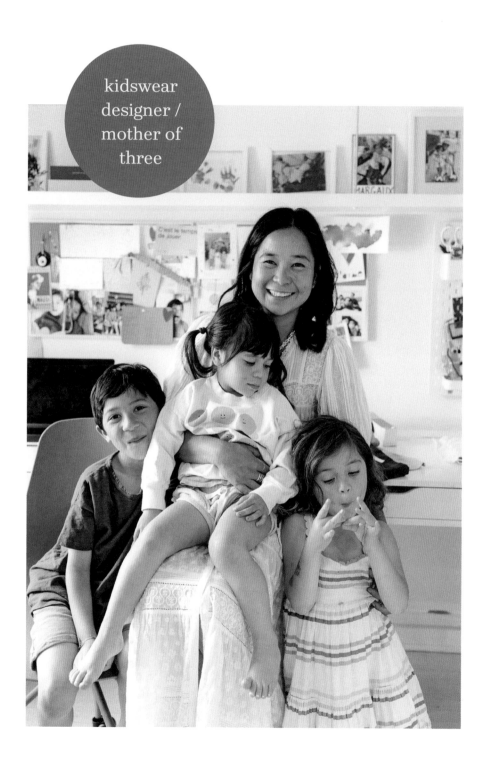

kidswear
designer /
mother of
three

Missteps like these made Veronique grateful that she started Les Gamins as a side gig while she was employed full-time and later consulting at a lifestyle brand for fashion and home decor. "I'm rather risk averse, so it gave me the confidence I needed to take the leap to launch the business," she says. But she recognizes that even this was a privilege. "I was fortunate to have had relatively easy pregnancies and was able to work the whole time," she says, an acknowledgment that some mothers don't have the luxury of health.

She was also thankful to have a full-time nanny, at least for the earlier stages of starting her company. "I felt guilty paying for childcare when I stopped working and consulting at my other jobs since I could barely pay myself, so we had inconsistent childcare for a while," she says. "I tried to cram in work during the few hours the kids were in preschool or napping and ended up working lots late at night, which was not sustainable for my mental and physical well-being. I also felt like I was never really present with the kids because I was often on my phone trying to get work done when I was with them and would get frustrated when I couldn't."

But as her children got older and spent more time at school—and she had more unfettered hours to handle the daily flow of Les Gamins—she came to realize that outsourcing work to others was a better use of her time and funds. "When I finally took the leap to hire people to help with some of the day-to-day of the business is also when the business took off, since it allowed me more room to be creative again," she says. And she landed on a childcare schedule that helped alleviate her guilt and maximize time at home and at work. "I try to schedule most of my work between 9:00 a.m. and 2:30 p.m., while the kids are at school, and spend the afternoon and evening with them. When work is extra busy, we have a wonderful

"Sometimes you just have to go for it. You can always learn, adapt, and adjust."

friend and babysitter who helps with the kids two afternoons a week. I then usually work for a couple of hours most nights once the kids go to bed. I still feel like I'm working to mostly pay for childcare, but I try to look at it as an investment."

She knows that schedule may be punishing for some, but it's what keeps her world spinning. "It's not for everyone, but it works well for me. I don't know if I really have an answer on how to overcome all of the obstacles, but regularly reminding myself of why I started this business in the first place— which was in big part to have a job where I could have some flexibility and spend time with the kids—helps."

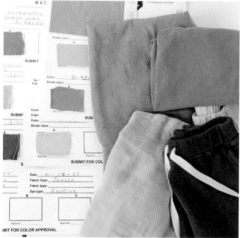

Advice from Veronique Nguyen

DON'T UNDERSELL YOURSELF. "I get uncomfortable talking about myself or the business and often try to deflect attention or downplay things. I've been trying to push myself to attend some networking events with other entrepreneurs and remind myself that I'm constantly telling my kids to believe in and be proud of themselves, so I should do the same."

BALANCE CAN BE A WORK IN PROGRESS. "I'm often working on my phone or laptop whenever or wherever I have a few minutes. But I'm trying to be more intentional about this and have some clearer limits so my kids don't see me in front of a screen so much. It's a tough balance. I want to be productive and try to get work done when I have some downtime, but I've also been trying to be more conscious about being present and not jumping on my phone to check and answer an email the second I'm waiting in some line for more than two minutes."

REDEFINE SUCCESS. "I've paused wholesale recently to focus on our direct-to-consumer business. It was a really hard, stressful decision since reducing sales streams doesn't feel like traditional 'success,' but this was the right financial decision. Making sure the business is sustainable is more important than just focusing on sales growth."

Veronique's Schedule

8:30 A.M.–12:30 P.M.	After a quick jog and breakfast, I start answering emails, reviewing sales, planning merchandise, and making marketing plans. I meet with order fulfillment to go over tasks for the day.
12:30–2:30 P.M.	Catch up with our West Coast manufacturers, digital marketing consultant, or photographers. Freshen up, pack after-school snacks, and get ready for pickups.
2:30–5:30 P.M.	I often split pickups with our babysitter. When big kids have after-school activities until 4:00 p.m. (a couple days a week), I work later. Otherwise I take the kids to the playground to burn off some energy before going home.
5:30–6:00 P.M.	Our babysitter takes care of Inès and gives her a bath while I help with homework and cook dinner. The big kids shower and get into pajamas.
6:00–7:30 P.M.	We try to do family dinners three or four times a week. My husband, Ben, has work dinners one or two nights a week, so I handle it all on those days.
7:30–8:30 P.M.	Kids' bedtime. Ben or I put Inès to bed while the other reads, helps finish up homework or piano practice, or just hangs with Zack and Margaux until they go to bed.
8:30–10:30 P.M.	Clean up, make lunches, catch up on more work, and a million other to-dos. I'm on the school board, so we also often have calls in the evenings. Then read and go to bed.

Roll with the Rejections

Crickets are the soundtrack of my life—only instead of producing a
comforting hum on a warm summer evening, they hiss deafeningly, like the
static from an old-timey television screen. I'm exaggerating, of course, but I
can't tell you the number of times I've sent out a pitch for what feels like the
greatest idea ever, only to have an editor completely disregard it (and me). I
follow up: nothing. This has happened with alarming regularity for the last
twenty years.

Many of us feel shame or anxiety around rejection, or see being rebuffed
as a signal of our diminished worth—so much so that it might keep us from
trying to do anything in the first place. But rejection is a normal part of the
process in the life of a freelance writer—or anyone in any profession for that
matter. Amanda tells me that for every brand that has chosen to collaborate
with her, three others have passed on her ideas. We even experienced
rejection when pitching this book to publishers. Three offered us a deal, but
ten—or was it twelve?—turned us down without even a meeting. Can you
imagine getting ten noes at once?

In the moment, it's only natural to perceive setbacks as failures. But
if you turn those hurt feelings into motivation, rejection can become a
road map for success. In that way, it is often the opposite of failure: It's an
opportunity to pinpoint what went wrong, refine your message, double your
efforts, and try it once more, with feeling. Rejection builds character and
resilience; it helps us pay attention to areas that might need work and gives
us real-world perspective that makes us better at what we do. We should all
be so lucky to fail fantastically every now and again. As mothers, we don't tell
our children to quit while they're ahead. If something doesn't work out, we
tell them to try, try again. It's fitting that we take our own advice.

WHAT IS SOMETHING YOU STRUGGLE WITH?

"Empathy and compassion. I work with clients who have often endured domestic violence and sexual assault, so I have found ways to shield myself from their emotions. While this initially felt cold, in the end it serves the client because I have to be able to rise above the emotions to figure out solutions."

LEONOR PERRETTA, LAWYER (PAGE 148)

"As I get older, I'm thinking about how I spend my mental energy and I'm a little more gracious toward myself. There's also the reality of accepting that this is who I am and understanding that there are fundamental things that are probably quite ingrained in who we are as human beings that we aren't entirely able to alter. I'm constantly figuring out how to work with those things in a more productive way."

NATALIA RACHLIN, PUBLISHER (PAGE 90)

"I'm often frustrated by being a woman in a tech field. It feels like we have to prove ourselves ten times as much as an agency run by men, and it's harder to get the trust and respect of men than of women. I used to want my team's work to stand on its own, and we didn't make a big deal in our marketing that we are woman- and minority-owned and -led. Now we're adding a bit more of that wording to our site."

ARIANNE FOULKS, DIGITAL CONSULTANT (PAGE 220)

"I really don't love the numbers part of the business. I'm lucky enough to have a friend who helped me set up my costing templates and Excel spreadsheets. I would be totally lost without her."

ALEX LAROSA, BAKER (PAGE 312)

"I struggle with taking on too many projects that don't make me any money. I love doing things for the community, but sometimes that work ends up taking a lot of my focus and I don't have enough time to keep my business growing and healthy."

AMANDA STEWART, KIDSWEAR DESIGNER (PAGE 130)

"I can be quite anxious and critical of myself and my work, and that's true of Natalia, too. I think sometimes it makes the work better because we're constantly questioning, but it also makes things a little bit harder when we're both that way."

MELISSA GOLDSTEIN, PUBLISHER (PAGE 90)

"Impostor syndrome. I've had an under-promise, over-deliver mindset for as long as I can remember, and while it has some good aspects, I also think it's been detrimental."

VERONIQUE NGUYEN, KIDSWEAR DESIGNER (PAGE 68)

the doughnut queen

Fany Gerson was working two part-time jobs—one at a tapas bar, the other at a hotel—when she had the somewhat crazy notion of opening a Mexican ice cream shop. The only problem: "I had never made one Popsicle in my life," the Mexico City native admits. Yet it didn't stop her from enlisting a friend, renting out a local bakery after hours, and spending her nights perfecting the recipes for her mango-chili, raspberry-hibiscus, and coconut paletas, often forgoing sleep to make sure everything froze in time to head out to her main gig in the morning.

"Popsicles weren't my passion—they were the vehicle. As an immigrant, I wanted to do something that was quintessentially American but with my unique point of view," she remembers. "I thought, *Let's test out the idea in the cheapest way possible.* Molds were less expensive than machinery, and since I didn't have the overhead of a factory or warehouse, we could keep it small."

Diving into unknown territory wasn't foreign to her. She had never written anything—"not even a blog post," she says—when she sought out an agent and pitched a book about Mexican desserts. "I was looking for this book about Mexican sweets, and it just didn't exist. I didn't have a platform or any kind of experience. The agent told me to write a proposal but not to hold my breath. We got a lot of rejections."

> "I get married to my ideas. My problem is editing. I always think I can do it all."

But eventually, Clarkson Potter picked up the book, and she spent her savings and more than a year couch surfing and researching confections across Mexico. (The trip was bittersweet: Her then husband, who was meant to join her in the journey, instead asked her for a divorce just two days before she left.) Despite the upheaval, the result was *My Sweet Mexico: Recipes for Authentic Pastries, Breads, Candies, Beverages, and Frozen Treats*, which was nominated for a James Beard Award.

It was upon her return that La Newyorkina was born. Fany signed up for a spot at the Hester Street Fair and, with her friend, made 850 paletas to sell throughout the weekend. They sold out in hours on the first day. By summer's end, she had quit her jobs and begun making plans for the following year, but she knew she had to find something to sustain her in the interim. That something turned out to be doughnuts.

For a few years, Fany was the cofounder and creative force behind Dough, a doughnut brand that helped launch the city's obsession with the fried desserts. But after parting ways with her investors over creative differences, she reemerged with Fan-Fan Doughnuts, a beloved Bedford-Stuyvesant shop that more accurately reflects Fany's culinary passions. Baked in small batches throughout the day, the offerings are based in cultural mash-ups that are unsurprisingly delicious: An oblong doughnut, what Fany calls a fan-fan, is filled éclair-style with yuzu custard and topped with toasted meringue; another is stuffed full of guava and cream cheese.

"It's about celebrating world cultures and creating a community-focused brand that makes people happy," she says of her

pastry chef /
mother
of one

work, which has weathered the closing of the Manhattan location of La Newyorkina and the flooding of the brand's Red Hook flagship, as well as every other kind of payroll and supply-chain issue. "It's also about what I want to put out into the world. I've always been a glass-half-full person. No matter what happens, I always come from a place of 'We're going to figure it out.'"

So it was when she became pregnant with her son, Gael—and lost her health insurance just before his birth due to her husband's preexisting condition. "There are always surprises," she says. When Gael was young, she had to bring him to the shop with her when she didn't have childcare, and she felt his resentment when she couldn't be with him because of the demands of operating two businesses in a city that never sleeps. Her compromise: She spent Tuesdays at home, checking in with her team by phone, and FaceTimed with him during the day when he was with the nanny. "It's hard to find time for the three of us. I just embraced the fact that there's never a balance and focused on the quality of time versus the quantity of it."

Now, Gael is the inspiration behind Fany's latest venture, Mijo, a partnership with her husband, Daniel, and an extension of the work they were doing during the pandemic, delivering reheatable meals to hospital workers. "Everything is a work in progress, but for the first time in a long time, we feel like we can breathe again."

After more than twelve years, Fany's paletas finally have a place on the shelves at Whole Foods Market, and Fan-Fan Doughnuts is beginning to hit its stride after pandemic-related fits and starts. "You have to be prepared for anything, but it's never going to be easy," she says. "The good thing is you have flexibility, but the bad thing is you're always on call. As an entrepreneur, your job is to be a firefighter, putting out fires so you can do the thing you want to do. And when you do that, it's a sweet life."

Advice from Fany Gerson

DON'T GO INTO IT FOR THE MONEY. "You always pay yourself last, and there's a lot of anguish if there's no money in the bank. Winters have always been a huge challenge for us with La Newyorkina. I'm constantly thinking, *Are we going to be able to make payroll?*"

DON'T GET ON THE BANDWAGON. "You have to choose something that you're personally connected with, and have an open mind about what success feels like. And you have to be honest about the why: Why are you doing this?"

BE PREPARED TO BE RUDE. "When I was writing the proposal for my book, I had to leave a friend's dinner party almost as soon as I arrived because I suddenly had an idea and I couldn't ignore it. I ran home and wrote all night. You need to give yourself permission to make your business your baby and do whatever needs to be done."

the stationery agent

There's no better white noise than the rumble of a bookbinding machine—at least according to Suann Song's second child, a daughter who spent her first four months being lulled to sleep at the warehouse where Suann produces her beloved line of stationery and appointment books.

"I had a swing in my office and I'd nurse and pump in the bathroom," Suann remembers. "I was deep in survival mode."

As a child growing up in the Seattle area, she played stationery store with her sister the way most girls play princesses. "I've always loved paper; I always had my little notebooks and stickers and ephemera," says the founder and CEO of Appointed, an American-made paper goods company. But it had never occurred to her that her passion could become her livelihood.

A first-generation Asian American, she was encouraged to frame success in professional terms: go to college, get a job. It's why she spent the earlier part of her career climbing the traditional corporate ladder as a marketer and public relations specialist while teaching herself graphic design on the side to satisfy her creative urges. It was all going well until shortly after the birth of her son, when a nightmare of a daycare tour forced her to rethink her path—and turn her maternity leave into a permanent one.

"I had every intention of going back to work," she recalls. "But in that moment, I

"Moms are always much harder on themselves than their kids are."

couldn't see the way forward in my current situation. "

So Suann fell back on her first love. She began working from home part-time, then enrolled in a letterpress-printing class for fun and found a sort of spiritual awakening. "In the first thirty minutes, I knew this was it for me," she says. She started small, designing cards and wedding invitations from her garage to build up her portfolio among budget-conscious brides while her son took blissful three-hour naps. "Thank God for those," she laughs.

As business picked up, she noticed a shift in the kind of work that was coming in. Brides who were happy with their wedding stationery began to hire Suann for other design jobs: restaurant menus and corporate letterhead and the like. She pivoted her wedding business into a full-service branding studio, all the while honing her skills and refining her personal style. She still yearned to make her entrepreneurial dreams a reality, but the timing was tricky: Now divorced, she no longer had a second salary to cushion the financial risk; her five-year-old son was becoming self-sufficient but was still impressionable; and she had recently begun dating the man she would later marry.

"I told him I had this idea for a notebook I didn't see on the market and said, 'If I don't try to start something now, I never will.'" He encouraged her to pursue it, so she spent eighteen months researching and prototyping, talking with industry veterans ("Men didn't take me seriously," she says) and reaching out to everyone she knew. A Kickstarter campaign provided $55,000 in seed money, but Suann also used her salary from her branding studio work to fund

stationery
designer /
mother
of two

Appointed's initial wholesale operations. "You really have to put yourself out there," she says. "I'm very comfortable behind the scenes; I'm really not comfortable asking for things from people. But if you're not going to ask for help, no one is going to ask for you."

Having a background in stationery and relationships that she could leverage to help reach her goals proved useful, but every day was a hustle. "It was a gradual grind," she says of those first few years. She arranged meetings with every good stationery store in every major city and carried boxes of notebooks in her trunk—just in case she could turn a stranger into a customer. It was in the company's third year that she had her daughter—and doubled down on those bookbinding machines.

Nine years on, Appointed has blossomed into the company Suann dared to envision. Spurred on by the Covid-19 pandemic, the brand has branched out into e-commerce and opened a storefront alongside its 10,000-square-foot (929 sq m) warehouse, and many of its twenty full-time employees are moms. No children nap there anymore, but Suann maintains her strong family focus. "I stack meetings on Monday and Tuesday afternoons so that I can work from home on Wednesdays. And I'm offline for school pickups and dinner from 4:30 to 6:30 p.m. every day, then after the kids go to bed I go back online to do some work," she says. She just doesn't have to do it from the garage anymore.

Advice from Suann Song

CRAFT THE COMPANY YOU WANT TO WORK FOR. "I never thought about what it meant to build a company culture, but it's a big part of what I do on a daily basis. We all spend a majority of the week with our coworkers—it's important to create an environment where people are happy and fulfilled. It makes the work better."

TAKE IT SLOW. "Because I began my new career as a hobby, there was very little financial downside to taking on work, and I could let the business grow organically without the pressure of making payroll or high overhead costs. Time also gives you the advantage of meeting more people in your chosen field, letting your network expand naturally, learning the ups and downs of the industry, and gaining experiences that will help inform your business plan down the line."

DON'T ASSUME YOU KNOW EVERYTHING. "Even if you've given yourself time to learn the ropes, you can't know it all. When I pivoted from the branding studio work to starting Appointed, I also transitioned from a service business to a product-driven one, a move that brought its own logistical, financial, and operational constraints. I felt like I was starting all over again because of the risk and the sheer revenue involved."

the traditional beauty guru

As a child in rural Wisconsin, Michelle Ranavat was well-versed in India's Ayurvedic wellness history. Her mom had been passionate about traditional medicine and art forms, and her grandfather was a collector of heirloom perfumes and soaps. But the skincare component never resonated.

"I experimented with it but I didn't really take it that seriously," says the maverick behind luxury Ayurvedic beauty brand Ranavat. "My mom wasn't obsessed with beauty products, and the kids at school just didn't get it. They'd say, 'Why would you put oil in your hair?—that's so gross.' And as a teenager, you're not shopping for beauty in an Indian grocery store. You want something that's cool and that connects with you."

Michelle studied industrial engineering at the University of Wisconsin–Madison (she comes from a long line of chemists) and later at Tufts University in Massachusetts before landing a high-powered job in finance at now-defunct Lehman Brothers in New York City. When Lehman went bankrupt, she went to work at her father's chemical company, where she learned the intricacies of large-scale production, supply-chain demand, and ingredient sourcing.

"I was already passionate about working with my dad, and so much of that touched upon the things that I wanted to do with my life," Michelle says. "I didn't have pressure to leave or pressure to find something of my own."

That all changed during her maternity leave, after giving birth to her second son.

"Success is being in love with your everyday."

While searching for a solution to postpartum hair loss, she came back to the hair oiling she had shrugged off as a kid. Before she knew it, a passing thought became an urgent need. "My head was clear, and I had the time to think about if I wanted to do something with this idea. When it popped into my head, the passion that I had for it was the catalyst. I started to realize that if I didn't find something that represented me, I could make it myself."

Using $30,000 of her own savings and relying on the skills she had learned as an industrial engineer, she started Ranavat from her garage and has steadily grown it over the last six years into the first South Asian skincare line to be picked up by Sephora. The slow evolution was by design: As the company's sole employee, she could maintain her stringent production standards and focus on the brand's identity yet still have time to spend with her young family. "I couldn't afford good people, so I waited," she says.

Now that her kids are older, Michelle spends a lot of her day managing her team as she continues to scale her business. Sometimes that means skipping a bedtime tuck-in or missing a school performance. In those moments, a babysitter and her husband pick up the slack, allowing her to do the work that keeps her fulfilled. "There are no Sunday scaries when you do something you love," she says.

There's also no mom guilt. "There are only so many hours in the day—you can always feel guilty about something," Michelle says. "I love empowering myself to say, 'If it's important, I'll make the right decision.' Could I compare my involvement to a full-time mom's? Probably not. But am I happy with the amount that I'm doing? Yes."

Advice from Michelle Ranavat

ORGANIZE WORK BLOCKS. "I like Mondays to feel like Sundays, so I clear the schedule and take that time to ease into the week. Tuesday through Thursday, I don't schedule meetings from 10:00 a.m. to 1:00 p.m. so that I can go through email, shower, and maybe do a little exercise. Then I'll have meetings in the afternoon. On Fridays I might schedule a fun lunch with a colleague or vendor, then have some meetings in the afternoon so there's no pressure to run around doing these things during the rest of the week."

BUILD UP YOUR RESILIENCE. "As an entrepreneur, you have to have a system of coping mechanisms because it's so hard and it takes so much to make it work. You have to have an optimistic way of looking at life—that's not always rooted in reality but sometimes comes in handy. And you have to be able to mentally push through the hard times. You also need a community of uplifting friends."

LEAN INTO YOUR MOM SKILLS. "You learn a lot being a mom, whether it's multitasking or embracing the idea that there are no boundaries. You learn to trust yourself and your abilities. So much of my day is accommodating the team and working around their schedules. I always feel happy and energized when we can work together to do our best."

the indie publishers

Anyone who's ever thumbed through a parenting magazine knows they'll find the usual advice on everything from lunch-box menus for picky eaters to tips for raising a confident child. While Melissa Goldstein and Natalia Rachlin have gleaned plenty of useful information from those kinds of articles, they also found the topics paled in comparison to the conversations the freelance writers, editors, friends, and moms of five kids under ten were having with each other over Instagram and email in the spring of 2020.

"I think we just felt like there's this presumption that if you're a mother, then the only conversation you're interested in having is a conversation about children," says Melissa, who lives in Los Angeles but had met Houston-based Natalia ten years earlier in London, when they both worked at a publication called *Nowness*. "Obviously, there's lots to talk about there, but we also felt like there was a lot of other stuff to talk about."

It was an observation that had always bothered them but became amplified within the unique situation of the Covid-19 pandemic. As freelancers, both women felt they had achieved a good balance in their work and personal life but struggled as they were plunged into stay-at-home motherhood—plus homeschooling. "We thought, *Why can't there be conversations about motherhood that are forthright and honest about what it means to be a mother in this moment, when we have more roles to balance and juggle than ever before?*" says Natalia.

As design journalists, they also took issue with the traditional aesthetics of motherhood. "We asked ourselves why we were having a hard time connecting with motherhood content, and we found one of the elements is that visually it wasn't stimulating to us," says Natalia. "We're both driven by how things look and feel, and how visuals expand the storyline." Adds Melissa, "We don't find motherhood to be soft or always superfeminine or pink. Why can't it look badass? Because it is."

Since there was nothing in the mainstream media that addressed that perspective, they decided to start *Mother Tongue*, a feminist indie magazine about the nuances of motherhood and its intersection with sex, politics, art, and culture—topics that mirrored the late-night discussions they were having online. Before long, making plans for the magazine's production became a full-time conversation. "It was such a lifeline for us, and we wanted to talk about it all the time," says Melissa.

But they vowed to take an alternative publishing path to the traditional newsstand model, opting instead for a crowd-sourced, direct sales strategy as much to minimize waste as to prove their concept. "In our minds, especially for a magazine about motherhood responding to the world we're in right now, we thought, *Let's make something that people want to keep, something that's*

> "We're not going to make a magazine about motherhood only to miss out on our own children's lives."
>
> —NATALIA RACHLIN

publishers /
mothers
of two &
three

"If we're being honest, there are lots of times when we are doing stuff with our kids and wishing we were working on the magazine." —MELISSA GOLDSTEIN

made responsibly, and let's not make any more than we need to make, any more than there's demand for," says Melissa.

Though they had each worked in the magazine industry for more than a decade, they knew little about how to actually build and print a publication. So they relied on a friend who had started her own indie zine for insight and resorted to old-fashioned research. "I was calling printers in Canada, in Belgium, in Berlin, having very random conversations," says Natalia. "It was an enormous education process, and I learned more about paper than I ever wanted to know, but at the same time those were the building blocks."

They started to build a brand identity, came up with the name, got a logo, and started piecing things together, not entirely knowing what Mother Tongue would be. "We were calling it a journal because that felt less scary," remembers Natalia. "Maybe it would be a one-off; maybe it would be this purely pandemic project. We had bigger ambitions, but we weren't letting ourselves say it out loud yet because we know that this industry is incredibly tenuous at the best of times—and this was in the thick of an unprecedented global pandemic."

Despite homeschooling, limited childcare, and all of the other obstacles moms faced during those dark years, they threw themselves into Mother Tongue, working while their children slept, making a small investment to get the business off the ground, and hiring writers and photographers, while reaching out to every friend they'd made over the last ten years for favors. "It felt so familial," says Natalia. "It was such a treat for us to pull in these people from various parts of our lives and see how they rallied around us. That was such a positive experience."

In the process, the pair's lives have become inextricably linked. They finish each other's sentences, and their texts wind around tasks related to Mother Tongue and then jump to conversations about television shows and weekend plans. Natalia always knows when Melissa is heading to the market because the service is terrible and her phone cuts in and out during their calls. "There's a franticness to our communication because it always feels like it's going to be interrupted or cut off," Melissa says. "We're constantly apologizing for being late to get back to the other because one of us took an hour to put our kids to bed. The funny thing is we both understand what's going on. We'll have a therapy session—I'm feeling this; you've done so much stuff and I haven't—but we're doing so much all the time. We want to give so much of ourselves because we feel we owe it to each other and we owe it to the potential of the brand. Neither of us has expectations for the other; we just have extremely high expectations for ourselves."

Their families are all in on the business, too. Natalia says her nine-year-old son always wants to choose the logo colors for the new issue, and Melissa points out that their husbands often drop into their Zoom conferences. "One of the most enormous privileges of this project is that it adapts to us," Natalia says. "It's been so satisfying to see that we can make it work even if I'm in Copenhagen with my family during the summer or Melissa is going to visit her in-laws in the UK. And that's also the beauty of there being two of us."

Though they can depend on each other to hold down the fort workwise, both women often feel like things slip through the cracks in their personal lives. "I have a nanny that helps my world go 'round and my husband is superinvolved, and it *still* feels that way all the time," Melissa says. Adds Natalia, "Part of me hates to admit that we all feel guilt around what we should be accomplishing and how we're spending our time. There's definitely loads of frustration. In many ways, this would have been a much wiser thing to do in a few years when our children are bigger. We would have had a lot more headspace and been a little bit further along in the shit show of it all. But that's life. Something strikes you and you go for it, and it's never the perfect timing."

"I think that's also intrinsic to the DNA of *Mother Tongue*," says Melissa. "It would be a different brand if we had a little more time and we were more clearheaded. Part of the reason why it resonated was that a lot of people felt that way, too."

Adds Natalia, "I think we felt like so many mothers. We were like, 'Hello, help—we don't want to totally disappear, seeing everything we worked professionally for those last ten years fizzle away overnight.' We latched on to each other and said, 'No, we're going to do something together for our own well-being. Let's not sit here and wait for all of this to be over. Let's make something now.'"

Advice from Melissa Goldstein & Natalia Rachlin

LEAN INTO THE DISARRAY. "My daughter has gotten into the idea of having snacks in the bath, and it's an easy way for me to get veggies into her before dinner and sort of lower the stakes," says Melissa. "The excitement of eating crudités while being partially submerged in water is a winning combination." Adds Natalia, "My house is in a perpetual state of chaos, and I've resigned myself to the fact that I will get to the bottom of it in, like, twelve years. It's quite funny because I love houses. I come from a design background. It's admitting that it's not going to be perfect, it's not the way I actually want it to be, and I'm 100 percent okay with that."

SET THE WORK ASIDE. "When it's your own thing, it literally never stops," says Natalia. "That process of having to negotiate with myself, that I cannot do this eighteen hours a day because I will drive myself crazy and I need to have time and space and energy for my family and myself, that's been a learning curve. There's always more that I could be doing, and I've learned to say, 'Okay, this is enough for today, and we'll resume tomorrow.'"

Always Have a Contract

If you don't watch your back, no one else will. It's your job to make sure you're being treated fairly, and a huge part of this is having a good contract, setting strict boundaries for your work life, and knowing when to stand up for yourself. I've had to learn this the hard way in my own career.

The first lesson occurred while I was living in Chicago. An acquaintance sent a photo over from a very well-known home decor store downtown. The showroom sign very strongly resembled a book cover I'd designed. In fact, it *was* my book cover! Someone had Photoshopped my text out and replaced it with their own. I was livid. And very pregnant. I reached out to the company and showed them the offending image compared to my own, letting them know very kindly, but also strongly, how I felt about the situation. They apologized and offered me $300. I did *not* accept. I knew the time it had taken to create that design, and the value of my time. I explained that this would barely begin to cover the fee, had I been hired. They understood and sent us a gift card that furnished our nursery as well as a portion of our new Chicago apartment—a memory I always try to summon when standing up for myself seems too hard or not worth it.

The second lesson occurred when I began working with a small company that has a large social media presence. They were warm in their welcome to work with their company and (red flag!) had us move forward without a written contract. I cringe when I think of it—I should have known better. After working with them for a few years, I suddenly received an out-of-the-blue email saying they'd accidentally overpaid me the previous year and that I now owed them nearly $4,000.

Mistakes happen, but this was a lot of money for us. I was weeks away from delivering my second child, and I was the sole provider as my husband was still in school. So they offered a deal: They would simply take it out of my royalties for the upcoming year. But this was income we were planning on, and to make matters worse, they simultaneously decided to adjust my royalties from 8 percent to 1 percent. They had every right to make this huge, and frankly unfair, cut because—guess who didn't have a contract? Me. I felt degraded and was embarrassed to be treated so poorly, but I agreed and continued with their proposed plan until my debt was paid off.

I shouldn't have been surprised when a few years later it happened *again*. (Cringe *again!*) I reached out to other artists they worked with, and the same thing was happening to them as well. I've since pulled my collection from the company, and learned to always, always, always have a contract. Your contracts will be your advocate and your safeguard when things get iffy. *Especially* if it's a friend or family member you're working with.

Here are a few more tips to ensure you have a good contract in place before starting a project:

- Spell out deliverables clearly. Be specific about what goods or services are included so there are no chances for miscommunication.
- Make sure you're only signing over the copyright to the final product, not all the iterations. This way, you can keep any work you create that isn't used by the client. Also include a limitation on how long the client retains the copyright, as well as a permission to use anything you create for portfolio purposes.
- As a self-employed parent, I always figure out how much time a job will take, and then add two weeks. It's better to deliver early than late. Should they need something within a tight time frame, add a rush fee into the contract so you don't have to negotiate mid-project.
- If you're creating physical material, make sure you ask specifically for produced selections of the pieces for your portfolio.
- I ask for half of my fee upon signing the contract, to ensure I get paid even if the project or partnership is terminated. This is the kind of language I use: *The client has the option to discontinue the project at any time. If the project is terminated after receipt of the first payment, the payment will not be returned. If design time has exceeded X hours, the client will be billed an extra X per hour of work.* And I make a stipulation that if they cancel after a certain point, they still need to pay me for work completed. I also add a clause that signals the client's responsibility for any fees associated with transactions via PayPal or wire transfer (and then suggest free payment options like a mailed check or Zelle transfer).
- Manage expectations. I conclude all of my contracts with this: *Once this bid is approved, a formal schedule with conflicts and holidays will be noted and delivered upon request. (A disclaimer: Amanda Jane Jones is a full-time mom and part-time designer. Occasionally, emergencies with children's health or otherwise might affect delivery timelines.)*

JAYCINA ALMOND

the model humanitarian

Like most of her millennial cohorts, Jaycina Almond is, in her words, chronically online. But she has made her time in the digital space count for more than just TikTok dances and viral memes. As the founding executive director of the Tender Foundation, a maternal nonprofit that provides emergency assistance powered by individual donations to Atlanta's single mothers without all the red tape that comes with traditional government assistance, she leans on her ability to tell a good story as much as her tendency to automate her life.

"I'm a big proponent of using all of the things that you need to make your life easier," says the model turned activist, who started with an idea for a self-care subscription box for expecting mothers and pivoted when she realized she was happily spending more time tracking down diapers for giveaways than curating the products. "Tech is what keeps us going. Our entire organization lives on Airtable, from our requests to our diaper bank inventory."

Being scrappy and efficient with her time and work processes is a lesson motherhood,

> "Since we don't take money from certain government entities, we don't have to play by their rules. We can run the company the way that we want to."

both her own and her mom's, has ingrained in her. Jaycina's single mom worked two, sometimes three, jobs to support her three children, then remarried and stayed in an abusive relationship because she couldn't imagine a scenario where she could make ends meet by herself. When, at the age of twenty, Jaycina also became a single mother, she was determined to not let that be her story. "I've always known I wanted to have something for myself because of growing up that way," Jaycina says. "Knowing the power dynamics at play and having a sense of gender equity, being able to have that freedom was important to me."

Taking advice from fellow creative friends, she turned to modeling, bringing her daughter on photo shoots and work trips because she didn't have anyone to watch her while she was away. Once Jaycina had more than survival money, she went back online to teach herself how to start and run a nonprofit in her own way, and the Tender Foundation was born.

"Most nonprofits spend their money on payroll and admin, but I didn't have a team. It was just me," she says. "And I always knew the power of branding and telling a story, and that if we leaned into that and the fact that millennials are now becoming adults who are engaged and care about the world, we could capitalize on it and generate revenue from there. I always had the mindset of being a small grassroots community organization."

She spent the next year with her laptop always open and an endless stream of Zoom calls providing the soundtrack to her pandemic experience. "I sacrificed a lot of time with my daughter," she says, recalling that her daughter watched episodes of

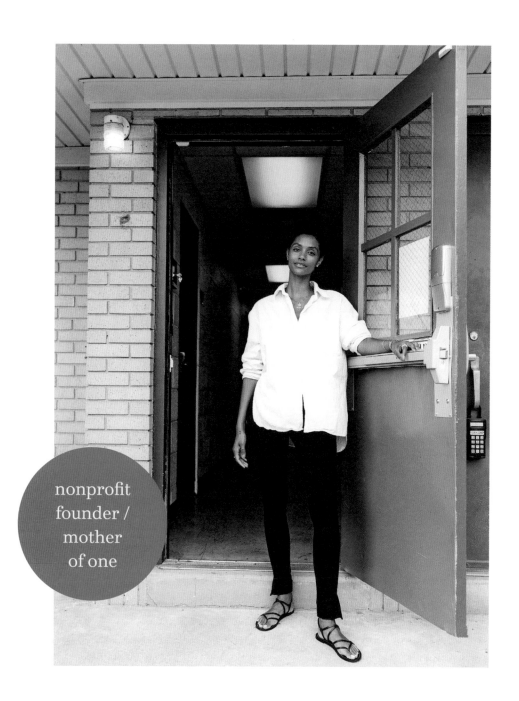

nonprofit
founder /
mother
of one

tender

We live in a world where s
hood is often stigmatiz
devalued. Motherhood is
Tender honors the streng
and love that goes int
work is guided by the
and rooted

re building a safety net for single
s living on the margins in Atlanta, so
they can invest in what they need -
housing to keeping the fridge stocked
d everything in between. Our mission is
help our moms focus on what's
rtant: their children.

a home, food in
ermore, r

> "Our moms are closest to the problems, but they're also closest to the solution."

Sesame Street while she made calls to donors and put out fires from her laptop nearby. "Looking back, I couldn't tell you what my kid was doing that year. But you do what you have to do. Now that we're not in scrappy start-up mode, I work from 9:00 a.m. to 3:00 p.m. every day, and whatever doesn't get done doesn't get done. After school, that's my time to show up for her and be the person she needs me to be."

Though her days are spent doing work she loves, Jaycina admits that some aspects of her job are harder than others. "I hate the power dynamics of fundraising, especially in corporate and more formal settings," she says. "I still have to get over my impostor syndrome. You feel like you don't have anything of value and get that inferior feeling because you're asking for money. It takes realizing that it doesn't have to be so transactional and that we do have something to give to the relationship."

In that way, Jaycina's work with the Tender Foundation is teaching her many of the same lessons about perseverance and advocacy that she hopes to impart to her daughter. "It forces me to become an assertive, direct person," she says. "It's a lot easier for mamas to advocate on behalf of our kids than to stick up for ourselves, but I have to lead by example. I've learned how to have a voice and how to use it to lift others around me."

Advice from Jaycina Almond

MAKE YOUR APPS WORK FOR YOU. "Airtable is a superintuitive spreadsheet but can also be a form or calendar. You can use it to build out anything. And Zapier is a really cool tool that connects these types of workflow-management platforms. I can automate Airtable to direct Gmail to trigger out an email to be sent. So for example, when a client submits a request, they get a confirmation that we received it and an FAQ."

KEEP IMPORTANT DOCUMENTS IN ONE PLACE. "Every piece of paper that we would ever need lives in a Google Drive folder, labeled clearly. It's a lot easier to do that from the beginning than to be two years in and realize you have to pull all of your accounting and marketing documents from all over the place."

LABEL YOUR INBOX. "This is big, especially if you're a one-person team. You can sort your emails and say, 'Okay, I'm going to work on accounting today, or marketing.' And then you're not even stressed out while you're doing it because within that window you can't see the other emails coming into your inbox."

the culinary historian

Growing up in a small village outside Mexico City, Wendy Juarez never imagined she'd be an entrepreneur. When the Salt Lake City cook was just a teenager, her taxi driver father discouraged her from starting a desserts business in her neighborhood. "He thought any sales transaction was shameful, so I was always afraid of offering services or products," she remembers. "I felt like a beggar."

Wendy's perspective shifted when she went to live with her mother in Utah fourteen years ago. "She taught me that selling food is a beautiful and honorable business," says Wendy, who was a single mom at the time and spent years making and selling tamales to friends before she and her mother launched Prime Corn, a catering business that operates both out of her home and from a local commissary kitchen, at the start of the pandemic. (Her mother passed away from lymphoma shortly afterward.) "It's not just the exchange of a product for money but rather a friendship where both sides care for each other."

That level of care is at the forefront of everything Juarez does. Prompted by a conversation with her vegetarian daughter and inspired by the meals of her childhood, she cooks authentic pre-Columbian recipes handed down from her grandmother—the same healthy, plant-based dishes that she prepares for her family on a daily basis. The menus incorporate superfoods that many Americans—and even second- and third-generation Mexicans—have never heard of: For every bean or chickpea there are nopales, huitlacoche, amaranth, and more. "Our vision is to invite and educate people, especially the new generations, to maintain healthy habits in a simple, affordable, sustainable, and delicious way, stemming from the point that pre-Columbian cultures survived that way for thousands of years."

Though cooking is second nature to Wendy, turning her passion into a business required a Herculean effort. Discouraged by an overwhelming amount of research into the required permits and licenses needed for starting a restaurant and working two jobs to make ends meet, she nearly gave up on her dream. But a friend introduced her to the Spice Kitchen Incubator, a program run by the International Rescue Committee in Salt Lake City that provides affordable access to commercial kitchen space, instruction on proper food-handling procedures, and financial support to immigrants and refugees who are looking to achieve economic independence. She already had a food-handling license and an accounting clerk certificate from Salt Lake Community College, but at Spice Kitchen, she learned how to price out a recipe and understand her target client, and built connections with other food-business owners who shared their real-world experiences in restaurant entrepreneurship. "Dreaming of something is so different from making it real," she says. "The logistics, the funding, the time commitment—they opened my eyes." Thus, Wendy pivoted from a restaurant concept to a catering and takeout venture.

> "My business is my joy, my connection with my inner child, my legacy, my passion."

caterer /
mother
of two

With a $5,000 grant, Wendy purchased the licenses, permits, and basic equipment she would need to start her business. She launched through Spice Kitchen's rotating café space, essentially a three-month pop-up where customers could preorder and pick up meals. Along with grants from local companies, that provided her with the money to reinvest for additional equipment and entry fees into festivals and larger catering jobs. "It has been challenging, but it's also been the door that opens other doors," she says.

Now, during any given week, you might find Wendy guiding home culinarians in a hands-on Día de los Muertos cooking class; giving lectures on equity and diversity at the Natural History Museum of Utah; or cutting and prepping hundreds of squash blossoms for a weekend food fair. She says business has grown exponentially. Sometimes, she's in awe of what she's been able to do with so little. "Going to bed with the feeling that I did something important for my family, my community, myself—that is amazing," she says.

That idea of success keeps her going on her busiest days and sustains her in moments when she has to compromise on time at home. "My business is like another child," says Wendy, noting that she often has to trade off with her electrician husband to make the timing and scheduling work for everyone, and she sometimes relies on her now teenage daughter for help at weekend food festivals and babysitting (Wendy also has a five-year-old son). "It's like a newborn taking all of my money and my time."

But her children have seen the benefits of Wendy's sacrifices. "She sells candies, makes jewelry; at one point she was taking a little table with fresh fruit outside to sell to the neighbors," says Wendy of her daughter's early entrepreneurial efforts. The proud mom uses each venture as an opportunity to teach valuable lessons. "She'll say, 'Oh, I didn't make money,' and I'll say, 'Okay, let's see what happened here.' Other times she'll say, 'Oh, I made $200 in four hours,' and I'm like, 'Oh girl, good job!' She's learning in a safe environment how to make decisions and be confident in herself. And it shows her that although I'm busy and can't be there sometimes, I'm trying to have a connection with her and be present."

> "It's very rewarding for me when people say, 'Your food reminds me of my grandma's cooking,' or 'You took me back to when I was seven years old.' I feel like I am the face of my people."

Advice from Wendy Juarez

SUPPLEMENT A SEASONAL BUSINESS. "Summer is my busiest time, so in winter I focus on my family and my other passion: holistic practices. I'm either learning or training or coaching people in groups or individual sessions."

TAKE ADVANTAGE OF TRANSITION PERIODS. "I was working sixteen hours a day and could barely manage to pay my bills and my daughter's babysitter. I was a single mom at that time and felt guilty for not being with her. Then I went back to school. I spent a decent amount of money on tuition and books to get an accounting clerk certificate and started my generals for accounting. But I realized I paid more money than I had to get a job that was barely paying more than the minimum wage. I thought that, being in my thirties, if I had to start from the bottom on something, then it should be my own business."

REMEMBER YOUR PURPOSE. "There are times when things don't go as I expected them to, when I lose money in a business instead of making it, when I work harder than my collaborators and make less money. There are times when they make mistakes that I have to pay for, when I want to cry, when I barely sleep a couple hours per day. But then I remember why I'm doing it. It energizes me when people try my food and tell me that it is so authentic they mentally traveled to Mexico from the first bite."

the style icon

The French have a saying, *Mieux vaut tard que jamais,* which roughly translates to "Better late than never." Clare Vivier was working as a journalist for the same French television station as her correspondent husband when she began sewing leather laptop bags out of her home in Los Angeles. Though she had confidence in her product, she had zero contacts within the fashion industry and was intimidated by the prospect of turning her hobby into a full-fledged business. So she continued to make one-offs here and there, selling them to friends and family, but the project largely idled.

It wasn't until after her son, Oscar, headed off to preschool, when she had the mental space to process everything she would need to do, that she decided to make a real go of it. "That's when I had the time to focus clearly and be intentional. When I look back at that period now, I think, *Wow, what a privilege,* and I loved it, but it wasn't all roses and rainbows," she says of the three years she spent as a stay-at-home mother. "I also felt like, *What am I doing with my life?* It felt like my career was passing me by, and making my own money and being independent was still on my mind. I wish that I had just been able to enjoy the moment, but I don't think I'm really wired like that. I always had this ambition to do something else."

With her son occupied from 8:30 a.m. to 12:00 p.m., she visited fabric stores to find the hardware and remnant leathers that she sourced for her bags and took on freelance production jobs to fund her burgeoning company. She also revived old talks with a family-owned factory downtown, bonding with the wife over her passion and ideas. "She loved that I knew how to sew and that I brought in these things that I had made myself. I think that was very endearing to her. But my sewing abilities weren't as great as my ideas were," says Clare. "She took me under her wing."

Clare spent her three and a half child-free hours there each day, soaking up as much as she could about the fabrication process and expanding the styles and inventory of bags on her website. "It's amazing how much you can get done in that time when you have to," she says. When days ran long, a neighbor pitched in to watch Oscar. "She was so helpful to me in those first few years," Clare says. "She never was the type to make me feel bad about leaning into that offer."

Through it all, Clare maintained a sense of nonchalance about the future. "I think I was able to do this because I didn't put a lot of pressure on myself to succeed," she says. "I believed in my product. I thought I could put something great into the world, but I didn't have funding; I wasn't spending anyone else's money. I would spend $50 on buying leather and make something and sell it, and then

> "I was doing it because it was something that I loved, and I thought maybe I could make a living doing it. I was doing it for myself and my own financial independence."

fashion
designer /
mother
of one

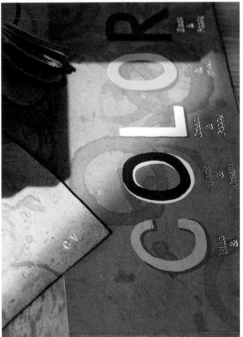

I'd make more bags. I had the luxury of not working full-time and not paying the nanny, but I can't be more clear that there was no money. And at the same time, I was taking freelance production jobs, so if the bag thing didn't work out I could always just do the production work."

It wasn't until six years later that things began to really take off: She sold 40 percent of her then eight-person business and opened her first store in 2012. "When I took on partners, my sales numbers were getting pretty high, and I didn't have any business experience. And I really wanted this to be a successful company and not just a passion project. I knew that I needed the business support. They let me run what I knew how to run—the creative stuff and how to tell the story of the brand—and then they were helpful where I needed them to be helpful: accounting, finance, HR, healthcare for employees, even just the structure of the business. I had never worked in a large fashion company before so I didn't even know the roles. I've just been learning this day by day over the past fifteen years."

At the same time, her husband, an investigative reporter who had traveled for work on stories and documentaries for many years while Clare was starting her business, decided to take a step back to be home with Oscar. Clare took the transition in stride. "I never felt guilty about missing anything because I read something early on that if children are cared for and loved they're okay, and I knew that he was," she says. "I knew that I was always available to him even if I was traveling. I tried to not have that cliché of what moms do to themselves. There were many family events that I missed because of work. And the world went on."

She also acknowledges how much her motherhood has informed the brand. "I feel like I'm so entwined with this business personally, but also motherhood is a huge part of who I am," she says. "I think that one

"There's no more important or noble work than raising children. You're raising intelligent, caring human beings that will one day go out into the world, and nobody celebrates parents for it."

of the best parts of being a mom is realizing that the world doesn't revolve around you and that you have to look out for other people and maybe put yourself second or third or fourth sometimes, depending on what is going on. That turns out to be a great trait for having a business and also really makes a great employee."

Today, her determination and willingness to adapt has turned Clare's small leather-goods company into an internationally beloved fashion and homewares brand, earning upwards of $16 million a year. But she doesn't rest on any laurels. "Success has always felt like a target that's constantly moving," she says. "The nature of business is that you're always looking to comp last year's numbers, and there's an amount of growth that I find fun and challenging. The fact that I can now provide livelihoods to over a hundred people is very rewarding."

Advice from Clare Vivier

MARKET YOUR STORY. "I realized early on that my blog was how I was going to tell my story. There was a nice creative community in LA in 2007, and it was a great way for us to talk about each other and create this wildfire. When I was starting my blog, I had that question of, 'Why are people going to want to read this?' And then I thought, *Well, I live in LA. Already that's big for a lot of people. I'm married to a French guy.* Check. *I'm a mom of a young kid.* Check. And then, *Interested in fashion.* It's so naive because now that reality TV and Instagram and TikTok are around, it's like, of course people are going to be interested in my personal life."

LEARN THE ROPES. "I always tell people as they're thinking about getting into this business, it's such a great idea to work for a bigger company to see the different roles.

It's completely doable to start a business without knowing the inner workings of a fashion company. If you have the wherewithal and the tenacity, you can do that. But it's an advantage to learn about the structure of these companies before trying to start your own."

MAKE A DIFFERENCE. "My mother was always so politically active and concerned with helping others, and that was very much instilled in all of us. It's wonderful to have a company that's been in a position to give back and have a voice on issues that affect women, our culture, and our community. We've been working with Every Mother Counts since 2015, and that has been a great experience. You don't have to be the biggest company to have a huge impact on raising awareness."

> "It's good to have a community of people who understand what it's like to own a business to commiserate with you but also help you celebrate the successes."

the design trendsetter

In 2018, people thought Sarah Sherman Samuel was crazy. At the time, the star interior designer and her husband were living in a two-bedroom house in Los Angeles that had started to feel a bit crowded since her second child was born. Despite being at the top of her game, and with her design studio and collaboration partners based on the West Coast, Sarah and her husband decided to pick up and move the family to her home state of Michigan.

"We wanted to give the kids what we had growing up: space and the ability to play in the woods and outside," says Sarah, who is known for bestselling home-decor lines with retail giants like West Elm and Lulu and Georgia. "I don't think we planned to do it so soon, but anxiety was running high. We were like, 'We gotta get out of here.'"

Not everyone thought it was a smart idea. "Instagram can be so wonderful for the community; it can also be so awful," she says with a laugh. "Some random stranger wrote, 'Why are you leaving now? Your career is just taking off.' And I thought, *What? I'm not leaving the world! I'm still able to work.* So that put a bit of fear in me. Like, *I don't know, maybe I'll fall off the face of the earth. I guess we'll just have to see what happens.*"

It wasn't the first time Sarah had taken such a life-changing leap of faith. Earlier in her career, she and her husband splurged on a fixer-upper cabin, the renovation of which

"Some days I'm a success. Some days I'm so far from it."

became the subject of her highly popular blog Smitten Studio and encouraged her to establish her design practice and take on residential interiors work. Spurred on by that initial success and after saving up for more than a year, she quit her job at a product design start-up to produce a capsule collection of picnic ware that she stored in her garage and sold on her website. Though she had no existing orders to fill, the baskets and linens quickly sold out on her site and opened the doors to collaborations with the likes of One Kings Lane and Pottery Barn Kids in addition to the relationship that she already had with Target.

"It's served me well having a design background but a different approach and having to come up with my own processes," she says. "It's definitely the harder way to do things, but you learn so much. Also doing all of the personal projects—the cabin and our house in LA—when you're so involved, it's basically like graduate school because you're learning in real time and real circumstances and all facets of it."

Like all of those leaps, the Michigan move proved prescient. "When the pandemic hit, I was set," she says. "People had to scramble to do what I had spent the last year figuring out. But it was hard. I thought it was going to make things easier, but it wasn't the case." Leaving Los Angeles meant losing childcare, a couple of employees, and an easy commute to meetings, site visits, and buying trips. What gets Sarah through the days is a carefully orchestrated give-and-take with her husband that's intended to be as equitable as possible.

"Everything has always been fifty-fifty, obnoxiously so, to the point where we'll be bickering about 'Well, it's my turn for this and

interior
designer /
mother
of two

"When both babies were little, my work was definitely my respite. It kept me sane to have something else to think about and break up the monotony of the early days of motherhood."

your turn for that,'" she laughs, noting that her husband went freelance after years of working in the advertising industry so that he could have the flexibility to co-parent. "Our conversations are always about having to make it fair, and there are plenty of arguments around what's fair and what's not. Life with small kids is basically that nobody feels like it's fair."

Now, nearly six years later, her gamble has paid off. Her children are thriving in Michigan, and her business, now a team of ten, is, too. Still, she continues to make sacrifices to accommodate her family. "I'm constantly turning things down to protect my balance." And work travel has become an Olympian feat in which Sarah adds an ever-increasing number of obstacles to make the trips as productive as possible.

"Archie hates when I'm away," she says of her son. "Whenever I travel, especially to LA because so much of my work is out there, I'm always trying to cram in as much as I can. This last trip, I had to coordinate the install of a client's house at the same time as shooting my outdoor furniture line with Lulu and Georgia. Within three days, I have to do twelve days of work because I don't want to be gone for so long."

It helps that when she's home, she's all in, whether she's drawing with her kids after dinner or doing school pickups or drop-offs. "I want to have a true relationship with my kids when they're older," she says. "I want to be able to have real conversations and talk about all the things. I want them to want to be close to me."

WHAT I'VE LEARNED

Advice from Sarah Sherman Samuel

GIVE YOURSELF A BUFFER. "I saved up one year of expenses before I left my full-time job to start my own studio. That financial preparation gave me enough time and mental space to launch my business and not feel the pressure to be profitable immediately. While making the transition, I took on all sorts of creative freelance jobs—graphic design (logos, websites, et cetera), event design, creative direction, and photography—which gave me the freedom to test out different roles and help shape what I wanted my studio to be. While I didn't know at the time how these jobs would help in the future, having that broad experience led me to develop the multifaceted studio we are today."

THERE'S NEVER THE PERFECT TIME. "Being an entrepreneur takes sacrifice, especially at the beginning. I launched my studio website when my firstborn was weeks old. I was in labor at home and emailing the final design files to the developer just before going into the hospital that night to give birth to Archie. I remember being thankful that I had already left my full-time job by the time I had my first baby because I had already gotten used to working from home and not having the social aspect of working in an office."

the dessert artist

Walk into BCakeNY's storefront on any given afternoon and there's a good chance you'll find a kid waiting for their parent's shift to end. "We've always had this open-door policy with our employees' families," says confectionery wizard Miriam Milord, whose children are fixtures at her Brooklyn bakery and have even been known to help out with a dessert delivery—so long as it's going to an NBA player. "Your kid doesn't have camp this week? Just let them sit here. Almost every day someone's kid is here."

In fact, during the Covid pandemic, Miriam did her employees one better: "We rented the bar next door and had the kids homeschool there," she says. "There was Wi-Fi, and we hired a substitute teacher to keep an eye on them so we could continue working. We're a small business so we can't have unlimited paid days off, but we try to offer what we can and are always flexible with schedules and childcare."

That flexibility proved crucial in her company's early days, back in 2008. Her first creation—a custom cake for a friend's baby shower—was so impressive it brought in a stream of orders that practically forced the former art restorer and gallerist to quit her day job and turn her new passion into a business. (She has since made cakes for the likes of Rihanna, Jay-Z, U2, and Jennifer

Lopez.) For the first few months, she baked at home out of necessity. She had just had her first son, and she had no seed money to invest in a kitchen space, let alone childcare.

"It was very much a scrape-together, eat-ramen kind of thing," she says of starting out, after teaching herself how to design cakes by studying at, in her words, "YouTube University" and using her earnings to invest in additional tools. To give herself time to grow the business while mothering, Miriam made an arrangement with another new-mom entrepreneur to tag-team watching the kids for half the week. "When I had the boys, I had this big play thing set up to keep them entertained so that I could email and promote and do all of those things to get my business going," she says. "It was a seven-day workweek, but at that point, it felt like there was no alternative because I had put so much of my own life and passion into the business. It *had* to work and it was *going* to work."

In a stroke of fate, Kris Jenner happened to see Miriam's cakes while scrolling through Facebook and asked if she could send one to LA for daughter Kourtney's first baby shower. "I remember saying, 'Sure, we do this all the time,' and then getting off the phone thinking, *How am I going to possibly get a cake to LA— and how am I even going to make the cake?*" says Miriam. "My approach was to say yes to everything and figure out later how to actually execute it, which worked most of the time."

When the cake appeared in a magazine, even more orders came in; she had to call a friend for help. "I was still playing catch-up on how to structure the business," says Miriam. "That's a mistake, obviously. It's better to be prepared from the start." But the money allowed her to hire a babysitter

> "The mom guilt is hard. What's the balance between what I'm leaving for them and what they need right now?"

cake
designer /
mother
of two

> "The responsibility of having employees is more stressful than having a boss."

and send her son to daycare, freeing up precious time to work on BCakeNY (though she and her friend, whose son went to the same daycare, were still trading pickup and drop-off duties). It also meant she could rent a share at a WeWork-style kitchen, then eventually open her own bakery with a storefront on a busy street in Brooklyn.

Today, business is booming thanks to Miriam's hard work and her mastery of a few key lessons along the way. "I wasn't very good at valuing my time in the beginning," she admits. "I would say, 'Well, I spent money on eggs and flour and this and that,' but I'd neglect the fact that I'd be working on a cake for two days." She also realized how to balance life and work with a more structured day and stricter boundaries. "I didn't want to be that mom at the soccer game who wasn't paying attention because I was on the phone the whole time. I've put a lot of intention into learning how to mom 100 percent and how to work 100 percent. I want to be fully in the moment either way."

enjoy
life
eat
cake

Advice from Miriam Milord

FIND THE RIGHT PARTNER. "My first marriage fell apart when I started the business," Miriam says. "We both tried to start businesses and didn't know how to manage the time and responsibilities, and there was a lot of resentment when I started to do well. It's a specific kind of person who will put their things aside to watch the kids or support you. It's important to find someone who can be in that supportive role, who can be an intern, a delivery guy—they're going to have to help you at some point. They have to come with a more flexible ego."

UNDERSTAND THE IMPORTANCE OF DELEGATING. "As an entrepreneur, you feel like you could be working 24-7. I often have this thought that if I worked eighteen hours a day my company would be doing even better than it is right now. That's the pressure. Once you learn how to trust other people, that makes a huge difference in your progress."

STICK TO YOUR SCHEDULE. "I wake up, work out, have time with the kids—all at the same time every day. On the weekend, I have certain work hours. For years, I'd skip my spin class for client calls, but now I won't do that. I really have to maintain those boundaries in order to be productive."

DON'T GLAMORIZE ENTREPRENEURSHIP. "I've been on panels where the women are perfectly made up with their crazy expensive bags. I'm coming in my sneakers from work because *that* is what entrepreneurship is like. I don't know when you had time to get your professional makeup done on a weekday. My counterpart was saying she enjoys not having a boss. I don't understand that. We have so many bosses: Our landlords are our bosses, our clients are our bosses, our kids are our bosses. I answer to so many people. I think being honest and realistic about what this team-no-sleep attitude does to women makes a lot more sense to me. It's long hours; it's stressed relationships. I want to tell everyone about how hard it is."

Don't Be Afraid to Ask Questions

It was 2015. I was eight months pregnant with my second child, swollen and feeling like my insides might slip out at any moment. Attempting to finance a self-proclaimed maternity leave, I was working feverishly to finish my outstanding projects when a well-known soap company approached me to art direct and shoot a two-day marketing campaign. I was completely unqualified (I'd been recommended by a very kind friend), but the pay was exceptionally good, and I knew it would mean more time with my sweet newborn. So I took the job with the caveat that I could give birth at any moment.

From the beginning, I was a fish out of water, but I was confident I could "fake" my way through it, even though I was a sweaty, limping mess; I barely even fit behind the tripod. As I clicked the last shot and breathed a very labored sigh of relief, the project manager said nonchalantly, "Once you have a second, just send me a link to all the RAW files." I started to panic. "RAW?" I asked, unfamiliar with the term. (For all you nonphotographers not gasping with your hands over your mouths, a RAW image file is the highest-quality image a camera can take, and it's the industry standard.) I had done the entire photo shoot in JPEG, a much lower-quality image that could be used only for web and social media. I was never hired again.

Looking back, I realize the thorn in my side was that I was too embarrassed to ask the questions I needed to, which, ironically, led to even greater humiliation. Damage to my ego aside, all wasn't lost. I left the experience much wiser, knowing not only how to run a two-day photo shoot but also how to ask specific questions. Being fearless about asking will help you get clarity on details such as technical requirements, timelines, materials, payment structure—any parameter you can think of. If you ask the right questions, you'll be prepared to do your best work.

That's the thing about running your own business: It's not going to be perfect, and that's okay. I've lost clients over being disorganized or being late. Mistakes help us grow; I do my best to learn from them. And you know what? When I've taken responsibility for my actions and honestly said, "I should have caught that" or "That was unprofessional, I apologize," I feel better and our working relationship is usually salvaged. If we give people grace to learn as they go, they will generally do the same for us.

WHAT LESSONS DO YOU HOPE YOUR KIDS LEARN FROM YOUR ENTREPRENEURSHIP?

"First, I hope my kids see that there are so many ways someone can earn a living for their family. You can choose to do something you enjoy. Second, I hope that as they experience a different gender dynamic at work and at home, they realize their lives can look however they want, and that they have responsibility for caring for their family regardless of how the world segments gender roles."

TRISHA ZEMP, PAPER GOODS PURVEYOR (PAGE 168)

"I want my daughter to know the importance of community and showing up for other people. We're stronger together. And I want her to see the merit in working hard and going after what you want."

JAYCINA ALMOND, NONPROFIT FOUNDER (PAGE 98)

"That my business is what gave them their mom. I grew up seeing my mom work really hard. The stress and distance she had to travel for work affected her mood at home. I want my kids to one day realize that being my own boss is what allowed me the space and privilege to be present in their lives."

CAROLYN SUZUKI, ILLUSTRATOR (PAGE 268)

"That it's okay to take risks. That you don't need to do everything perfectly right away. Just keep on doing your best, learning from mistakes, and adapting. That failure is okay and success takes on different forms. That hard work is important. And that work can be fun!"

VERONIQUE NGUYEN, KIDSWEAR DESIGNER (PAGE 68)

"I hope they see the beauty in the ups and downs and the fact that slow times for my business meant more time with them, while busy times meant a temporary pause in our family time but led to great rewards, such as a much-needed family vacation. I hope they know their mama was able to do something she was passionate about while also being able to be there for them."

PRISCILLA VEGA, MEDIA STRATEGIST (PAGE 34)

"That it's important to have a lot of identities so you're never too much of one thing (including Mom)."

SHANNON WATTS, ACTIVIST (PAGE 60)

the self-published success

Just ten days after giving birth to a baby girl named Ida, Justina Blakeney—the author, designer, and blogger behind the digital juggernaut Jungalow—had a strange compulsion. In the midst of a rough recovery from an emergency C-section, she began grabbing things at random off the shelves of her living room and setting up a small tabletop photo shoot. "I felt like I needed to do something that gave me those creative juices back," she says, even if it was just for a few minutes.

Though she appreciated her new role as a mother, it was clear that she really needed to get back to her work. For personal and financial reasons, maternity leave was not an option, and she had always been a worker, even if that work trajectory could hardly be described as linear.

After studying world cultures at UCLA and enrolling in a yearlong design course in Italy, she stayed abroad for seven years, performing odd jobs to make ends meet. In a stroke of fate, it was a self-published book— *99 Ways to Cut, Sew, Trim, and Tie Your T-Shirt into Something Special*—that launched her career. The book was picked up by Random House and turned into a series that had her writing fashion books and hosting workshops for the next six years. The editor and fashion writer then taught herself how to use digital publishing tools, calling herself a "creative for hire." She'd design a logo, then a website, then art-direct and style social campaigns for small female-owned businesses; eventually, the clients would commission the design of their shops and even their homes.

But while Justina thrilled in helping people share their stories, she realized ultimately that it was her own story she wanted to tell. Her passion for writing led her to start her now famous blog focusing on content creation and brand partnerships in 2009, until she was mostly working for herself instead of clients. Her fifth book, *The New Bohemians,* became an instant hit and a *New York Times* bestseller, establishing her as an authority in the home decor space, fortifying her design practice, and turning her blog into the digital powerhouse it is today. (On Pinterest alone, Justina has 1.4 million followers and more than 10 million views monthly.)

Of course, when it rains it pours: Just as Jungalow was taking off in 2012, Ida arrived. During that newborn phase, Justina's work and play were so entwined because she was still working solo and didn't have the luxury of an "out of office" sign in the window; at that time, she *was* the office.

But she is the first to admit how lucky she is when it comes to the village that has helped raise Ida, including her stay-at-home-dad husband, Jason, a freelance writer and editor who could work from anywhere. "You're probably not going to believe this,

> "When I had my daughter, it became clear that I really needed, wanted, and appreciated my work. I also needed, wanted, and appreciated being a mom."

interior
designer /
mother
of one

"Be all in for the long game. Then day-to-day setbacks don't shake you."

but Ida is nine, and we've had a babysitter that we've had to pay only *once* in her entire life," Justina points out. That's because the couple chose to settle in Los Angeles near family to have easy access to three sets of grandparents who live in the surrounding areas, all of whom were eager to help with their grandbaby from the start. It has been a unique blessing, especially given how little rhythm or structure there is to Justina's weeks.

As Jungalow grew, that proximity to home became a constant. Though she's been offered multiple television show deals, she has declined them without hesitation, preferring to limit time away from her family. Ida has become such an integrated part of Justina's daily work and office life since birth. "She'd be here every day if she could," Justina

laughs, adding that her office has been just a block away from home for the majority of Ida's lifetime. "She is our eleventh employee." So it was when Justina was a child, spending days at her own parents' residential treatment center for mentally affected young women. "I grew up steeped in their work environment," she says. "It feels second nature that Ida would be very involved and present."

Today, the business is more than just Justina. She currently employs ten people (four of whom are mothers) and contracts with a handful of freelancers and printers in an office she describes as "colorful, maximal, messy, and full of stories and music and fun." Now, of course, she can afford to take a few days off, but given how much joy surrounds her, why would she want to?

Advice from Justina Blakeney

EXAMINE YOUR RELATIONSHIP WITH MONEY. "When my business was starting to take off, I needed to build out a team and hired three employees at once—and then ran out of money within six weeks. Most of my money was coming in quarterly from licensing and partnerships. I ended up having to take out a loan, which felt like a failure because my parents taught me to pay with cash and to never borrow money. You buy what you can afford. It took me out of my comfort zone to apply for a loan and get a credit line. But the deeper I got in the business, the more I learned that everybody is working on borrowed money. This is how the US economy works. It's scary! Even now, I have a built-in discomfort around having high limits on my credit cards. But I've learned how to do financial projections and cash flow. The biggest takeaway was to ask lots of questions, talk to lots of people, and learn what I needed to know."

BUILD UP YOUR EQ. "Having people skills is the number one, most important thing in business and in life. Being able to read people, having empathy, being able to share, to be open and connect with other humans, is everything."

HIRE A LAWYER. "Early on, I made a lot of mistakes with legal stuff. I thought I could read contracts on my own. But I'm also very low-key and chill; I'm not litigious. I tend to think other people have that same orientation, but I learned rather quickly that's not the case. Having a lawyer you trust and who understands your business is worth the money."

LEARN FROM YOUR FAILURES. "You can't let setbacks bury you. If what you want to do is lighting you up inside and you're seeing small successes, you can build on them. I'm much more of a pivoter than a quitter. Along the way, there have been facets of what I do that I've left behind, but I think of it as growing. It's a really important part of entrepreneurship and of motherhood. If you're trying stuff out and it's not working, try something else."

"Self-confidence is key. In the creative world, but also in general, presenting yourself in a confident way makes others believe in you."

the shopkeeper

Three hundred dollars—that's all it took for Amanda Stewart to start her business, only she didn't know it was her business at the time. The stay-at-home mom was living in Berkeley, California, when she saw an ad for a screen-printing workshop in San Francisco. Thinking it might become a fun creative outlet, she enlisted a friend to join her.

"I thought I would like being a stay-at-home mom, but it wasn't for me," says the founder of children's clothing company Mochi Kids, who quit her job in banking when her son Stephen was diagnosed with autism at eighteen months. Though she spent much of her time fulfilled by helping him reach his milestones, many of them delayed, there were also some depressing moments, especially after she had her second baby and was doing the same routine every day—"feed, burp, repeat," she says—while she was deep in the newborn phase. "It just felt so monotonous," she admits. "I was always doing things like knitting, sewing, crocheting, cooking—anything that gave me a sense of accomplishment and self, because it was like I was living in *Groundhog Day*."

But the screen printing stuck and soon turned into a much more practical endeavor

than she had anticipated thanks to Stephen's very particular preferences. Like many two-year-olds, his interests ran from science and nature to Thomas the Tank Engine. So she tried to create designs to reflect that: a volcano, a cactus, the solar system.

It turned out they were hits not only with her son but with friends and relatives. She made shirts for her husband's family reunions and started hosting screen-printing classes that earned her enough money to buy supplies and her own equipment. Her husband, now an architect, was in grad school at the time, so there were practically no savings to dip into. And even though she didn't have a real space to increase production to meet the demand, she began to think her clothing-making hobby had some business legs.

"I was screen printing in the corner of my kids' playroom whenever I could—nap times, nights, weekends," she laughs. "It was great because I had no overhead, but I didn't have a formal way to accept people's payments." So she launched an Etsy shop in 2015 to allow friends and family to order and pay for her designs, but she was surprised to find that other people were also ordering. A couple of years later, she added a Shopify and personal website, enticed by their promise of greater functionality and customization, all the while still not realizing that her small home operation was, in fact, a legitimate business that could sustain her family *and* her creative needs. A Kickstarter—and baby number three—came in 2018 to give her the funds to manufacture a full clothing line. "It was a very slow evolution of turning my hobby into a business," she laughs.

In 2020, when she began to outgrow her basement fulfillment center and supply-

> "In the early years of my business, I did feel bad about missing some things, but I have so much flexibility now that it kind of balances out."

kidswear designer / mother of three

"Social media has democratized small businesses. We can see inside of them, and what we're seeing more and more is that women and moms are running them."

chain shortages exacerbated by the Covid-19 pandemic kept her sold out of much of her regular inventory, she added a small selection of toys and gifts to her digital shops. A year later, Amanda saw yet another phase in the evolution of her business: Instead of moving to a fulfillment center to meet demand, she acquired her first small-business loan and opened a brick-and-mortar store in downtown Salt Lake City. "I made a promise early on to not use any of my family money for my business—I just kept reinvesting profits back into the business whenever I could. Borrowing was nerve-racking, but I felt like people had been cooped up for a year and a half and were ready to feel more of a sense of community and connection. So the timing was right for me."

Three years later, and almost ten years after unknowingly starting her business, the gamble has paid off. The Mochi Kids store offers Amanda's signature kidswear and a collection of well-curated toys and gifts, but also book launches for local writers and a small studio space for community events and in-store celebrations. "I'm sure we could have grown faster doing it another way but instead we have grown very organically," Amanda says. "Someone recently said, 'I can't believe you're still doing this,' and I said, 'Me neither!' But it's been fun figuring it all out."

Advice from Amanda Stewart

Amanda operated her business online for six years before she decided to open a brick-and-mortar location. Though she made the transition in large part to help build a parent community after Covid upended personal relationships, lots of other factors went into her decision. Here are a few things she suggests considering before making the jump from the web to the neighborhood.

LOCATION

- Will there be enough foot traffic to justify merchandising and barcoding product?
- Are there competitors in the area, and if so, where are they located?
- Are there any territory conflicts with brands you want to carry?
- Does your target customer frequent your intended location?

DEMAND

- What will set your shop apart from other stores in the area?
- Do you have a niche that fills a need in the community?
- Do you have enough demand to provide the capital and cash flow needed to open and run a store?

DESIGN / FUNCTION

- Does the space offer customers a rewarding experience that online shops don't?
- Does owning a physical store satisfy a need—for instance, office or storage space, a fulfillment center, or a photo studio for digital marketing campaigns?
- Does a store give you the opportunity to diversify your business by providing space for events, classes, and workshops, for example?

"I don't consider myself to be a very well-connected person, but I have a loyal customer base, and that has made all the difference in terms of connecting me with people and projects."

the fast-casual pioneer

Einat Admony was just two hours postpartum when she learned that the posh New York City restaurant she was working at had abruptly let her go. That the news came from a colleague rather than her boss was only mildly indicative of how toxic the environment had become. Fortunately, the Israeli chef had a backup. A year earlier, she and her husband, Stefan, had opened a 200-square-foot (19 sq m) falafel counter in Greenwich Village, based on nothing but her nostalgia for one of her favorite foods and a tip she received from a friend who owned the café next door to the then vacant storefront.

Though the couple wasn't completely out of their element (he was a server at Bouley; she had worked in acclaimed restaurant kitchens like Bobby Flay's Bolo and David Bouley's Danube), they had no business plan—or even the slightest forethought about what they were doing. "I was complaining that there was no good falafel in the city or anywhere," she remembers. "So I thought, *Okay, I'm going to do this for two or three months, and then go back to fine dining.*"

She and Stefan pooled together $30,000, plus some money from a friend and cousin, and opened Taïm on a hot summer day in July 2005, all the while working their full-time jobs. "In the beginning, Stefan handled all of the day-to-day operations. I would come in early, from six or seven in the morning until eleven, to create, prep, and improve recipes," she recalls. "I was learning and understanding the fast-casual market in real time and fine-tuning the back of house before heading to my fine-dining job each day."

It was a lot of sweat, but Einat was used to being scrappy. A former soldier in the Israeli military, she came to New York with just $200 and the clothes on her back. But the art of feeding people, a passion she inherited from her aunt as a girl, had always paved her way, even when hardships threatened to break her. "I'm not a quitter," she says. "Even at the hardest moments of my career, when I was almost bankrupt, I never questioned doing this. I knew what I had. If you have good food, you're going to be successful."

Still, the success was slow going. After giving birth to her son, Liam, she and Stefan operated Taïm in near obscurity for another six months, relying on loans from family to pay employees and on their own determination to keep the shop from closing. "Liam was sitting on the counter or on my back while I was working all of the time," Einat says. "Many friends would support me, coming for an hour or so to watch him so I could help more. I felt lucky to have that support."

A glowing review from a food critic at *New York* magazine finally put Taïm on the map, setting off a firestorm of culinary praise from every newspaper, tour guide, and would-be critic posting on Yelp. Customers—including the actor Robin Williams, who bounced an eight-month-old Liam in his carrier while he waited—lined up around the block. And Einat and Stefan silenced any haters who had questioned their fast-food gamble. "All these people made fun of me for doing falafel, but look at burgers now, pizza," she says. She's having the last laugh.

In recent years, Einat has parted ways with Taïm, opting to focus on fine dining at

"My path makes my kids stronger."

chef /
mother
of two

her award-winning West Village restaurant Balaboosta, which, like Taïm, is a family affair. Her son, Liam, now a teenager, often stops by for lunch; her daughter, Mika, helps develop recipes at home; and Stefan is still handling day-to-day operations. Though her ambition and drive are still there, life has taken on a happy rhythm for Einat.

"Success is so many different things," she says. "When I was younger, I thought that a Michelin star would mean success, a James Beard Award, establishment recognition. Now I know that no award can define what I am and who I am. I have a beautiful marriage and a beautiful family, and I'm doing something I love. What else is there?"

Advice from Einat Admony

SHAKE OFF THE BAD VIBES. "For a long time, I felt like there was a boys' club in certain circles. I never felt like I wasn't respected, but it seemed like the men always got so much more recognition and no one realized that it was harder for me. They had wives who took care of the kids, but I was the wife. But feeling the bitterness is not a healthy thing for me. Over the years, I've learned to put all of that negative energy aside."

ESTABLISH BOUNDARIES. "I cook five days a week, but I don't ever want to work on Friday nights. I always have

Shabbat dinner with my family, and I always cook. If I have dinner with my kids, I'm not answering a phone. They're teenagers, so they're always trying to keep their phones on the table, and it's not happening."

CONSIDER COUPLES THERAPY. "Marriage is hard and very demanding, especially when you're working together. There was a lot that was unfair: My husband was making sure that everything ran smoothly, but all of the press and attention, all of the glamour was about me. It's good to talk through it."

the dream team

For the owners of the woven-textile fashion brand Ace&Jig, Cary Vaughan and Jenna Wilson, ten-day trips to India (where artisan partners weave all of the yarn-dyed fabric used for the brand's clothing and accessories) were frequently in the cards. "It is always a logistical nightmare getting out the door," Jenna laughs. "Cary's claim to fame is that she pumped and froze 199 ounces (5.9 L) of breast milk for Paul when he was seven months old. On our way to the airport, we'd be texting lists to our partners or parents or whoever was helping out. It's a lot on the family to have the moms missing in action for that long. But once we walked into that airport, we'd go straight to the bar for a farewell family cocktail."

And then they'd get down to business, refining fabric designs and checking on color and texture quality. But motherhood always found a way in. "We have so many great breastfeeding stories," Cary says. "Once, Jen's breast pump broke in India on the way to the airport, and we drove around to all of these places looking for another one but also trying not to miss our international flight home. We finally found a manual breast pump, which looked like it was a toy. Jen basically had to hand-pump the whole twenty-four hours home."

Most of the time, none of it fazed the pair, who say they were used to the sometimes feverish pace of business. They became friends as interns at the retail shop of a small fashion brand in New York City, doing everything from dressing celebrities to working with store buyers. They individually moved on to a few other brands, learning all the ins and outs of the fashion business and making the connections that would later help them start Ace&Jig. "We were running around the garment district, making friends with all of the trim vendors, delivering packages to get the last international UPS pickup in the Times Square Toys"R"Us, and leaving work anywhere from 10:00 p.m. to 12:00 a.m.," Jenna remembers. "Then we'd go out with friends and wake up the next morning and do it all again. We had so much energy back then."

Yet for all of their spirit, starting their own business proved challenging. They had rented, in their words, "a teeny section of a basement room" in a collaborative workspace in the East Village and, inspired by their shared love of antique textiles, dreamed of making their own fabric and garments from their library of lace and textile remnants. But finding time to work in their studio while putting in overtime at their day jobs kept their dreams at bay.

It wasn't until Cary's daughter, Alice, was nine months old and Jenna was newly pregnant with James (the Ace and Jig in the brand's name) that they finally decided to quit stalling and dive in—with a significant pivot. "Between the demands of working and little ones, we didn't have the time to create one-of-a-kind garments, but we did have the time to design one-of-a-kind fabric," says Jenna. "But not from antique cloth. We decided to work with master weavers in

> "Being a mom is similar to running a business: lots of curveballs and lots of fun." —JENNA WILSON

India, who have the technical skills to make woven yarn-dyed textiles that hopefully evoke a beautiful nostalgic feeling. We were going to make fabric stories." And using their connections and the knowledge they had acquired leading up to that moment, they did just that, designing free-flowing garments that eschewed hardware for a more organic, simple shape and construction.

After nearly fifteen years, Cary and Jenna are sometimes surprised but always proud that they've made it this far in terms of the longevity of the business. "We started when we were pretty young and it was the perfect time, but the industry has changed dramatically," says Jenna. "We feel like every week now is a crash course on all the new things—for example, there was no social media when we started. Five years ago, we were sold in about 150 boutique stores worldwide, and now we are only sold on our website. Things change quickly."

But they are equally astonished at the well-adjusted teenagers they have helped to grow. "There have been many times of doubt and insecurity," says Jenna. "There have been many failures. We have had to press pause on work for family concerns that arise. We pick each other back up and work through it all together, and we like to think that we are stronger and more resilient for it." However, there have been just as many instances when they've had to compromise their family time. "This pretty much happens daily," says Jenna, who now works out of a studio in Portland, Oregon, while Cary works out of one in Brooklyn (yet they spend nearly six hours a day sharing a screen and ideas from across the country). But they say they have "no time for regrets, only radical acceptance." Says Cary, "Our kids and partners know we work hard, and they respect that."

So Cary and Jenna—especially Jenna, who spent the first ten years of the business as a solo parent with two small children—embrace the chaos in life. "That was extra messy, extra

> "Policies and benefits that enrich quality of life are a priority to us, and so is work-life balance. We try to clock out promptly at the end of the workday and keep after-hours work boundaried as much as we can." —JENNA WILSON

bonkers, and at times extra thrilling," Jenna says. "Shortcuts are king. We skipped a lot of baths; now we skip a lot of showers. Who needs haircuts? We still eat breakfast on the way to wherever we are running late to. We have stains and wrinkles. There's clutter, but we aren't minimalists anyway. Baby carriers while doing everything is the workout." Cary adds, "Jen and I are multitasking queens, but we can't do it all. I definitely try to split as many household duties as possible with my partner. The key is making them take ownership for the category. For example: dental. The loophole is he didn't realize dental includes orthodontist," she laughs.

But on this point they both agree: Amazing babysitters deserve all the awards.

Advice from Cary Vaughan & Jenna Wilson

GET YOUR FINANCES STRAIGHT. "We have never taken any outside funding. We started the business with small savings we each had, and then fought hard to get approved for a line of credit with a reasonable interest rate, which has been helpful ever since. Small short-term loans from family members helped out in the early days, too. When we first started, a friend recommended the Amex small-business Plum Card. It has been so helpful for cash flow throughout the years. We have sixty days to pay and get a small discount if we pay early. This is not a paid ad, but every small business should get one of these. Between years six and seven, our business started to be able to finance itself, with our line of credit helping to smooth out the wildly fluctuating cash flow that comes with having to invest in raw materials up to one year before having finished clothing to sell."

BUILD STRONG BONDS. "We have a weekly hour-long 'team tea' where we talk about non-work-related stuff. We are a very close group and have been there for each other through life's ups and downs. All of our employees have been with us for over five years, and a few of them for more than ten! We are *tight*. We really enjoy each other's company, and our team is so kind and funny that even the most mundane spreadsheets aren't so bad at the end of the day."

IT PAYS TO BE A JACK OF ALL TRADES. "We do most of the business operations, finances, and legal stuff ourselves and have a couple of trusted professionals we have worked with forever that we outsource some things to (bookkeeping and shipping, for example). We all wear all the hats here since our team is so small, and luckily we like wearing the hats. There's never a dull moment, and plenty of curveballs, but it's never boring!"

"As business owners, things sure do pop up, generally when you are on a vacation with your family. You do the best you can, but you have to go with the flow, too." —CARY VAUGHAN

LEONOR PERRETTA

the legal advocate

For the last five years, immigration lawyer Leonor Perretta has taken a day off from work every week to tend to one very important piece of business: her granddaughter. "When she is with me, I am focused almost entirely on her and what she wants to do," says Leonor, who came to Utah from Uruguay with her family in 1972, at the age of six, and learned English by watching *Sesame Street* and *Mister Rogers' Neighborhood.* "Because I take this day off, I sometimes have to do some work in the evenings or weekends to catch up, but it is worth it to be able to enjoy her. I so value our time together."

At fifty-eight and nearing retirement, Leonor works much less than she did when she first started her law firm, as a divorced single mother of two. Though there were times when she wanted to be a full-time mom—and she was for the first two years of her oldest children's lives—she knew that she could provide a better life for them (and herself) while doing something she loved.

So she scrimped and saved to put herself through law school, attending classes while the kids were in preschool and relying on her parents for help in the afternoons and evenings. In fact, she only applied to the

University of Utah because of its proximity to home. "I knew that I would need my parents' help with the kids to succeed in law school and, more important, as a mother," she says. "My main concern was to make sure that law school and my career would not get in the way of my kids and their needs." When she got home, she was in full mom mode until they went off to bed, at which point she went back to studying.

Once she graduated, Leonor landed a job at a small law firm but knew almost immediately that working as a new associate wasn't going to peacefully coexist with having two small children at home. She also knew nothing about immigration law at the time—it wasn't a course listing in the late 1990s—but the firm pushed her into the practice, so she leaned into learning, buying treatises and poring over laws to become an expert on every detail of every case. Fatefully, two attorneys— another immigration lawyer and a criminal lawyer—approached her to share an office with them when she had just a year under her belt, so she took a chance and left to start her own immigration law firm. "It was a great fit and a good way to go into business for myself as we were just office sharing, and I'd have someone to help me set it up," she says. "I was actually not looking for this at the time, but a door opened and I went through it."

Being self-employed changed the game for Leonor. She could choose the types of cases she took on, hire her own team, adjust her schedule when family needs demanded more of her time, and achieve her managerial goals faster than she might have had she stayed on the corporate law track and waited to become partner. She also says the flexibility made her a better parent. After she remarried, she

> "It was a bit scary going out on my own, but my philosophy has always been to not let fear stop me from doing what I think is right."

lawyer /
mother
of three

and her husband were better able to juggle childcare so that she worked only three days a week for the first year of her third child's life, offloading cases to other attorneys at her firm. And when work was particularly busy, her kids would join her in the office after school so they could drive home together. (She later bought the building she currently works in and expanded into the one next door as her business grew to a team of sixteen.) But she also avows that sacrifices were always part of the calculus.

"Early on in my career, I made many choices not to participate in events that other lawyers would because I needed to be home with my kids," she explains. "I chose not to join Law Review or go to parties and extracurricular activities at law school because my children needed me. If I was involved in professional organizations after law school, I attended meetings and events only during the workday and not in the evening."

What professional doors those events might have opened is hard to say, but Leonor doesn't dwell on the past. "I have three happy, healthy, well-adjusted, and educated kids. They admire my accomplishments, and my daughter, especially, always tells me that if she can become half the woman she thinks I am, she has done well."

Now that her four children (she also has a stepson) are grown, Leonor has pursued other interests that she says she never would have while her kids were little. She currently teaches a class at her alma mater one semester a year, mentors new lawyers through the Utah State Bar, and though she has always been diligent about emphasizing her physical well-being, she has dialed up the intensity with an exacting CrossFit schedule and annual competitions. Then, of course, there's that granddaughter. Leonor says, "I just want to be Hazel's favorite person, and I work toward that goal every time I see her."

Advice from Leonor Perretta

DITCH PERFECTIONISM. "All working mothers struggle with trying to be a perfect mom, wife, and career woman. I am no different, especially since I am a perfectionist, which is something I have had to let go of somewhat in order to give myself acceptance. I accept that I am neither a perfect mom nor wife, nor a perfect attorney, but I try hard at all three."

DECOMPRESS BEFORE YOU GO HOME. "I realized early on that I needed transitions between work and home in order for both to go smoothly. By the time I am done with my workday, I am often stressed. I don't want to take that stress home, so I plan my schedule so that I can go directly to CrossFit from the office. I work out hard, release all the stress, and feel I can go on to my home life. When I am mentoring new attorneys, I emphasize that point. Maybe a twenty-minute walk, stretching at the office, yoga, running, meditation—anything that helps release stress and at the same time takes care of your body. After the transition, you are ready for your day at home."

DON'T LISTEN TO THE NAYSAYERS. "When I was applying for law school, several people tried to discourage me. They said that as a single mother, I would not make it through, and if I did, as a non-Mormon woman in Utah, I would never find a job or be successful. My parents, on the other hand, always encouraged me and believed I could do it. I proceeded with the plan I had had since I was a child. Once I make up my mind to do something I think is right, no one is going to persuade me otherwise."

"Balance is crucial when you are trying to raise a family and be good at what you do at work. My husband and kids come first, and I surround myself with people with similar beliefs."

Planning for Maternity Leave

With all of my children, I allowed myself between six and eight weeks of maternity leave. Usually though, I'd work a couple of hours a week, jumping on email and making sure things didn't fall through the cracks. Though it's not the twelve weeks (or more) of hands-off time that some companies offer, I much prefer the flexibility that self-employment provides after the eight weeks is up. It's a trade-off I'm happy to make.

Currently, four states (California, New York, Massachusetts, and Washington) as well as Washington, DC, offer some sort of financial assistance for self-employed mothers. For those of us in the *other* forty-six states, preparing for maternity leave takes a lot of planning, saving, and flexibility. I started making my clients aware of my pending leave at around the twelve-week mark. That may seem a little early (and uncomfortable, as I know what it's like to lose pregnancies late), but it gives colleagues enough time to plan accordingly and creates a much more compassionate work environment. Yet even given the advance planning, with each pregnancy I lost clients (only single male ones ironically; the women and fathers usually understood the struggle). You just have to be prepared for some people to not get it.

I'd also advise starting leave two to three weeks *before* your due date. This allows for early arrivals and lagging projects. I didn't set that early end date for my first maternity leave and ended up having to finish some projects at one week postpartum. Lesson learned.

In the lead-up, I always try to set aside a portion of each paycheck into a savings account to help tide my family over while I'm not working. If you start sooner rather than later, even if it's a little bit at a time, it can be extremely helpful once the baby arrives. It's usually still a very tight time for us financially, but I've never regretted making room for a leave. Those newborn snuggle-filled days are some of my favorite memories, and I wouldn't trade that time for anything.

After a leave, it's always hard for me to get back into the swing of things. I get anxiety and impostor syndrome mixed with postpartum depression. But I've learned I can start small. Not everyone needs to know when I'm back to work. I can start with my top-priority clients and work from there. Just take baby steps, and ask for help and grace as you get back into a rhythm.

WHEN DO YOU GET WORK DONE?

"When I'm trying to go to bed and I'm thinking a thousand things, I'll voice text to Notes so I don't have to have the screen in my face. And then I wake up to the funniest messages. I'm always like, 'What was I talking about?'"

SARAH SHERMAN SAMUEL, INTERIOR DESIGNER (PAGE 114)

"Sometimes when I need to get work done during the daytime, we'll go to an indoor playground. The kids get to play to their hearts' content while I work on my laptop and dole out snacks as needed."

MICHELLE LEAVITT, PAPER GOODS PURVEYOR (PAGE 168)

"I usually wake up when the world is silent—at, like, 2:00 a.m.—and I'm reading, I'm writing, I'm running things in my head in bed so that when I really wake up in the morning, I'm ready to go."

ADRIAN LIPSCOMBE, ACTIVIST (PAGE 164)

"I can't function without the Notes app on my phone. When inspiration strikes, I write literally anywhere: on the sofa, while watching *Bluey* with my six-year-old; at the playground, pushing my four-year-old on the swing; in the checkout line at the grocery store. The only work I do at my desk is after my daughters go to sleep, and it's copying and pasting and editing all of the snippets of phone text that I've sent to myself."

JENNIFER FERNANDEZ, WRITER

"I've definitely taken my laptop while I wait at my kids' track practices to work on nonprofit stuff, or sent emails from my phone while I'm waiting for my kids to get out of school. It's about making every minute count."

KIMI MATSUMURA, NONPROFIT FOUNDER (PAGE 226)

"I'm always working on the go. Sometimes it's on the subway or at a nearby coffee shop, but my kids have intensive sports schedules so I tend to be most productive during their long evening practices, catching up on emails and checking off preproduction tasks from the sidelines."

HEATHER MOORE, PHOTOGRAPHER (PAGE 202)

"I bring my iPad almost everywhere I go, so if I have an opportunity to mark up drawings or documents, I take advantage of that time. My wife thinks I'm a terrible driver, so I do a lot of work sitting in the passenger seat of our car. Even during a fifteen-minute ride, I'm able to get a lot done."

JULIE PURPURA, INTERIOR DESIGNER (PAGE 174)

the wrap star

Elle Rowley knows what disapproval feels like. "One time I got on a plane and posted a quick pic of me heading to an event somewhere," recalls Elle, who launched the celebrity-favorite infant carrier brand Solly Baby while she was pregnant with her second child. "A comment from another mother popped up right away that said, 'Wow, you leave your kids a lot.' I slumped in my chair and hid my face; the tears would not stop coming. It was a difficult work season, and I was already particularly sensitive and sad about traveling as much as I was. I don't think anyone would've said that to my husband if he were on the plane."

She composed herself, but the criticism hit Elle especially hard. "Solly Baby was fueled by my motherhood," she says. "Becoming a mother rocked my world and my confidence for a bit, but over time, it gave me a newfound boldness to try new things and explore parts of myself that I hadn't before."

One of those things was sewing. Elle had only basic skills—and a used serger machine that she purchased for just $50 on Craigslist—but after a bad experience with a commercial baby carrier with her first child, she dreamed up something more comfortable for herself and a pregnant friend. And then she kept going, selling her wraps on Etsy and at pop-up shops for three years to pay rent while her husband, Jared, was still in school. Every time she made some money, she'd put it back into the business, but mostly the couple self-funded with credit cards and small family loans in the early years. "I'd sew wraps in the sewing nook of our duplex apartment while my little ones napped and ship the wraps after they'd wake up, but I could feel there was more potential there."

Then the wraps took off on social media, Jared joined the company instead of going to business school, and the true learning began. "I'd had a lot of jobs but zero real experience or understanding of what it would take to start, much less run, a business," Elle says. "Looking back, I still can't believe I did it. I was completely unprepared, but I was open and teachable. I would say my willingness to talk to everyone and anyone I could about business was my biggest asset."

Solly Baby made its first million in 2014 and has since been worn by millions of parents and celebrity moms like Anne Hathaway, Serena Williams, and Pink. The company now makes up to $20 million a year. Of course, there were always difficult moments. "In the beginning, I was very sloppy with my working hours, but over time I have become very intentional," Elle says. She also admits that the company might have grown faster if she had prioritized it over family in certain instances, but that wasn't a compromise she was willing to make. "I think many people would be surprised by the opportunities that I've turned down over the years simply because I knew that it would be too hard on my family or me."

Yet she's content with the course she has laid out for herself and relishes the time she

> "Having babies and starting a business creates an opportunity for growth that few experiences ever could."

baby carrier
designer /
mother
of four

spends at home with her four children. For years, she and Jared happily (and sometimes unhappily) juggled childcare responsibilities, switching off mornings and afternoons to get work done. "It took us five years to get a real flow, but it was worth it," she says. "My hope is that it'll be that much easier for my daughters and son in their future families, having watched us work together." And while Solly Baby's warehouse is just down the road, she finds herself working from her room at least one day a week. "What can I say? My bed is *very* comfortable," she jokes. "I also really love working from home. I know I'll be interrupted a million times, and it can make the line between family and work a little blurrier, but I'm okay with blurry."

She's also content with the unexpected life she's created for her family. In 2021, she and Jared sold the majority share of the company—they retained 100 percent equity until that point—and are currently minority stakeholders who serve on the board in various capacities, from reviewing the company's past performance and future projections to supporting the brand's philanthropic efforts, namely a family center for Mayan mothers and babies in Guatemala. "I love that my kids can listen to my husband and me solve problems and take calls and make decisions and have epic fails and dream up life together. It's a part of our family culture that I am unapologetic about."

Advice from Elle Rowley

Elle started Solly Baby on Etsy because it offered her a gentle entry into entrepreneurship. Here's why it can work for you—and how to know when you've outgrown it.

THE CUSTOMERS ARE ALREADY BAKED IN. "One commonality that almost every small business has is limited resources and bandwidth. Etsy made it feel like I had a partner, but one without equity or feelings, which made life a lot easier in those early days. It gives you built-in marketing and immediately put me in front of a massive audience that I never could have found on day one on my own. Finding your 'top of funnel' is one of the greatest challenges in any e-commerce business, so to have that built in at so little cost was miraculous."

IT STREAMLINES YOUR OPTIONS. "I found that the design limitations around setting up my storefront on their site reduced the decision fatigue and got me up and going within a few days. Etsy was the easiest, cheapest, and fastest way to launch my minimum viable product."

IT FOSTERS CONNECTION WITH YOUR CUSTOMER. "Marketplace sites give you time to get to know your customer and how to talk to them. Receiving so much customer feedback was instrumental in continuing to develop the product until it was everything I and my customers wanted it to be."

IT TELLS YOU WHEN YOU'RE READY TO LEAVE. "My friend Susan Petersen, who started the baby moccasin company Freshly Picked, had just moved away from Etsy to her own website, and when I asked her why, she said, 'I had been watching where my traffic was coming from on Etsy, and I told myself that as soon as more than 50 percent came from my own marketing efforts, I'd take the leap.' I followed her example and am so grateful I did. That 51 percent was such a great litmus because it meant that I knew how to have a relationship with my customer, and now Etsy was going to start hampering my growth, not create it. It was time to flap my proverbial wings and go out on my own."

> "If I had put the pressure on myself to be like other entrepreneurs, then that would've been really stressful, but I made a conscious decision to be myself."

AMBER LEE

the video vanguard

VISUAL COUNTRY
BROOKLYN,
NEW YORK

When the cost-benefit analysis of attending an international networking event scales heavily in favor of the latter, Amber Lee usually finds herself visiting one too many airports.

"My parents have been extremely helpful in those moments where I've had to go to a conference," says Amber, a single mother of one and cofounder of Visual Country, a video production company that's worked with a range of big-name brands like Gucci, Amazon, M&M's, and Marriott. "Last summer there was one in Cannes. It's where all the television networks are, where all the people who are buying the shows are. So I had to take Bennett out of school; fly him from New York to Toronto, where my parents live; fly from Toronto to Cannes (and there are no direct flights); fly back to Toronto to pick up my son, and then fly home to New York. Just to go to a conference. I didn't have anyone local I trusted to be with him for that long, and that's a lot of responsibility anyway for a babysitter. And it's a lot for him, too. There are tons of things that I wind up not going to."

Not that Amber is complaining. She persevered to become a mother, undergoing two rounds of IUI and one of IVF over a

three-year period before her son, Bennett, was born, all the while managing the finances and day-to-day operations of Visual Country with her then life and business partner Meagan Cignoli, the company's creative director. But motherhood was a curveball. The couple had decided early on that they didn't want kids, but Amber's perspective shifted as she entered her thirties and the business took off, while Meagan's remained the same. "I was met with this hard decision of being with a partner that wanted the opposite life," she says. "We were together for eight years, and one of the reasons we stopped being together is that I went and had a kid on my own."

Thankfully, there were no hard feelings or professional repercussions. "It was very tough, and the business was not easy because there was a lot of uncertainty around whether we could make this work," Amber says. "The one thing we were always good at was being honest and communicative with each other. We're still the best of friends and business partners. We vacation together, she has a relationship with my son, and I have a relationship with her partner."

While all of this was happening, business was doubling year over year. What started as a passion project for Meagan—creating playful yet chic stop-motion videos on the now defunct video app Vine between fashion styling gigs—turned into a lucrative career move that brought in a million dollars in the first year, and that brands increasingly wanted in on as social media began to take off in 2013. When Meagan founded Visual Country, Amber was working at eBay—and not particularly eager to leave, though she was doing accounting and legal tasks for

> "I don't think I'm designed to not work. I've been fortunate that I love what I do. I like to do it in my free time when I don't need to do it."

stop-motion
artist / mother
of one

Visual Country on nights and weekends and the studio was humming with full-time work and employees. "There was a hesitancy because it was a good job and we were a little scared of working together. We were both very excited, but the business was also very overwhelming and led to a lot of burnout because all we wanted to do was talk about it, or one would want to work and the other wouldn't, and that would be a source of frustration." But in the end, Amber says they were well-matched partners, as Meagan focused on the creative vision and Amber dealt with the clients, finances, and strategy. "We really trusted each other and had a good balance of skills."

Once Bennett arrived, Amber, now a majority owner of the company, had to reinvent her working style. She had always been so hands-on—she says she was drawn into an HR dispute on the day she got home from her C-section delivery—but had to accept that she couldn't maintain the same level of intensity toward her career. "In the end, Ben comes first, so as a consequence, work has suffered. It's sad to admit, but the reality is the business got harder, and I often had to tend to him instead of getting to that thing I wanted to finish."

Amber says most people are sympathetic to her situation, but it's still a bitter pill to swallow. "It's adjusting to the acceptance that sometimes you don't have a choice but to put the work down," she says. "At some point, you're going to have to send an email that says, 'Sorry, I couldn't get this done, and we'll get it done tomorrow.' Most of the time it's okay. Since Covid-19, people in the corporate working world have a little bit more flexibility and understanding of the people who have lives outside of work, but sometimes you get someone who doesn't get it. And that's hard because it takes sucking up your pride and pushing aside all the moments in your career when you were very able to show up because all of a sudden you can't."

But for all of the juggling, Amber wouldn't change her choices. "I've always operated a little to the beat of my own drum," she says. "I grew up in a very nice home, my parents are still together, and it was a pretty ideal upper-middle-class life in Canada. A big part of me wanted that, but I knew that it would look different. It wouldn't be 'two kids, two parents, two pets in a small town.' It's Brooklyn, in an apartment, a business owner, traveling with my child when I need to. But I'm okay with that."

"We didn't know anything about stop motion, but Dolce & Gabbana wanted a campaign, so we learned. It was a little bit of luck and a lot of work and seizing the opportunity."

Advice from Amber Lee

HIRE A CONSULTANT. "We were expanding to kids' content, which I didn't know anything about. There are a few conferences that all the kids people have been going to for thirty years. So I'd go to them. Someone would mention a consultant in a panel talk, and I'd google them and email them. They helped me understand the industry, how to pitch a television show, how to get in the room with network execs that could make that a reality. It's almost impossible to become anything overnight on your own; it takes finding people that you can invest in, and who will put time into helping you get where you need to go."

DON'T DEFER YOUR PROBLEMS. "One time I was feeling very defeated, so I called Meagan and said I was going back to Canada to see my family. And she said, 'Just know that all the things you left are going to be here when you return, so you need to figure out how to make things work where you are.' In this situation, I needed to not wake up at five or six in the morning, so I had my nanny come early two days a week; I got to say goodbye and go back to sleep until nine. Meagan's callout gave me permission to ask for something that wasn't immediately obvious to me that I could ask for. If there's a problem, I can't run from it. I need to find organization here on my own every day. There are always limitations— money, time, people—but I'm trying to get creative to figure it out."

ADRIAN LIPSCOMBE

the black-food evangelist

40 ACRES & A
MULE PROJECT
AUSTIN,
TEXAS

Before the start of each year, chef, city planner, and community organizer Adrian Lipscombe chooses one word to guide her efforts for the coming months. In 2020, that word was *legacy,* but it has become a constant refrain in every action that she takes. "For me, everything is about the future and what our children are going to be left with. That is a thought in my head every single day," says the Texas-born mother of four.

A few years before that pivotal New Year's Eve, in 2016, Adrian and her husband had accepted an opportunity to open a restaurant in La Crosse, Wisconsin, with a revolutionary approach to revitalizing the community based on her studies of urban planning and gentrification as a doctoral student at the University of Texas at Austin. To complicate things further, they had welcomed their second son just a few months earlier, bringing him in a carrier during the restaurant's construction and then switching off carrying him on their hips before he was old enough to go to daycare.

"But I never looked at it as a restaurant because of the community impact," she says of her goal to create a gathering space

"I want the kind of life where my grandchildren run to their parents and ask, 'Did Grandma *really* do this or has she lost her mind?'"

for sharing ideas. "We were the catalyst. I wasn't coming in and saying, 'This is what needs to be done in the community.' We wanted their voices to be heard." She gave locals a platform to articulate their needs to city council members at neighborhood events, fostering a sense of shared values and accountability, and a dialogue began to take place. "Someone said they needed better crossings at the street corners, someone else said they needed better lighting; some leaders said, 'Hey, we need a farmers' market.' It was the community's perception of what they needed." In the five years that they operated, Adrian says the changes to the area were palpable as goods and services proliferated. "You saw single-family homes being bought up because now people were able to walk to buy their fruits and vegetables; they felt safe. There was the perception of a revitalization. We were trying to get people to realize their worth but also trying to get the city to realize how valuable this area is."

Despite all of the good they were doing for the community, Adrian woke up one morning with a startling realization: "La Crosse has some of the most organic farms per capita, sort of along the lines of California, and we got to see and know those Hmong farmers and the Indigenous tribes that were in the area. But there were no Black farmers." She began researching and found that less than 2 percent of US farmers were Black, and there were fewer than five registered Black farmers in that area of Wisconsin. "We started to see that there was this huge injustice and think about how we could fix it," she says. Her solution: buying land through established channels and partnering with existing organizations to educate a new

activist /
mother
of four

generation of Black farmers. "My whole thing was, 'I don't want to reinvent the wheel; I just want to make the wheel go faster,'" she says.

Thus 40 Acres and a Mule—based on a post–Civil War government order for land redistribution, enacted and then immediately overturned—was born. Using proceeds from a GoFundMe campaign, she partnered with five chefs and purchased land in South Carolina's Gullah Geechee region with the goal of preserving the techniques and culinary history of Black farmers and protecting Black foodways. Plans to erect a heritage center on the grounds dedicated to sharing stories of Black agriculture are currently in the works.

In the meantime, Adrian has returned home to Texas, giving lectures, hosting pop-up dinners, and fielding calls from like-minded organizations that want to partner with her initiative. She recently participated in a conference call with the USDA and White House aides—her kids were playing on the ground just out of screen. (She met President Biden in Wisconsin while she was pregnant with her youngest and kept those connections.)

That Adrian has managed to raise four children in the process is as much a testament to her resolve as to her boundless energy. "Half the time, I don't think I'm busy enough," she laughs. "I'm able to be home because a lot of my things have been meetings. But the way that my mind works, I don't think I ever could have been a stay-at-home mom. I like the idea of it, but I want to help change the world. Being a stay-at-home mom only provides that I would make sure my children would change the world."

But she also knows her limitations and admits that she couldn't do it all without the help of her husband, who works remotely and has the flexibility to be with their children while she's doing that important work. "I often wake up when the world is silent and think things could be a lot easier if I just worked an office job. But I did that,

"As mothers, we're multitaskers. We're doing a lot more than just holding a role in a business."

and I wasn't happy. I wasn't able to make the changes in the world that I wanted to."

In both her work and home life, Adrian hopes she has been a worthy model for living a life of purpose—*purpose* being, not coincidentally, her New Year's word for 2023. "My kids have all been raised in the kitchen," she says with pride. "When we had them, one of the first things we did was garden. We had beehives; we built an aquaponic system in our yard. We wanted them to know where our food came from." In Adrian's book, it's all intended to serve a greater purpose. "We only have a short amount of time here—a short amount of time to learn but also a short amount of time to teach. I want to make sure that when I leave this world, my children are handed knowledge and empathy and humanity, and the humility to move forward in meaningful ways for themselves and their communities."

Advice from Adrian Lipscombe

SET BOUNDARIES AND STICK TO THEM. "When we had our restaurant, it was open seven days a week for every meal. But I was missing having dinner with my family, so we stopped dinner service and got a little more of our life back. Now, my phone goes on silent at 7:00 p.m.; I really have to look at it to do something. And I won't take a meeting until after 10:30 a.m. because I have to go to the gym. Sometimes it comes to a head when things run across each other, but those are sacred moments within our family that we're holding dear to."

OUTSOURCE TIME-CONSUMING TASKS. "Handling social media is like a full-time job yet it's also hugely important when you're talking about branding and storytelling. But I don't need another program to learn. If anyone has money to spend, I'd advise you to spend it wholeheartedly on social media."

KEEP CALM. "Doing things on your own is a lot of pressure and a lot of anxiety, especially if you're doing something that you don't see out in the world. But if you're freaking out, who's doing the work?"

the sister act

There's nothing more frustrating than knowing exactly what you want to buy and not finding it on store shelves. But realizing that product doesn't even exist? Sisters Trisha Zemp and Michelle Leavitt saw that as an opportunity when they came up empty-handed after searching for a planner to gift their mom for Mother's Day. "What made matters worse was that the two of us couldn't even agree on what the perfect planner would look like," says Michelle, a former dancer and mom of three girls. "Trisha thought it should have lots of open space and plenty of to-do boxes for projects. I thought it should have a detailed hourly schedule. As we drove home from the mall, we realized that the perfect planner would be one that our mom could make for herself. We quickly hopped onto Google, only to find that such a thing did not exist. From that moment, we started brainstorming, and the idea of Golden Coil was born."

Eager as the two recent college graduates were, finding a printer that could produce each customizable planner on demand at a reasonable price proved challenging—and delayed their launch for nearly a year. The pair contacted hundreds of printers, most of whom laughed them out of the room. But they finally connected with one who had the technology necessary to realize their vision, and they launched Golden Coil on Kickstarter when Michelle's firstborn was only five weeks old. "We knew we couldn't move forward unless others believed in it, too," Michelle says. During their thirty days on the platform, they raised $105,006; an investor matched the fundraising goal, bringing their initial investment up to $200,000. With the printers and investors lined up, they were ready to go.

"One of the greatest aspects of running a business as a partnership is having two people's skills at your disposal," says Michelle. "I work behind the scenes, making sure everything runs smoothly—from employee management to data organization to daily goals. I'm very organized. I'm the child who would pull everything out of a closet just so I could put it back in a better way." That leaves Trisha to handle all of the creative aspects of the business. "Any video, photo, planner layout/page, or web page has been thoughtfully created by Trisha," says Michelle. "She comes up with our most creative ideas and has been instrumental in creating the brand that we have today." The other secret to their success: outsourcing. Because the printer binds, packages, and ships planners directly to the customer, the daily operations that Trisha and Michelle engage in are related to management, marketing, and social media content creation.

Outsourcing also gives Trisha the flexibility to be fully present in her other entrepreneurial effort—as a successful,

> "We sometimes laugh that we always want to sell our business in December, but when March rolls around, the thought of leaving is unfathomable."
>
> —MICHELLE LEAVITT

paper goods
purveyors /
mothers of
three & two

self-employed stop-motion animator who has worked with the likes of Warner Bros., PepsiCo, and T-Mobile. And it gives her time to include her two boys in her work, whether they're helping Trisha prop for a project or coloring alongside her in the studio.

"I have an open-door policy—I want the boys to feel welcome," she says. "My oldest has grown up being my studio baby. He often starts working on a little art project and then brings it to me and says, 'Mom, I made this for our videos!' Or when we meet new people, he likes to pipe up all the time. They might ask, 'What do you do for work?' And he will say, 'We are artists.' I love that he feels like a big part of what our family does."

That's because for the first three years of her elder son's life, Trisha's studio was in her basement. The ease of movement allowed her to work and mother more seamlessly, but as her businesses grew, so did the need for some separation. So she and her husband bought the townhouse next door and moved the family there so they could maintain operations in their original home. "If there's something that needs to be done with the production company, my husband or I can attend to it while the other takes care of the kiddos," she says. "And when I'm done with work and want to be with my family, I just walk over. I can pop home for lunch, or pop in at the studio when my little one is napping. With the two distinct spaces, I can now be more present in each space."

Yet no matter how busy things get, there's a prevailing belief that family comes first, a sentiment that is also important to the sisters when it comes to running Golden Coil. All of their staff are mothers to multiple children. "We make sure our employees know that if they need time off to care for sick kids or go to appointments, they don't even need to ask," Michelle says. "They set their own hours so they can navigate their family time accordingly." Trisha and Michelle hold themselves to the same standard, even if

> "I could have allowed motherhood to become my whole identity. But starting Golden Coil at nearly the same moment gave me room to let something else be a part of me." —MICHELLE LEAVITT

Michelle says she often finds herself "playing Tetris" with her responsibilities as a mother and business owner. "Trisha and I often step in for each other when we have to," says Michelle. "When one of us is postpartum or going through a significant difficulty, the other will fill in the necessary space for Golden Coil. To know that we can focus on what we need to as a family and not worry about work in those times has been a blessing."

Despite their success—in 2020, just four years after launching, Golden Coil had its first six-figure day (and made an additional $1.2 million) after a TikToker posted about one of the brand's planners—both sisters remain humble in the most endearing way. "I don't necessarily feel like a female founder," Trisha says. "That is exactly what I am, but my view of a female founder is this glossy, well-put-together woman running a team of employees, and that is just not what's happening over here. It's a no-makeup mom with a topknot, wearing athleisure in her basement and getting stuff done. It's not superglamorous, but it is really fulfilling and a lot of fun."

Advice from Trisha Zemp & Michelle Leavitt

WHEN WORKING WITH FAMILY, PUT YOUR RELATIONSHIP FIRST. "Trisha and I have been inseparable for most of our lives," says Michelle. "We were concerned that being in business together could harm our relationship. So before we even began, we agreed that our relationship came first, and that Golden Coil would never get in the way. Nearly eight years down the road, that's remained true. When something comes up, we remember our priorities, and it helps us iron out any issues in a really honest way. Another promise we made early on was to make all of our business decisions together. If a situation ever came up that one of us didn't feel comfortable with, we would talk through all the details and find another way to accomplish what we'd set out to do. This has encouraged us to be really creative! Making our decisions as a team has strengthened our relationship and helped our business grow into something we feel secure and safe in."

HAVE SOME PERSPECTIVE. "Early on in our business, Trisha and I did have the 24-7 mentality," says Michelle. "We were in the trenches answering every social media comment and customer service email. We allowed ourselves to be run by our business instead of the other way around. One day, we just sort of realized that there were no life-and-death situations when it came to planners. An email could wait until the next day, and a comment could be resolved after bedtime. It gave us so much freedom to remember that we had a say in how and when we needed to be available. Now, this is how we run things. Family always comes first, and everything else can wait if it needs to."

IT'S NOT ALWAYS GOING TO BE FUN. "I remind myself that everything builds on itself," says Michelle. "What's done in the less interesting parts of business work is what makes the big, amazing stuff possible. This brings a lot of intention to what I do and helps me meet every task with full effort."

FIND THE MOTIVATION. "Knowing that every moment I am working, I could be spending time with my family motivates me to be extremely productive when working," says Trisha. "Instead of dragging my feet on a task, I try to work as efficiently as possible so I can go home and spend time with them."

DON'T FEAR FAILURE. "When starting Golden Coil, I called my dad in a panic and told him how terrified I was to create a Kickstarter with a large goal and not see it fulfilled," says Trisha. "He expressed to me that failing is an excellent teacher, not something to fear. It is a part of innovation, and not trying anything new would be worse than trying and failing at it."

the hospitality expert

When it comes to seizing the moment, few have embraced the concept as wholeheartedly as Julie Purpura. "I got fired on a Friday, posted on LinkedIn that I was starting my own firm that afternoon, and received an email that evening about a project," says the Chicago-based hotel and restaurant designer, who spent fifteen years working at various design firms before striking out on her own with Avenir Creative. "On Monday, we got started. I was scared shitless but refused to fail. I also remember thinking that every day felt like Christmas morning. I was so excited to design and grow and see what I was capable of on my own."

Enthusiasm aside, Julie says the accelerated timeline forced her to start the business on the right foot, beginning with a lean budget that helped her scale the company without borrowing money or raising outside funding. "For the first three years, I didn't pay myself, and my wife's salary supported us," she says. Her wife continues to enable Julie to run her business, working from home and staying with their five-year-old son, Sebastian, when Julie has client meetings out of town. "Any money I made was put back into the company to buy laptops, build a website, rent a space, hire part-time staff. I wanted to hire a full-time employee and offer benefits, but I didn't do it until I had three times my monthly expenses in savings."

> "You have to be okay with a to-do list that never ends."

But the fast pace also took a toll. "I worked eighteen-hour days for those first three years, and it became unhealthy," she says. "I put a lot of pressure on myself to become successful." Case in point: In 2019, Avenir had been working with the Hyatt hospitality chain on the development of a new hotel brand. "I remember my wife in the delivery room, about to give birth to my son, with me hanging off my laptop answering emails," Julie says. "That was a really intense moment as an owner, and I will never put myself in that position again."

Ironically, it was motherhood that taught Julie how to balance her work and home life. "Since I owned Avenir prior to having a son, I had to learn how to carve out time away from my business to be a mom," she says. "I've always been motivated and career driven. Now, I make more time for my family. I work less, and I've finally started letting go of responsibilities and trusting other team members to do those tasks." She also began outsourcing to ease her workload, hiring a part-time human resources consultant to help with onboarding new hires and navigating healthcare and 401(k) updates, as well as a remote accountant and a firm that produces all of the company's 3D models and construction drawings.

But sometimes she does mix business with leisure. "We go on a lot of 'adventures,' which is basically going to antique furniture stores," she says of weekend day trips with her son. "I love the shop Dial M for Modern. The owner, Tim, is a friend of mine who happens to have very long, flowing, curly blond hair. I told my son he's a real-life merman, and that's how I trick him into vintage furniture shopping with me." Now, that's taking care of business.

interior
designer /
mother
of one

YELLOW

Advice from Julie Purpura

GO TO THE OFFICE. "Working from home is very challenging. Most of the time, I really need to put my head down and concentrate, or I need to be on calls, which my son loves to make himself a part of. Thankfully, the office is only a few miles away. When I need to review presentations or drawings on my iPad, I can do that working from home after my son goes to bed. I work about one night a week until 1:00 a.m., catching up on deliverables."

MAKE A SCHEDULE THAT WORKS FOR YOU. "Our team works ten hours a day from Monday through Thursday, so we are able to have Fridays off. When we have deadlines, our team puts in extra hours, but I make it a priority for everyone to work as close to forty hours a week as possible."

LEAN ON YOUR EXPERIENCE. "Working for others, I learned the complex design and management process that goes into programming a hotel and restaurant with a team. I learned how to be a good communicator, how to develop file structures and internal organization to keep everything in its place. This was all important background for starting Avenir."

Just Say No. (But Also, Say Yes!)

There's a really great song by the 1960s supergroup The Zombies, in which they pretty emphatically repeat the word *no* a whopping sixty-three times. Over the years, that little ditty has become a bit of an inside joke between my husband and me because, classic people pleaser that I am, I could learn a thing or two from that chorus. I never say no to work. Or at least that used to be the case.

Almost all of the mother founders in this book told me that at the beginning of their careers they said yes to everything. Though we may disagree with a lot about "hustle culture," the truth is that sometimes you have to hustle to make growth happen. In my first freelance year, I accepted every assignment that came my way, both because I took a volume-based approach to financial success (my mantra: The more stories I take, the more money I make), but more significantly, because I have a debilitating fear of letting people down.

So I wrote hotel and destination roundups—"Seven All-Inclusives with Out of This World Pools"; "Eight Great Weekend Getaways in New England"—for way longer than I should have. Of course, I was grateful to have those stories to lean on when I was starting out: They helped me pad my bank account, build up my portfolio, and create content that I could use to market myself and hopefully drum up more assignments. But after a few years I started to question my thinking. Roundups like these are neither well paying nor particularly esteemed portfolio pieces. And though I had hoped that these editors would remember that I had done them a solid by knocking these assignments out of the park and bring me along for the ride if they ever went to, say, *Vanity Fair*, I'd yet to see that pan out. If I'm being really honest with myself, I was afraid that people might forget about me and assignments would dry up. But accepting those kinds of projects only brought more of them, and they were taking me further away from getting the long-form narrative stories I really wanted to write.

The problem with saying yes to everything is that it's a drain on your time and energy. Sure, money is money, but taking on projects that don't bring you closer to your career goals keeps you from being able to say yes when really big, good projects that you truly want come along.

For me, this was that project. When Amanda reached out to me on that fateful day in March, I knew that this book was everything I had been looking for but would never be able to make time for if I didn't clear my schedule. And so, I finally figured out how to say no. I turned down lucrative writing assignments, knowing that this project would be much more fulfilling and in line with my future goals. And since then, I've found that the assignments will always be there, I might just have to push a little harder to get them. I've learned that saying no is freedom (as is setting boundaries—more on that in Amanda's essay on page 288). You have to say yes to everything until you don't, and only you will know when that moment arrives.

the best-tressed mom

Running a company together can test even the strongest bonds of sisterhood. That's why family therapy sessions became a necessary business expense while laying the groundwork for Striiike, the Beverly Hills salon and beauty studio that Ashley Streicher launched with her sisters, makeup artist Jenn Streicher and eyebrow expert Kristie Streicher, in 2014.

"We had a lot to bring to the table—we all had our own businesses that were growing independently—but figuring out how it all worked together in a way that was equal and fluid was a little bit more difficult, especially because we didn't have a plan," says the hair stylist to the stars, who spent her career buzzing around Los Angeles as a freelancer, creating red-carpet looks for the likes of Mandy Moore, Kiernan Shipka, Alison Brie, and Sarah Paulson. "We are very close, but at the end of the day, having Striiike made us better partners and sisters because we had to get some communication out."

Still, there were hiccups along the way. "We ended up going through several business managers because of how finances were split between the three of us," Ashley says, noting that Kristie needed the physical

> "Now that my son's in school, I'm a lot more productive in a relaxed way. I don't even know what I was doing before this. I was totally just winging it."

space, therefore paid more rent, while she and Jenn traveled to clients so paid more for transportation costs. "Having a clear plan and specific job titles within the ownership would have saved some *big* family fights." And they struggled to balance their creative yearnings with bottom-line thinking when it came to training a team of stylists and planning community-building events. But the sisters always maintained a strong work ethic and were used to being industrious to make things happen. The business managed to grow even when oldest sister Jenn became pregnant just after opening: "She's a natural-born hustler, so I think she worked more than she probably needed to," says Ashley. "She just strapped her son on her back and kept going."

When Kristie became pregnant six years later, Ashley and Jenn were able to manage the business while she was away, hosting wine and beauty nights and other client-building events. But watching her sisters grow into their motherhood gave Ashley a framework for what to expect when she eventually decided to start a family while maintaining her career. "I'm grateful that I was at least a little prepared mentally," she says. "I waited until I was ready, and even still it's crazy."

When the Covid-19 pandemic hit in 2020, and in-person operations had significantly slowed down, Ashley felt she had more latitude to reconsider her life and make some big transitions that had seemed unimaginable even a few months earlier. She moved back to her native northern California, bought a house with her partner, and had a son, Ansel, in 2021. (She is also a stepmother to her partner's eleven-year-old twins.) "The world had changed, and so I felt okay just letting myself be with him," she says of her extended

hair stylist /
mother
of one

maternity leave. "I don't think the previous me would have done that." The break also gave her time to consider her next steps. She had been consulting with brands like R+Co, Garnier, and Vegamour before her son arrived and decided she wanted more of that freedom. "Things are crazy again in a whole different way, but I feel like it's more my choice now."

She still cuts hair at Striiike for a week out of each month and caters to her celebrity clientele as needed, leaving her partner and the grandparents, who live nearby, to tend to Ansel when he's not at school. The separation is good for Ashley. "I thought that I was going to be the kind of mom where I could just bring him everywhere and have him on my back while I'm cutting hair, but that's not the kind of kid he is and apparently that's not the kind of parent I am," she says. "My time is better spent when I'm working without him. It's much better that he stays home and in his routine. But I only just have gotten used to being away from him. I'm a control freak, and it was hard."

Thankfully, her latest venture, a departure from both the beauty world and her sisters, keeps her close to home for the rest of the month. With her partner's family, she somewhat spontaneously purchased a hundred-year-old fruit orchard. "The way that it unfolded was all so seamless, and it just kept moving forward," she says. "Having gone through it with Striiike, I knew so much more for my new business. What I've also learned from the first time around is that owning a business should be hard work but it also shouldn't be *too* hard."

In fact, what she feels most these days is excitement. She's expanded the existing bakery's operations and added an artisan makers shop at the Orchard at Apple Lane, and she's started welcoming local schools for educational field trips and hosted dinner party events for industry friends; her partner is the on-site arborist. And no matter what she's doing or who she's entertaining, her sisters are, of course, always among the invitees.

Advice from Ashley Streicher

USE YOUR OWN MONEY TO AVOID COMPLICATIONS. "Jenn, Kristie, and I invested our own money into Striiike. We scrambled to get our pieces of the pie together and agreed for the first year nobody was going on vacation because we all needed to continue working our 'real' jobs to fund our new business. We leased this beautiful space but had to gut the whole thing. But then at that point, we had no more money, so we had to barter with the landlord: 'We need you to not charge us rent for three months, and we're going to fix this place up and it's going to be worth it.'"

HAVE A PLAN. "Not having a business plan didn't work out in a lot of ways, but we got through it. Could it have been easier? Yes. It just creates a bit more chaos, and starting a business is already hard, so I definitely used that lesson when starting a new business with the Orchard at Apple Lane."

FIND YOUR PEOPLE. "The thing that saved us is that we always worked with a lot of great people. Start finding the people you trust and who believe in you, the people who can help you and be part of your business and equally invested. It's like parenting. You don't want to do it by yourself. Find your community."

the fashion plate

Every February Sherri McMullen misses the first couple of days of Paris Fashion Week for one very important reason: her son's birthday. It's not ideal for someone whose job is finding and acquiring the newest pieces by emerging designers from across the globe for her destination fashion boutique, but the founder and CEO of McMullen in Oakland, California, wouldn't have it any other way.

"I prioritize my son and I don't feel guilty about that," Sherri says matter-of-factly. "There's always going to be another fashion week. I'm at a place in my career where I can set my own schedule, and I'm embracing that."

It wasn't always so. "There were times, especially in the beginning when Frederick was born, when there was this fear of my business failing," says Sherri, a single mother who relies on her co-parent when she's away on buying trips about four times a year. "I had built this business for eight years, and we were in a groove, and I felt that if I wasn't at the store every day, it was going to come off the rails."

Part of the reason the stakes seemed so high was because she had self-financed the store, scraping and saving to make her dream happen when others doubted her determination. "Financing the company was the hardest thing because I could not get funding from banks," she says, despite her credentials and experience as a former buyer for Neiman Marcus and Williams-Sonoma Inc. "I was thinking, *Here I am. I have a business degree, I've studied accounting, I have a business plan.* In my mind, I was the perfect candidate to get a loan for this." It wasn't the first time her credentials had failed her. "Being a Black woman, I was one of the few in the building in a position to buy and make decisions about product," she says of her corporate life. "Every company I worked for, I saw few people who looked like me. I felt like I had to work two or three times harder than some of my counterparts just to be recognized. I had a very strong, growing, profitable business, but I felt like I wasn't getting the recognition that I fully deserved. That's when I was really thinking, *Is this satisfying me?* and *How much longer am I going to be able to sustain this work life?*"

Despite the setback, Sherri rallied friends and family and was able to pay back $50,000 (with interest) in personal loans in her first three years in business, then continued to secure infusions of money for the boutique (and pay them back) whenever things got tight.

"I had to become incredibly resourceful throughout the process," Sherri says. "I was coordinating with contractors to build out the space, and they were still laying down flooring just two days before the store's opening. The invitations were already sent, and I was thinking, *Oh my God, are we going to be able to pull this off?* Thankfully, my friends came to the rescue, helping with everything from merchandising to hanging fixtures, since we didn't have the budget

> "As women, I believe we should have something for ourselves that brings some type of grounding or fulfillment."

boutique
owner /
mother
of one

"My son understands how important McMullen is for me, and that makes me happy."

for any staff at the time. Our fixtures and furniture were mostly secondhand, sourced wherever I could find them. Despite the tight budget, we somehow made it work."

The anxiety of it all forced her into making decisions she wouldn't dream of making now, including an abbreviated maternity leave (two weeks) and even sending out newsletters from her postpartum hospital bed. But those moments also revealed her own resilience and the strength of her commitment to her business. "I definitely feel like I did something that I'm proud of," she says. "I've been able to continue to run this company on my own for sixteen years." She currently has a staff of ten people, including a head of partnerships and marketing. "I'm at a really good place where I can take time off if I need to."

Like the team that now supports her, motherhood also encouraged her to slow down and appreciate her hard work even more. "I felt like I was on this wheel, working nonstop, constantly traveling all the time," she says. "Having my son changed everything. Everything that I was doing had a different meaning. Now, I think about my son seeing me, a working mother owning my own business, and how powerful it is for him to know that he, too, can own his own business and do anything he wants to do."

Her son is older now, but she relishes the time she spent with him on the clock while he was young. "Having him crawling around the store or in the sling, traveling to New York or Paris with him on buying trips—that was just part of our world," she says. "Those times were challenging, but I have no regrets."

WHAT I'VE LEARNED
Advice from Sherri McMullen

GET HANDS-ON. "There's nothing that I don't understand about my business—I've touched every part of it. Even if there's something I don't know, I'm going to look into it, research it, and figure it out."

ASK FOR HELP. "It was really scary at first, because as a single mother I didn't have a lot of options in terms of getting someone to be with my son while I was working. When I wasn't carrying him in a sling at the store, friends helped out with visits and stroller rides to a neighboring garden. Anything so that I could have two hands to type out an email."

FIND YOUR NICHE. "At McMullen, our focus has always been on curation. You can have a great business if you have great service and a differentiated, highly selective assortment of products. If you combine those two things and do it in your own way, you can succeed. From the outset, I was passionate about championing young and emerging designers. While contemporary and high-end brands were prevalent, there was a gap for those just starting out. These designers were true artists, offering well-crafted products with a distinct point of view. They simply needed a platform to showcase their talent."

the mother-daughter team

The trials and tribulations of mother-daughter relationships have been fodder for books, movies, and television for obvious reasons: For all of the unconditional love, the conflicts can be pretty spectacular. But that threat didn't stop Joyce Zhu and her mom, Jane, from starting Numa Foods together.

When Joyce was traveling across the country as a management consultant for work, she found herself in places often described as food deserts, areas where there was little access to healthy snacks and meals. For someone suffering from an autoimmune disease and a sweet tooth, as she was, the options were few. So Jane did what any mother would: She whipped up batches of Joyce's favorite childhood candies using a fourth-generation recipe for low-sugar, high-protein milk nougat taffies made with all-natural ingredients, and sent her daughter on her way. Joyce began sharing the candies with friends and coworkers, who all raved about them enough to encourage Joyce to seek out others who might pay to try them. She and Jane took them to local New Jersey farmers' markets on the weekends, and the reactions there were just as positive. Before they knew it, Joyce had plans to quit her consulting job and pursue Numa full-time.

But not everyone in the family thought it was a good idea. "Initially she had a very difficult time with us," says Jane. "We weren't sure if it was the right thing for her. As a mother, you always worry about your daughter's future. You want her to have a good career, a good relationship, and you see your friends' children have boyfriends, get married, find good jobs. Your daughter has a totally different path, and you feel unsure. *Is she going to waste her time?* Those thoughts were always in my mind."

But Jane and her husband eventually supported Joyce's decision—and she came out of an early retirement to help her daughter turn Numa into a first-to-market product unique to the US commercial landscape. The family invested $100,000 in an 800-square-foot (74 sq m) facility in Pennsylvania, a couple of stand mixers, and a flow wrapping machine—Jane and Joyce imported and installed all of the machinery themselves, with many support calls to their manufacturers in China—plus bulk orders of real ingredients like coconut and maltose (brown rice syrup).

"Being a family-owned company with few connections, we rolled up our sleeves and basically bootstrapped this whole business," says Joyce of their hands-on process for launching Numa. "We're probably unique in that my mom and I have outsourced very little and done everything ourselves up till now. Looking back we would have loved to, but with the nature of our product, it wasn't an option."

Naturally, mistakes were made. "We spent a long time figuring out how to scale that recipe and get it from our home kitchen to a batch that was twenty times larger," says Joyce. She recalls one instance when they spent two weeks in that small room, attempting to get sugar syrup to boil to the

> "The learning curve is quite steep, and we're both climbing it together." —JOYCE ZHU

snack food
makers /
mother &
daughter

right temperature. "We thought we were going to die," laughs Joyce. And mother and daughter haven't always seen eye to eye. "We definitely have had our fair share of fights where tensions were high across the business," she says. "In those moments, it was most important to separate for a day or two and sit with our own thoughts. Eventually, we'd get back together when we could talk more reasonably about it. I would say friction is natural with any entrepreneurial partner relationship. It works for us because we have very complementary skills, where my mom is in charge of handling all of our vendor relationships in China and Vietnam, and then I do almost everything else."

But through it all, what has kept Jane and Joyce going is their commitment to each other and the shared knowledge that the business has brought much more nuance to their already strong bond. "The fact that I've been able to evolve my relationship with my parents on a much deeper level has been very rewarding," says Joyce. "We've always had a good relationship, but we have a deeper understanding now than ever before."

The feeling is mutual for Jane. "Before, it was just a mother-daughter relationship, and in terms of being business partners, the roles are changing," Jane says. "I found that Joyce has other capabilities that I never knew about. I see another side to her. And I've learned how to adjust myself to support her. I give her my thoughts, but in the end, I follow her decisions. When you are in business, you have a lot of time in the dark, in emotional situations—how do you control your emotions? I've learned a lot from her. So, in six years we've come to know each other very well. Not only like a mother and a daughter but each as a person. Our family has a stronger relationship because we support each other. It is a beautiful thing."

Jane's also learned how to be a better parent in the process. "Lots of parents think

> "I think nothing I've ever done in my life has taught me so much at such a high rate and on such a personal level."
>
> —JOYCE ZHU

of their kids as kids, not maturing, always the same," she says. "You worry that their opinions are different from yours; you think they're wrong because they're young. This is all wrong. Each generation has their own time and vision. You just need to trust them."

Advice from Joyce Zhu

LISTEN TO YOUR CONSUMERS. "Our customers are the heart and soul of the whole business. We read every single Amazon and website review that we receive, and we've done so much recipe refinement based on consumer feedback. We also like to speak with people at in-store demos and pop-up events. Doing that has been the key factor to actually growing the business."

PRIORITIZE COMPASSION. "All of our workers to this point have been non-English-speaking immigrants, many from China, and they come and do very tedious manual labor that can be hard on your body. We understand that because we did it ourselves. Formulating how we compensate them can be very difficult for a small business, especially when margins are fluctuating. Partly because of my mom, we always led with heart and were very conscientious and thought of these laborers as a part of our small family. And that has paid off in spades because of their commitment to the company."

HAVE A MEDIATOR FOR DIFFICULT DECISIONS. "When we can't agree on something, we'll sometimes go to my dad. I can overthink and hold a lot on my plate all the time. My mom is a people person, and she is very boisterous. My dad is levelheaded and strategic and logical, so he often is a good mediator between the two of us."

the design mom

In the fall of 2008, while most of the country was melting down over the subprime mortgage crisis, Gabrielle Stanley Blair was busy practically begging bloggers to attend her brand-new conference in Salt Lake City called Altitude Design Summit. "We made zero money that first year," says Gabrielle, the writer behind Design Mom, one of the original and most transformative blogs of the early aughts. "But it was incredible. The very first panel was Maxwell Ryan from Apartment Therapy, Heather Armstrong from Dooce, Grace Bonney from Design*Sponge, and Jean Aw of NOTCOT. You couldn't have had bigger names. And then Ben Silbermann—who had a little website called Pinterest, which was just in beta—was walking around trying to get people to check out his website. SFGirlByBay was there. It was just insane."

By her own account, Gabrielle was simply trying to re-create the friendly camaraderie of her comments section. The former ad agency art director had attended mom blog conferences in the past and was moved by their rah-rah spirit, but had been disappointed by the lack of design content creators present. So her sister Sarah, who had experience in event planning, suggested

they team up to start a conference of their own. Making use of empty assembly rooms in hotels booked for the Sundance Film Festival, the sisters planned a week of events to help bloggers connect and learn from each other about social media strategies and the merits of WordPress versus Squarespace. But almost from the beginning, Alt Summit, as it came to be known, was ground zero for creative, mostly female entrepreneurs and influencers striking deals and taking their digital businesses to the next level.

"We had all of these photos from the first Alt Summit, so there was momentum for the next one," Gabrielle says. "Sponsors, speakers, and publishers would come to meet these bloggers; there were ad executives and network executives trying to recruit new names. Ben Silbermann came back as a keynote—Pinterest had just taken off because he had gotten people from Alt Summit to use his website, and they were populating it with millions of images, just the most gorgeous content. It was so lovely. Everybody wanted to be at Alt Summit."

Eventually, everyone was. Jessica Alba, Martha Stewart, and Joanna Gaines all made appearances. But back in 2006, when Gabrielle was just beginning to dip her toe into the blogosphere, she could never have imagined that her maternity-leave hobby would give rise to the leading business conference for creative entrepreneurs. When she had her fifth baby at the age of thirty-one, she was already in the habit of dispensing wisdom to her friends and family about everything from the coolest kids' shoes to the best potty-training strategies. Stuck at home with a newborn and a toddler, she realized that she could help a larger audience

> "I was nursing and writing. I was working in the cracks, in the in-betweens. I would squeeze it in where I could."

blogger /
mother
of six

> ## "I could probably grow Alt Summit ten times bigger than it is; I could have fifty employees. But I am unwilling to make that sacrifice because of what it would do to my family."

while banishing baby blues by satisfying her creative itch and launching a blog.

"I obviously had experience having babies at that point, so I knew I was going to be facing postpartum depression unless I had something creative going on," she says. "So I was thinking, *What can I do that's creative that has no time or schedule constraints? Maybe I could do a design blog.* And then I was thinking about what I could write about. I was working in design and I had such an identity as a mother. So I decided I was going to look at the world through a design lens. I knew right away Design Mom would be a great name for me, and my tagline from the beginning was 'The intersection of design and motherhood.'"

But she ended up writing about all sorts of things. Politics, gun violence, elections—everything was fair game because motherhood touched everything. "I loved discovering that I could talk about whatever I wanted," she says, noting that she found her voice the more she practiced. She also loved that she could do it at her will, whether that was while feeding her baby in the dead of night or while her toddler and newborn napped in the middle of the day, and that connected her to a world of mothers who

were going through exactly what she was in real time.

"It changed motherhood for me in an amazing way," Gabrielle says. "I found motherhood challenging and fulfilling in certain ways but also so frustrating because there was no acknowledgment of what you did in a day. At a job, I got a paycheck and a promotion and someone told me, 'Good job' and 'Five stars.' You get this validation and acknowledgment. As a mother, you get zero. Blogging changed that. To be able to write about something I'd done with my kids that I felt so good about, all these other mothers recognize that as an accomplishment. But in normal everyday life, you tell that to your spouse and they're like, 'Okay.' It was delightful."

Within a few months, Gabrielle was trying to figure out how to make her blog a full-time gig. To teach people how to comment on her posts, she created the first-ever blog giveaway and implemented a bit of coding to track the number of people visiting the site. "It blew my mind," she says of learning that hundreds of people were clicking through daily, not just the three that she would see commenting. "It changed the way people thought about Design Mom. And then the numbers just took off from there."

As the site grew, she courted advertisers; bought her sister out, then took over and expanded Alt Summit; wrote a book called *Design Mom: How to Live with Kids: A Room-by-Room Guide*; and moved from New York to Colorado to California to France, where she currently lives, bringing her readers along for the ride. She says she was able to do it all—with six kids no less—because her husband also worked remotely for a Washington, DC–based educational firm after getting his PhD, at a time when that was the exception rather than the rule, and has shared all of the home and child-rearing tasks. "There are years where it's not feeling very balanced," she says. "Sometimes he's in a building phase or I am. Anytime you can see something amazing happening in my life, my book just came out or whatever, that means I've dropped the ball on something else. That's something I've gotten used to. There's always going to be laundry; there's always going to be dishes. The idea that you can cross these things off a list is silly."

In the end, blogging has allowed her to make the most of both her creative career and her motherhood, even if it does sometimes come with twelve-hour workdays. With her flexible schedule, she's been able to write another book, the bestselling *Ejaculate Responsibly: A Whole New Way to Think About Abortion*, her manifesto on reproductive rights. And her

children have traveled the world with her. "Overall, I'm really happy with the decisions I've made," she says. "It's meant so much time with my kids that other kids don't always get, and a great relationship with my spouse, which is also great for your kids if you can manage it. There's just no way I write *Ejaculate Responsibly*, which is really important to me, if I keep working in New York as an art director. But it is relentless at times. Some people that build a thing have an exit strategy. I wish I was a genius businessperson like that, but I'm not. I'm in it for creative reasons. I don't think I would have been happy in another scenario."

Advice from Gabrielle Stanley Blair

MAKE MISTAKES. "I feel like the two biggest strengths of the internet are speed and changeability. If there's something you want to do, do it fast, and don't worry, because it's changeable. When I would do signage and letterhead, if there was a typo, there was no money to reprint that. But if you make a mistake on a website, you just change it the next day. No one is watching yet as you're building. Anyone reading it at first already loves you. If you don't have a good writing voice yet, it doesn't matter. Start. Start it today because you can. If you don't like it tomorrow, you'll change it."

DEVELOP A THICKER SKIN. "From the beginning, there has always been someone saying I'm doing it wrong or I'm not representing moms correctly, or Mormons, or women in business. I'm always making someone mad. I have had to get to a place where I remember

that these people are literal strangers to me. Usually, I'm pretty good about managing it, but every once in a while I'll get a comment that digs at me, and it's probably because I recognize the truth in it and don't know what to do about it."

WRITE, EVEN IF YOU'RE NOT A WRITER. "I wasn't in writing classes, but I was writing so much. You end up crafting hundreds of blog posts a year, so you're going to get better and learn how to express yourself better and see what people respond to. That's true of any kind of writing, whether it's Twitter or Instagram or Substack. You don't want to have to defend yourself because you said something poorly or didn't say it clearly, so you're forced to learn. Learning how to write as clearly as possible is almost like a defense mechanism. I was trained in the real-life school of that."

"The energy at Alt Summit is so good. You have all of these very successful women sharing every secret they've ever learned and holding nothing back. It's amazing. I love amplifying women's voices."

the portrait artist

Heather Moore thought that she would thrive as a stay-at-home mother. When she and her husband moved to small-town Texas after college for his work, she put all of her energy into getting pregnant and starting a family. But when the moment arrived, she was faced with a harsh reality. "I just couldn't sit still," the mother of two says. "The hours of nursing on the couch felt endless. It felt like I was in the same spot for the majority of the day, which made me anxious."

To pass the time and keep her spirits up, she decided to focus on her new daughter, Penelope. Wanting to document her growth in a more personal way—and without the cheesy bows and headbands that were a hallmark of the early 2010s—Heather turned to photography, a childhood interest that had been a diverting pastime with her brothers growing up but never managed to take hold as a hobby. "I genuinely had zero knowledge; I never took a class in high school or anything. I just thought that since I was spending so much time on the couch, I could figure out how to use an entry-level DSLR," she says of the camera she and her husband had purchased just after their wedding and then promptly forgot about.

She looked up videos on YouTube and read online tutorials, propping up her perfect sleeping subject on the Boppy to test where the natural light was hitting, then troubleshooting her sometimes-blurry or dark photos. Heather shot every day for a year until she landed on a style and point of view all her own, and never missed an opportunity to expand her knowledge. "I was up nursing at 3:00 a.m. and thought, *This is a great time to have my laptop out and figure out Lightroom and Photoshop*," she says. "It just became a true obsession."

Slowly, Heather started shooting senior portraits and birthday parties around town, eventually building up to weddings. When her husband got a new job in Dallas, they picked up and she started building her business again. But she struggled to make a profit. "A lot of my clients were small local businesses, and people didn't know the value of photography then," she says. "I didn't know the value myself. I just thought that it was okay to charge little to nothing because that was what people would be willing to pay."

Yet small brands across the country increasingly took notice of her work—and the beauty of her historic home—on Instagram and sent their products for her to shoot. One client was based in Brooklyn, and after a fateful talk with her younger brother, who had just finished a photography internship in the city, Heather started to believe that her childhood fantasy of living in New York was a possibility. Her husband found a job at Bloomberg, they sold their house, and nearly six months later, they were Brooklynites. "I developed this delusional sense that I could

> "A lot of times people enter a situation with a set idea of what's possible. The truth is there are no limits. Anything can happen if you dream it."

photographer /
mother
of two

make it as a photographer in New York," says Heather of the confidence her early partnership with a children's toy company in Park Slope gave her. "I thought, *Oh, I have one client*. It was that special one that gave me that hope." Quickly, other brands followed, including Gap. Every night, after saying good night to her son and daughter, Heather and her husband would promptly set to work rearranging the living room furniture to make space for shoots, then move it all back again before the next morning. "We were extremely scrappy, and my living room was my studio," she says.

Though she was thrilled to have accomplished a lifelong dream that she had never imagined possible, Heather admits that hustling so hard for volume—many small shoots for little pay—took a toll. "The late nights were piling up, and the lack of profitability was adding up, and I was like, 'What am I doing?'" she recalls. "But we loved it here so much. My kids flourished here. I just kept pushing. I was determined to make this work, but I was so burnt out."

The turning point came when her social media snaps got the attention of an agent with a sage business strategy: "They wanted to get me to a point where I was letting some of the smaller stuff go and taking bigger jobs that may not come as frequently but were worthwhile because they were higher paid," she says. "That was a huge transition for me. I started to feel like I was regaining balance. I was so much happier and yelling a whole ton less. I was actually enjoyable to be around. Looking back, I had been losing my mind trying to make it all work. It was just like a weight lifted off my shoulders. I thought, *This is why we live here— so that I can enjoy my career but also create a great environment for my family.*"

And that's what happened. Campaigns with Target, Birkenstock, GapKids, and Olay have sent Heather across the country. While she's away—and even when she's shooting in Brooklyn—her husband, who now works remotely for Netflix, takes care of things on the home front. Client introductions have given her children opportunities to appear in photo shoots for J.Crew and Casper. And Heather has finally found the fulfillment that comes with being a good mother and developing her sense of self outside motherhood. "I realized that I can have a career and a happy family," she says. "I've developed so much more of a friendship now with my kids. Not everybody is meant to be in a traditional situation."

"I feel guilty leaning on my husband so much, but when you're self-employed there's nobody else to lean on when last-minute jobs or meetings come up."

Advice from Heather Moore

DRESS FOR THE JOB YOU WANT.
"When I was shooting for mothermag, they were sending me into the homes of extremely successful women who were living a life that I was not living. It sounds so silly, but I would do a lot of research on their careers and interests and style and would tailor my look to make sure I would stand out or be a little bit different. Presentation matters."

EMPOWER YOUR KIDS THROUGH WORK. "My kids were my muses, so they're all over my social media. I always ask permission if it's a little more personal. But they love what I do. It's afforded them a lot of opportunities to participate in work. Quinn did a J.Crew campaign last year, and we all modeled together for a Casper shoot. It's been a great college-fund building source for them."

ALWAYS ASK FOR A BUDGET FIRST.
"Within two to three months of being in New York, Gap reached out. It was a social media shoot—nine Instagram squares for Halloween—and I had no idea how a proper photo shoot was run. So I called my younger brother, who had just graduated from photo school, in a panic. I had to set up an estimate for them, and he told me to always ask for the budget before you give them your rate. So I did that and my jaw dropped. I was like, 'Oh my gosh, there's real money here!'"

the motivator

Growing up in a conservative religious community, Sara Bybee Fisk heard plenty of horror stories of child neglect and moms shirking their responsibilities when working outside of the home. A leader of her church went so far as to say that "no success could compensate for failure in the home." It was a sentiment that was often reinforced by the attitudes in her own family: "My mom was so sad when she had to go back to work because of family finance needs; it was always a regret," says Sara. "My dad felt like he failed."

And so, though she had a degree in elementary education and spent four years in the classroom before getting married, Sara became a full-time stay-at-home parent, raising her five children for seventeen years and homeschooling them for ten. Yet she always longed to have a career. She finally decided to take a chance and start working as a life coach once her oldest went off to college, investing $18,000 in a certification course and working at the school she attended before diving in on her own. "Having my business has felt like giving birth to something that was just for me, just because I wanted it," she said. "Building it was amazing for my self-concept."

In addition to a distinct sense of purpose, her business also gave her character-building

> "Learning how to hold neutral, judgment-free space for other people allowed me to do the same for myself."

resources she never imagined for herself. "I had to learn new skills, feel uncomfortable emotions, and fail over and over again," she says. "I had to learn to sell, to use new tech. I feel strong, powerful, sovereign, and so capable in so many ways that are completely unexpected. Making money—knowing that I could support myself—and then excelling has been incredible."

To do that, she's put everything she had into her business. She found mentors to help ease her through the process and took a coaching job for very low pay to get the on-the-ground experience she needed. "Working for the Life Coach School was a huge break for me," she says, noting that she relied on her mom and babysitters to help watch the kids so she could flourish. "It gave me hours and hours of back-to-back coaching each week, so I got good really fast, and I learned to be exact and concise, to communicate effectively, and to say difficult things with grace." People began to take notice. "Although I had a noncompete, I was offered other teaching opportunities that drew on my expertise—I turned them down—and made a name for myself in that small pond. When I quit, my first private clients were all people I'd met through the school."

But as rewarding as the experience of entrepreneurship has been, it's also been incredibly difficult, forcing Sara to examine aspects of her own life in order to help others overcome their obstacles. "I made myself my project and designed a curriculum to stop people-pleasing," she says. "It was six weeks long and very basic, but then I started testing it on me. Then I tested it with a group of volunteers, and now it's iterated to become what I do as a coach." On figuring out how to

life coach /
mother
of five

"This is a marathon, not a sprint. You'll have help, you'll feel alone; you'll feel like you know exactly what you're doing and also feel completely lost. You'll weep and worry and reincarnate and rise hundreds of times."

balance home life with her husband, who is himself a self-employed entrepreneur, she says, "We are unlearning a lot of traditional gender roles, and we've had to have lots of discussions about how much I was doing before and how my job is limiting that now," Sara says.

She also says that being a coach has had an unintentional effect on her motherhood: It's made her a better parent. "It's given me a great way to frame talking about failure and success," she says. "And sometimes my kids even let me coach them."

Though Sara is now the breadwinner in the family, and the business is thriving, she admits that it's still hard to find equilibrium between her professional and personal life. "I've tried to make my work compatible with being a mom, and it's an endless balancing act," she says. "I don't always like how I balance things, but I see it as 100 percent individual. I've had to tell my kids that I can't do things that they want to do because I'm working." But ultimately, her children understand the sacrifice. "They are incredibly proud of me, and they notice how hard I work," she says. "They are my biggest fans and supporters."

Advice from Sara Bybee Fisk

SEEK OUT WISDOM FROM WOMEN. "My role models are other female entrepreneurs in the trenches with me. Sometimes they are 'ahead' of me on the path, sometimes we are walking side by side, and sometimes they are 'behind' me. I also listen to other women—so many different female voices in pop culture, politics, and the arts. I've listened to enough men to last me a lifetime."

PROTECT YOUR TIME. "I let all my clients know what my business hours are and stick to them. If I respond to them outside of business hours, I want it to feel like a pleasant surprise and not something expected. In the beginning, I was constantly sneaking off to my office to get more work done, but I've learned to think about it as a marathon and take regular breaks to let my brain rest."

BE KIND TO YOURSELF. "My rule is that I never, ever beat myself up for any reason. I make the best decision I can with the knowledge I have, knowing that I might regret things or wish I had made a different decision. But I will never layer self-criticism or self-judgment on top of regret. I'll just try and learn and make decisions where I think I'll like the outcome more next time. Messing up is part of being human, and I'd rather not do it—but when I inevitably do, I will be really kind and generous with myself and try and make amends."

Advocate for Yourself

I was raised to believe that being a martyr to motherhood was the noblest way to live. I assumed that once I had my children, I would lose myself. But as I got older, it became harder to imagine a future where I wouldn't be able to do the work that sustained me. Though I love my children dearly, I couldn't help fighting for a version of my life in which family and work could coexist the way I wanted them to.

For self-employed mothers, some of the most important advocacy you can do will begin in the home. One of the biggest arguments my husband, Cree, and I had during our first year of marriage, when he was in law school, was about work. Dreaming about life after graduation, he naively said, "Won't it be great when I get a job? Then you won't have to work." Well intentioned as he was, I felt slightly betrayed. I cried and reminded him how important my work was to me. Since then, we've had an understanding that we would work toward our professional goals side by side. No martyrdom, just teamwork—in our work *and* family life.

Cree is fair, kind, and supportive, yet to this day—more than ten years later—I still have to advocate for myself and my job and remind him that even though mine is more colorful, our work is of equal importance. Any time things start to feel out of balance in our life, I vocalize the issue and we readjust to make sure we both have time for our kids, our work, our relationship, and our goals. Cree cleans; he cooks, changes diapers, grocery shops, and has days with the kids just like I do. He cuddles the kids to sleep *and* he works. He is praised for this by peers and often treated much like a four-leaf clover—something I happened upon by luck. It makes me want to pull my hair out. He is an equal contributor because we *chose* to structure our life like this—together. This type of behavior from a man or partner is admirable, yes, but it could also be the standard—no extra praise needed. My children's lives are enriched because we both have time with them, and they also see both parents as contributors in different ways. We aren't unique. I see this change happening all over the country, and I'm empowered by it.

the globetrotter

When it comes to traveling with kids, there's always a fair amount of schlepping involved, but Carol Lim acknowledges that her partner's itineraries weren't like most. Though she was based in New York, the cofounder and CEO of It-girl clothing brand Opening Ceremony (she was also the creative director for French fashion house Kenzo for almost a decade) spent almost seven months of the year in Paris; the rest of the time she was bouncing between far-flung locations like Shanghai, Hong Kong, and Barcelona. As a result, her partner, a documentary filmmaker who lived in London, clocked lots of hours in the air, shuttling their daughter between New York, his home base, and Paris and beyond.

"It was crazy," remembers Carol, "the number of times where we were like, 'Why are we doing this?' Well, the alternative is we're not together. You have to weigh the ease of some of that against the time that you have to bond with your child, so my husband made that happen. If he decided he didn't want to travel, it would have looked a lot different. Those are decisions we made as a family. Not every family is lucky enough to have that choice, but we did at the time."

For Carol, there was never a question of grounding her career for motherhood. "I have always loved working. Even as a young teen, I asked my parents for a letter so that I could start working earlier than fourteen. I loved making my own money and having the agency to do whatever I wanted with it. So once I had children, it didn't surprise me that I wanted to go back to work soon after. My job gave me the space to really be present as a mother when I was back home."

When she wasn't traveling, Carol left the office by 5:00 p.m. every day, was fully in the moment at home, then got back online at 9:00 p.m., after the bedtime routine. "You begin to quickly realize that everything can wait for a few hours, and it made my time in the office even more productive because I wouldn't be available those few hours," she says. She also cut back on travel as much as possible once her second daughter arrived. "I didn't want to be gone, especially with two kids and especially because I felt very indebted to my husband, so I really cut out anything that I didn't think was important for the business," she says. "Had I not had children, I would have done so much more."

Enforcing those boundaries was helped by the fact that her mom flew out from Los Angeles to pitch in, whether that was in New York, Paris, or wherever, and her cofounder at Opening Ceremony, Humberto Leon, had a similar perspective on parenthood and the kind of life he wanted to build for his twin children, who were born between Carol's daughters' birthdays. "He and I would take turns," she says. "We were in the same boat in terms of what's going to pull us away has to be meaningful."

Once back home, she'd throw herself into family life as much as she could, doing the school planning and volunteering for the PTA to hasten a sense of balance. "I think even if I didn't travel, that's a little bit my nature—I'm

> "You have to integrate joy throughout the day and not feel apologetic about it, or it's not worth it."

fashion
designer /
mother
of two

hyperorganized and I obsess about certain things," Carol says. "That felt like an easy way to integrate into the rhythm of family life. My husband is always like, 'You don't have to volunteer for everything,' but it's my way of being around the children and seeing a little bit about their world when sometimes I'm gone for the entire week. I just want to come in and join life."

Now that Carol is back in her hometown of Los Angeles and she and Humberto have sold Opening Ceremony (though they still serve as creative directors), she says she's begun another chapter of her motherhood, one in which she's much more present. "My mom always said you can have two jobs, you can have three, but when your daughters turn ten you need to be present because that is when the hard work begins," she says. "It's so funny, but I think that's 100 percent accurate. As they become teenagers and navigate this transition in their lives, there's so much drama. Not that I can fix anything (nor do I want to), but I'm just there so when each of them wants to come to me they can. I feel like it would be a really hard time for them at this point if I was traveling as much as I did when they were younger."

Carol's transition to primary caregiver— her husband was previously working from a home office but has increasingly taken more jobs away—has naturally brought up questions of contentment. "When you've built and run a business and had a family, you're juggling all these different aspects in terms of defining who you are. I used to easily say, 'I'm a career woman, I'm focused on my job and my company,' and then you add motherhood to that, and as certain things evolve you begin to wonder, *Is that all that I can be?* I often think I have more to give."

But Carol wants to be extremely intentional about starting something new—and she doesn't want it to stem from a need to keep up with everyone else or relive her past experiences. "I'm thinking about how to approach every single opportunity in a way

"I want to continue to learn and be challenged, and if I can do that in a thoughtful way, I know that it will help me be a better mother."

that doesn't feel negative. *Why am I going after certain things? What is it that I'm trying to do? Is the intent to maintain a certain status, or is it something I actually want to do?* I think it's hard for women to feel okay with just being like, *Wow, I have time. This is okay. And maybe this is why I worked so hard to get to a point where I could hold space in my mind to do things outside of just that.*" In the meantime, she's taken up volunteering and mentoring young entrepreneurs as well as some consulting work, and she continues to question whether she'd want to jump back into corporate life or entrepreneurship. "There is an allure to being back on the wheel; there is an adrenaline rush that comes with that. I always have to ask myself, *Is that worth it?* And right now it isn't. When you think of everything you're going to have to sacrifice to do that, it becomes pretty clear."

WHAT I'VE LEARNED

Advice from Carol Lim

TAKE STOCK. "I make a list right before bed every night and then send it to myself. It helps me remember everything that needs to be done, both personal and professional, and prioritize or delegate if needed."

BLOCK YOUR TIME. "My first daughter was in the NICU for six weeks, and a bizarre silver lining was that every night, I would come home and I was able to sleep. Having time to recover physically, and then mentally being prepared for her to come home, gave me the sense that if I organized myself, I felt better about the things that I could do. At that moment, I was still kind of working both jobs, so I really learned how to separate my time. To this day, when I get home I never look at my phone. I'm just there. And then when my daughters go to bed, I can check a few things."

OWN YOUR WORK TRAVEL. "My husband likes to tease me because I had this crazy way of accounting for the days I'd be gone. I'd be like, 'I'm actually only gone for a day because I still see you the day I leave.' When I would do that, I already felt like I was in trouble. I know a lot of working moms feel the same way when they present to their partners. Having gone through that, I would say, 'Don't do that to yourself. This is your work, and you're choosing to do this.'"

the art liaison

When her children were young, Tallia Feltis was a stay-at-home mother who spent most of her days visiting art museums, libraries, and children's museums to help nurture her little ones' creative development and teach them the general principles of being a good human. "I have always loved creative spaces—those were places I felt really supported as a parent," says Tallia.

It turns out that in the process, she was also doing valuable field research that would later fuel her entrepreneurial ambitions. When her children were eight and six years old, Tallia founded the Neighborhood Art Center in downtown Provo, Utah. The nonprofit's mission: to make art accessible to everyone and inspire a lifelong love of art in every kid who visits the studio. "When we moved to Utah, I really missed having that community connection and dreamed of starting something that would fill that void, but it felt like such a big, unattainable project."

For a long time it was, but she says having both of her kids in full-day school was the game changer. "Once I had the space and time to think about long-term projects and start dreaming stuff up, it all happened really fast," she says. "It only took about four months

from when I decided to do it to us opening our doors, which is kind of wild when I look back at it. But at the time, I was focused and excited about what we were doing, and we just worked really hard to make it happen."

It helped that Tallia had a built-in blueprint for programming that would draw families to the space. "By taking my kids to so many museums, I learned what I liked and I could see firsthand what kids engaged with and what didn't interest them," she says. "This knowledge helped me set up the art center in a way I knew would appeal to kids."

Though she purposely limited her time at the center (a former portrait studio that she renovated with $7,000 of her own money), the two days a week she was on-site were an adjustment for her family, who had grown accustomed to her being home. "My husband had always participated in household duties like cooking and cleaning," she says of her partner, an entrepreneur who owns a local catering business. "But it was never fifty-fifty because I was the parent who was home all the time. Starting NAC was the first time I was away from home for big chunks of every week, and he was the primary parent with the kids. I felt guilty for being gone at first. It took a lot of conversations and a lot of figuring things out. I knew things were working the first time one of the kids needed something and automatically called out for Dad instead of Mom. That's when I knew we were really sharing the load equally."

Today, she keeps the same two-days-per-week schedule and tries to maintain a healthy attitude toward work and her mental well-being. "I don't let my job be a 24-7 thing," she says. "I knew that if I went all in every day, I would burn out fast. I have always guarded

> "Before becoming a mom, I didn't realize how hard I would have to work to preserve myself and my goals and ambitions."

community
art leader /
mother
of two

"One thing I wish I could have told myself before starting out would be to just do what you want to do."

my free time, and I will put off almost any work until the next day if it means I can go to bed on time."

Sometimes, she admits, that decision has hampered the organization's growth, but she doesn't view that as a negative outcome. "I haven't grown the Neighborhood Art Center as aggressively as I could have because I've always wanted to be able to spend time with my family and have free time to do what I want."

She continues: "It's easy to fall into the pattern of believing that growth is the only measure of success in a business or organization. NAC has grown slowly and steadily, and I am proud of everything we have accomplished, but from the beginning there has been a lot of pressure to always do more, and I have had to actively fight against that pressure. I started NAC as a community-building project, and if I was depending on it for income, my choices would be very different. But it is much more fun and enjoyable when I'm not always worried about growth and progress all the time. If things are going well, it's okay to just let them keep going. You don't have to keep adding things to your plate."

Advice from Tallia Feltis

DON'T START TOMORROW IF YOU CAN START TODAY. "I knew if I put off opening, I might have been able to get some kind of start-up grants and donations eventually, but it felt easier to start first and then apply for grants later. And don't try to live up to anyone's expectations, because that takes all of the fun out of what you are doing."

FAKE IT TILL YOU MAKE IT. "Before I started NAC, I had zero work experience in nonprofits or art education. I just really liked creative community spaces and wanted to build one. I had no idea what I was doing. I looked up a lot of stuff on the internet about starting a nonprofit and made some studio plans. I have learned a ton along the way and also pretended I knew what I was doing a lot."

GIVE YOURSELF AN OUT. "A lot of hard moments stem from feeling like I am not doing a good enough job running the center. One way I've found to feel better about things is to tell myself that I don't have to do anything I don't want to do. If there is a program that is too hard to run or an event or activity that isn't producing the results we want, we can just stop doing it. I realized that when I hold myself to an inflexible standard, things start to get harder, but when I give myself (and NAC) the space to change and adapt, things are so much more fun. It's your business. If something is hard, make it easier."

ARIANNE FOULKS

the dot-com mom

AEOLIDIA
SEATTLE,
WASHINGTON

Arianne Foulks isn't like a *regular* mom, she's a *cool* mom—at least according to the kids who attended her older son Desmond's middle school (he's now in high school). When he asked her to speak at career day one year, not only did she upstage a dad who worked on augmented reality for Meta—the sixty-hour workweek didn't do him any favors—the website design and development expert managed to impress kids who didn't even know her son.

"The next day, Desmond said that now everyone in his grade knew who he was, and kids that he didn't know told him his mom is cool," says Arianne, who started her strategic design firm Aeolidia to help small creative businesses scale up. "Thinking about my job from a thirteen-year-old's perspective was really fun. I feel superlucky to be doing what I do and to have turned into such a brave and confident individual. Thirteen-year-old Arianne would barely recognize me."

But that's not entirely true. Growing up in Seattle, teenage Arianne was already laying the groundwork for her future livelihood in the mid-1990s, when she became the writer, art director, and marketing manager of her

"Success is spending my days doing meaningful work. It's having time for family, friends, and myself. It's putting some good in the world and lifting others up."

own zine. Stories about her favorite music and comics eventually reached hundreds of readers and generated money for the zine's creator with sold advertising spots. Even Sub Pop, the indie record label that made Nirvana famous, bought a full-page ad. "Creating my zine gave me a solid background in the variety of tasks needed to put a publication together," recalls Arianne, who printed it at her local copy shop and snail mailed it out to fans. "I'd spent years learning storytelling, design, graphics, layout, promotion, sales, and fulfillment. This 'jack of all trades' type of experience translated closely to all the things you need to do to make a website."

Her analog production method went digital in college, where she began experimenting with coding, clip art, and Adobe Photoshop, using the school's computer lab as her office. "I found designing and coding so enjoyable that I would redesign my site regularly, and since I knew so many bands and record label owners through my zine, it seemed like I was always helping someone put their website together," Arianne says. Small creative companies also needed help. One friend introduced her to another, and before she knew it she had a booming freelance business outside of her job at a web hosting company, where she polished her customer service skills and later applied them to her own clients. "I had no business plan, or any plan at all at first," she says, noting that there was little overhead or need for internal or external funding for her business. "I was doing something for fun that other people valued and wanted to pay me for."

Ironically, business really took off when Arianne decided to start a family with her now ex-husband. "It was having children

digital
consultant /
mother
of two

that led me to expand my team with new employees," she says. "Babies didn't give me the hours-long blocks of time I needed to create a website, so I started hiring designers and developers, and eventually project managers." The changes transformed her day-to-day responsibilities but also her approach to the work itself. "When I hired the first web designer to replace me, I was worried that I wouldn't like my job anymore. Very quickly, I realized I loved all the ways my job grew, and was glad never to sit in front of that intimidating blank white page in Photoshop again. I started to focus more on marketing and relationships, and steering our ship."

Arianne says a lot of her success came down to hiring people who were better at what she did than she was—and flexibility. She was fortunate to always work from home, and she had childcare help from her father, who watched her two sons (Calvin is sixteen) during work hours—and sometimes outside of them. "I've nearly always had a break every week from parenting," she says of her father's support, "and I can always take time away from work to take my kids to the doctor or the beach. Owning my business while parenting has felt easier than having a full-time job outside of the home. I was lucky to be able to set my own schedule and slow down work as needed during busier times of child-rearing."

Yet there is often tension between her wants and the needs of her family. "I always, always, always feel torn between work, my husband, my kids and stepkid, and my extended family and friends—don't even mention hobbies," she says. "I never feel like I've got the balance right. The nice thing is that I know there isn't an ideal way to do this, and it's not that I'm failing at anything. I'm just doing what I can do at any given time and shifting my attention to where it's needed."

In the end, it all runs smoothly for Arianne because her approach to her work and her home life is surprisingly similar. "If business is always easy, you won't innovate in the way you would if you were having a problem," she explains. "In the same vein, having children has challenged me to grow in ways that help my family life and my work. My kids don't let me force decisions on them, which is *hard* but also great for my empathy, patience, and ability to collaborate. I'm always ready to be in the wrong when clients come to me with complaints, and it's the same when my kids get upset with me. Not needing to be right helps me slow down and try again."

She goes on, "I run my business like I run my family, for better or worse: I get a group of great people together and sort of throw them in the deep end, and we learn from our mistakes together. In both work and family, I choose my battles, respect individuality, and encourage independence." Very cool, indeed.

Advice from Arianne Foulks

REFRAME YOUR PRIORITIES. "Seth Godin says that often when you say 'I don't have time for this,' what you mean is 'This isn't a priority to me right now.' I heard that when my kids were young, and I loved it. Saying that I don't have time for something makes me feel out of control. Saying that the very same thing is not a priority feels purposeful and strategic—and it's true!"

TURN TROUBLES INTO LEARNING EXPERIENCES. "I had been trying for a couple of years to see if we could design websites more quickly, but wasn't getting anywhere. During parts of the pandemic, it was very hard to sell our usual high-ticket projects. Our solution was to offer a Website In a Day service. We stripped out the extras while providing a thoughtfully designed website using our best practices. This emergency-driven service is now our Website In a Week. Even a very complex custom project can begin with this quick way to get up and running. What seemed impossible in 2020 is something we do regularly in 2024. Without the push of tough times, we wouldn't be there."

DON'T BE SEDUCED BY FLASH. "The way I built my business was by putting one foot in front of the other over and over for twenty years. That's not sexy or exciting or particularly interesting to talk about. I've seen businesses grow quicker and bigger than mine, and felt a twinge that I haven't taken enough risks or pushed hard enough. Then time passes, and I find out they're deeply in debt and are closing the business. Slow and steady and authentic is working for me."

GO EASY ON YOURSELF. "It's easier to mentally compile the list of things I feel guilty about as a parent than the list of things I feel proud of. Women shoulder so many expectations from society, family members, and themselves. It's almost impossible to not feel like you're falling short. The truth is, though, the 'proud of' list is probably more important than the 'guilty about' list, and we should all take time to appreciate that list as well."

"One thing I'd tell myself before starting out: You can afford to be a bit less cautious. I'm always hiring a new employee after needing them for a long time, which is a strain and stretches everyone else thin."

Arianne's Schedule

In keeping with her ethos to work smarter, not harder—and bolstered by studies that link long hours with diminished productivity—Arianne's team has shifted to a thirty-two-hour week. She says the move has benefited her team "from a balance and burnout perspective," but it's also just good business. "What we produce is better, our time at work is purposeful, and our profitability is strong." Here's how you can do it, too.

MEET LESS. "Fewer meetings, shorter meetings, fewer people in each meeting," she explains. "We also try to not have a meeting whenever we can: 'This meeting could have been an email' is a meme for a reason."

MINIMIZE ADMIN. "We worked together to figure out what work we do that's truly important. There are areas where we still want to get an A or A+, but for some things we're now willing to put in a C amount of effort. Others we quit doing entirely. It's important to bring our best to our design and development projects, so most of our cuts were to admin tasks."

ESTABLISH SYSTEMS. "We spent the prior year creating a templated task, tutorial, and scheduling system in our project management software. We also use the Entrepreneurial Operating System (EOS) to run our business," she says of the software that provides tools and processes to help identify problem areas and streamline her business strategy.

ENCOURAGE FEEDBACK. "We asked every person on the team to report back to us with anything that they suspected might be a waste of time, then we worked together to optimize or remove those tasks. For instance, for every project our designers were tasked with creating multiple graphics for our portfolio. In reality, we only ended up promoting a handful of projects each year. We now create these graphics as needed, rather than proactively."

SET EXPECTATIONS. "We knew our schedule could be a surprise for the shop owners we work with, so we put together an explanatory message for them. We emphasized that they wouldn't lose any of our time or see our work drop in quality. Instead, we let them know that we are constantly building the skills needed to complete their work more quickly than before."

the autism advocate

As a stay-at-home mother of three young children, Kimi Matsumura says she had plenty of reasons not to start a nonprofit. With a degree in education and little experience as a community organizer—even less that qualified as business acumen—she felt uncomfortable calling the shots for anything besides her kids' bedtime routines.

"I hate being in charge of things. I'm much more comfortable as a follower," says Kimi, who was raised in a conservative Utah home and was taught that being a mother was the highest calling. "But I was coming to the point in motherhood where I was starting to get a little freedom back. Two kids were at school all day, and one was in preschool for a couple of hours each day, so I started to feel like I wanted to use that time to create something that would help other people and also help me develop my own sense of self and purpose. And I was really feeling the lyrics of *Hamilton*: 'God help and forgive me, I wanna build something that's gonna outlive me.'"

That something wasn't immediately apparent, but when her second daughter received an autism diagnosis at the age of three, Kimi became increasingly disturbed by the lack of credible health resources available for families trying to navigate Chicago's serpentine network of support services. In 2016, spurred by encouragement from her husband and buoyed by the community outreach and business plan work that she had done for a friend at the Joffrey Ballet School, she founded Chicago Autism Network, a 100 percent volunteer-run nonprofit that, against all odds, has raised more than $300,000 for families struggling under the weight of their own diagnoses.

"I had one year as a high school teacher, two years at the Joffrey as a teacher and administrator, and a few months of volunteer work writing a mission plan," Kimi recalls. "But writing up the Chicago Autism Network's business plan helped me clarify my vision for the organization. I was incredibly inexperienced, but I am building this organization as we go."

For Kimi, that means utilizing as many spare moments as possible without compromising her time with her children. "I'm a really bad delegator, so I end up doing a lot—social media, parent workshops, grant application management, et cetera," Kimi admits. That means doing nonprofit work on her laptop and phone wherever she can, from the pickup line at school to the bleachers at her kids' sports practices.

In the end, though, her family comes first. "The nice thing about being in charge is that I can commit as much as I want to," she explains. "If one week I get twenty-five hours of work in, that's great. If the next week, I only have time to do social media, that's fine, too. I sometimes wonder if I gave a little more

> "I wish I would have realized at a younger age that being a mom and having a career are not mutually exclusive, and that having a career could strengthen me as a mom."

nonprofit founder / mother of three

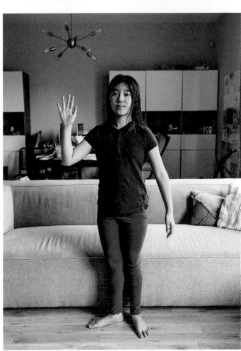

time to Chicago Autism Network if I could get it to grow faster, but I'm very content with my balance right now. I typically tell people I'm available between 8:30 a.m. and 2:30 p.m., and the rest of my time is reserved for my family. But there are definitely weeks when I put in a full forty-plus hours, and my laundry piles up and we eat more instant meals than usual. But I love the flexibility of calling all the shots. Being able to say, 'I'm not working today because my kid really needs some extra attention' is invaluable."

Also priceless are the unexpected skills she's picked up while running the organization. "When I envisioned the future before I was a mom, I thought that work and motherhood had to conflict with each other," she says. "While they definitely do fight for your time, I think motherhood and running a business can be complementary endeavors that add strength, depth, and clarity to each other. For the first year and a half or so, I would be trembling before, during, and after every single board meeting. I was just so intimidated and nervous about being in charge that I would literally shake. Now, I feel more confident in presenting my ideas, leading discussions, and proposing changes. The increased confidence has definitely helped me be a better and more deliberate mom."

That focus on family became even more important in 2023, when Kimi was diagnosed with clear cell sarcoma, an ultrarare form of cancer with a bleak prognosis. But while she has slowed down in the last couple of years, she's not slacked off. "When things get hard, I often question if I should keep going forward with this," she says, "but I see the community rally around our mission and feel energized to continue this for as long as I can."

WHAT I'VE LEARNED

Advice from Kimi Matsumura

Kimi taught herself how to draft a business proposal when she was working with the Joffrey Ballet School, but she perfected her method when she established the Chicago Autism Network. In her words, here are the most important components of a good business plan.

STATE YOUR MISSION. "In your opening, often called the executive summary, share an overview of your purpose and processes. Though this comes first, it's often easiest to write it last to ensure you've concisely covered all the important points."

EXPLAIN HOW YOU WILL ACCOMPLISH IT. "To be thorough, you may want to address these questions: What are your programs and/or products? Who is your target audience/ideal customer? Who are the key people in your operations?"

HIGHLIGHT WHAT MAKES YOU DIFFERENT. "Share your market research on potential competitors and what makes you stand out."

OUTLINE YOUR PLANS FOR GROWTH. "Detail where you want to go and how your marketing/program strategies will get you there, as well as your start-up costs and future projections."

TANYA AGUIÑIGA

the conceptual artist

LOS ANGELES,
CALIFORNIA

Los Angeles artist Tanya Aguiñiga learned the hard way not to mix work and parenting. A couple of years ago, she was invited to Oakland for a feminist exhibition, but childcare was, as ever, an issue: Her husband was traveling for work, and her sister, who lived next door and helped out with the babysitting, was busy. Since Tanya had been itching to share her work on a deeper level with her ten-year-old daughter, Io, she figured she'd just bring her along this time. But once they arrived, the museum hosting the show had plans for a press conference, with all of the artist interviews and video segments that entails. A former student of Tanya's who was now working at the museum offered to watch Io, but when she was pulled away to work, the curator called her own nineteen-year-old daughter to take over.

"My daughter was like, 'I hate this. Why am I hanging out with a stranger?'" recalls Tanya. "She said, 'All these strangers keep coming up to me and talking to me like they know me, but I don't know who they are.' They were adults that I'd been working with for

two or three years, who thought they knew her because they knew me and they'd heard so much about her. It was weird, and she was really unhappy. But going to exhibitions—that's me doing business. I have to be able to network, so I made the decision that I have to be by myself. Now, I just do my thing and bring her casually to see the work rather than have her at openings."

Though it requires extra juggling for Tanya, that boundary means her time away can be more efficient and productive. "If I take her with me, I'm in a totally different mental and emotional space," says Tanya, whose work often deals with trauma and difficult life experiences. "It's hard for me to be vulnerable the way I sometimes need to be in conversations about my work in front of her."

In fact, Tanya has always needed that separation between her professional and home life. When Io was born, Tanya took an eleven-week maternity leave, using money from commissions and pieces that she sold in the lead-up to the birth to support the family during her time off. (She and her daughter receive health insurance through her husband's full-time work.) Her leave might have been longer, but she says she had a bad case of postpartum depression and needed to get back to work. "My mental health is so much better when I'm in the studio and actively making things and talking with people about stuff," she says. "For the first three years, I stopped traveling for residencies and exhibitions so I could be home and figure out how to make enough money from my studio practice while having a child."

To make that happen, Tanya relied on family and friends, including two studio managers and her two sisters who lived

"Now that my daughter is older, I don't go on longer trips because I miss her. It's less 'Can I swing it?' and more 'Do I really want to be away from my family for that long?'"

artist /
mother
of one

next door at the time. But for more regular childcare, Tanya entered into a complex nanny-share system: She'd get a few hours two or three times a week to start, then she'd drop her daughter off at other houses as more moms joined the share; sometimes, the nanny would come to her house for a solo session. "Later on, our nanny worked for us full-time, and then at some point we were sharing again so I could split the cost, and kids would get dropped off at my house. A lot of the caretaking is me coordinating."

For the most part, Io is okay with it all, but Tanya's commitment to her work sometimes causes friction—and requires her to turn to negotiation tactics. "She gets sad when she doesn't have enough cuddle time, but I remind her why I'm doing something, and she'll say, 'Okay, but then I want a scalp massage,'" Tanya recalls with a laugh. "Or I'll explain that I need to go to the studio this week so that I can have the whole week off with her next week. She gets bummed, but she knows that we have to work for our money. And I think she understands that some of the work that I do isn't just to make money—she sees that there are certain things we have to do as humans to be part of a peaceful, helpful society."

In the end, Tanya says all of the arrangements she's made around her work time—shortened trips, declined offers, scheduling headaches—are worth it because through it all she's maintained a sense of autonomy that a more structured job wouldn't allow. "Sometimes I wish I could take a month off and be in a different place with my family; I wish I could have dedicated family leisure time. But I'm also so driven to make things that I don't even know if I could do that. Being in the studio making stuff is where I find a lot of peace."

WHAT DOES SUCCESS LOOK LIKE TO YOU?

"Fulfillment, feeling like I am translating and alchemizing some creative expression from within me and bringing it to this world. Like I'm doing what I'm supposed to be doing and feeling invigorated by how much I'm giving."

KAREN MORDECHAI, ARTISAN FOOD PURVEYOR (PAGE 242)

"Being able to produce something that someone actually wants to pay their hard-earned money for. It's not about being rich. Making my business self-sufficient as a way to support my family is success."

TIA CIBANI, KIDSWEAR DESIGNER (PAGE 246)

"Being present in everything that I do and not feeling like I need to be doing something else. It's about feeling grateful and content that I have this moment to share with family or friends and letting that sink in."

CAROL LIM, FASHION DESIGNER (PAGE 210)

"Being in charge of my own schedule. Following the things I am curious about. Having the space to be creative. Saying yes to the things that matter to me; being able to say no to the things that don't. Living a slower life, and spending time with my family."

TRISHA ZEMP, PAPER GOODS PURVEYOR (PAGE 168)

"The ability to relax and dream. To be able to have long meals in spectacular places with people I thoroughly enjoy. To sleep in and take naps. To live without fear. To not get caught up in the things that don't matter."

BEATRICE VALENZUELA, FASHION DESIGNER (PAGE 304)

"Freedom. Being able to make the choices that are right for my family and feeling good about my life. The *existence* of a choice is a big success."

JAYCINA ALMOND, NONPROFIT FOUNDER (PAGE 98)

Money Talk (Please Talk About It!)

Most women have been raised to treat money talk as "unladylike" or rude, but that type of thinking is as old as the patriarchal system that's holding us back. Being financially fluent and stable is feminist, and talking about it is empowering. In 1870, Victoria Woodhull (one of the first female stockbrokers) asserted, "Woman's ability to earn money is better protection against the tyranny and brutality of men than her ability to vote." And as one of my favorite financial feminists, Tori Dunlap, says, "Having money means having options."

What is it about money? No matter how much experience you have or how much you think you're worth, financial conversations always bring about so much hand-wringing. The best way to start feeling confident about financial talk is to keep an open dialogue with people you trust. My friend Mika Rane, the illustrator, started a group for some local art entrepreneurs; we have a text thread and also meet monthly where we make art, share work, discuss rates, and talk industry standards. It's a safe place to bounce ideas off of each other, get real-world evidence on best practices, and also help each other know our worth. I highly recommend doing something similar with entrepreneurs in your neighborhood or related industries.

One of the most empowering blog posts I've ever read was by designer and entrepreneur Jessica Hische. I was just starting out in the freelance world, and she posted about how much freelancers should be bidding projects to large companies. I'd been bidding jobs in the one- to two-thousand-dollar range. She was bidding projects in the *hundred thousands*. I was dumbfounded but also so impressed with her. We were similar ages, in similar fields, and she had the guts to charge what she thought she deserved. And I didn't. Because of her honesty and vulnerability, the next time a large advertising company approached me to collaborate with them, I worked up the courage to bid the job at $60,000—and got it, a trip to London included. Now let me just say, I don't go around bidding things at that rate every week, but I share this because Jessica's being brave enough to talk about money empowered me to charge what I felt I was worth. So talk about it!

the strength trainer

As a parent of two neurodivergent sons, Kelita Hollins says she has to be more forward-thinking than most to ensure a prosperous future for her children. "Our goal is to raise independent men, but we also need to address what that independence looks like for someone who's on the spectrum," says Kelita, a fitness professional who coaches trainers and clients across the Chicago area. "My husband and I realized that we need to create some generational wealth so that we can continue to live our own lives but also be able to help our children down the line."

That's much of the motivation behind why they strove to think bigger than their day jobs as trainers (they met at a Bally Total Fitness). So when a friend approached them about KidStrong, a new science-based milestone accelerator that focuses on functional movements, character building, and cognitive development for children, they jumped at the chance to become franchise owners of the Texas-based brand, even though it meant learning on the go about the business side of running a fitness center and putting a big chunk of their savings into it. "We saw KidStrong as a way to help our kids become more well-rounded and increase that body awareness, especially for the little one," she says of her son Max, who is autistic. "But we also realized that this is something that other families need, whether their kids are neurodivergent or not, and we felt like we could support them and build a community with it. When you think about it from that perspective, the zeros don't hurt so bad."

But like most entrepreneurial endeavors, nothing has gone according to plan. The space was vandalized, pushing back the opening date, and construction costs have proven higher than expected (hence all of the zeros). Impatient members crack jokes on the location's Facebook page about how the gym will never open. "I just had a little breakdown with my husband the other day because that hurts, and I was like, 'I don't have anything left emotionally,'" Kelita says. "It's mentally draining, and it's easy for me to say we could just get three heavy-hitter clients to train. There are times when I want to throw my hands up and say, 'Does anyone want to buy this off of us?' But my husband always reels me back into the now and the importance of what we're doing. We've come too far, and I know this is going to be life-changing for families."

In the meantime, it's been life-changing for her own family. They put vacations on hold for two years and cut back on date nights and outings, embraced cooking at home, and got creative with quality time. "We have Fort Night Fridays, where we build a tent in the living room," she says. "We try to make the small things big things." And she's using the opportunity to teach her sons lessons in financial literacy. "Learning the value of money is something that we didn't get growing up because we were living paycheck

> "I love that my days don't have to look and feel the same. If something comes up with the kids, I am able to be there for them."

athletic coach /
mother
of two

to paycheck, so to be able to give them that is a big deal for us," she says. "Sacrificing the frivolous spending has definitely been worth it. We had to scrape up all of our coins, but we'd do it again in a heartbeat."

That's because she sees the gym as something that's much bigger than her family. "When you become a parent of a child with special needs, it makes your world that much smaller," she says. "I feel like I have to be an advocate for other moms, for other Black and brown neurodivergent families that don't get the assistance that they need. We've been in the midst of so much chaos and turmoil, and if I can do one thing that is going to benefit my community, this has got to be it. These little guys are going to be adults, and I just can't imagine someone not treating my child with respect. I've got to do something now to try to advocate that change for the future."

WHAT I'VE LEARNED

Advice from Kelita Hollins

UPGRADE YOUR OUTREACH.
"Building a community is much more than newsletters and happy hours. Understanding the neighborhood helps you better serve it. For instance, when creating a schedule, it's important to know peak traffic times— how easy is it for most members to get to your locations?—and school pickup and drop-off windows. Are there veteran coaches in the area that potential citizens gravitate to? If so, hiring that individual will allow your member base to grow exponentially. You can learn about what people need or want just by being willing to listen to them and creating a culture of constructive feedback."

CHOOSE PARTNERS WISELY. "Our original business partner lives out of state, and we quickly realized how inefficient that was. In the midst of construction, we met our future (now current) partners as they were in the process of diving into another KidStrong opportunity in the suburbs. We met with them to discuss some questions they had regarding build-out, recruiting, et cetera, and after working with the franchise and meeting again, we decided that being a team would be most beneficial. It has been a relief to have business partners that have previous experience with owning similar businesses and share a common goal."

BANISH GENDER STEREOTYPES.
"There have been a lot of role reversals in our marriage. There were times when my husband stayed home, and that was great to show our kids, especially boys. Our schedule revolves around what the boys need, and we try to prepare them as much as we can if there's a schedule change. Lately, my husband and I will have dedicated time that we spend with each child to make up for any disappointments."

the dinner party host

When it comes to creating boundaries between her work and personal life, Karen Mordechai admits that blurred lines have suited her best. As a graduate student at New York University and the International Center of Photography, she examined her heritage through the cooking of her maternal ancestors in a visual essay that became her thesis. In adulthood, she inadvertently started Sunday Suppers—the communal dinner party series that launched a collection of cookbooks, classes, events, and gatherings around the world—after photographing and posting pictures to her blog of a private dinner party with friends she hosted in her Brooklyn apartment in 2009. And when Karen's daughter, Sophia, arrived two years later, there was no question that she'd be there for every part of the process.

"I just merged Sophia into my work," says Karen, who continued to host dinners through her ninth month of pregnancy, then took two months off before getting back to work. "Shoots were paused for feedings, and I remember putting her in a BabyBjörn rocker on the dining room table while I cooked and styled food. My work, mothering, and life balance are all communed. Sophia and my husband, Ken, are key players in all of it."

Eventually, Karen moved the dinner parties to a studio across the street, allowing for at least a little separation as Sunday Suppers kept growing. And grow it did. People emailed (and snail mailed) from across the world to reserve a spot at her table, and she began to collaborate with other chefs, florists, designers, and more as the meals became larger in scope. When Sophia was two, Karen was asked to write a cookbook, which she likens to "mothering two beings." But she says she was giving so much of herself to Sunday Suppers that she became entwined with the business. "We had the most amazing opportunities, but it was also very hard to say no to anything; there were a lot of yeses," she recalls. "As a new mother, wife, and woman, I was over-giving to everything around me. I later learned this to be a crutch that I leaned on in my youth—to produce and create and go at an accelerated pace."

Seeking some respite, the family moved to Los Angeles in 2015, and after writing two more cookbooks, Karen scaled things back, though she continued to host global dinners for nearly three years. "It was uncomfortable for me, but I did not fill in the space immediately," she says. "When I was ready to create again, my intention was to do it differently, to build a brand in a resourced and resilient way."

The result is Le Marké, a gourmet marketplace for sustainable goods (for now, organic hand-harvested olive oil and vinegar) presented in refillable bottles and carbon-negative packaging. It's a convergence of food, community, and product that embodies the creative spirit that made Sunday Suppers so beloved—without demanding so much of Karen's physical and emotional well-being.

> "I surround myself with strong females. They are soft and full of love, and they offer generous and boundless support."

artisan food
purveyor /
mother
of one

"My north star is being connected to myself, which in turn allows me to be a good mother *and* businessperson."

Instead of taking everything on herself, this time around she says she is building a mature brand that aims for a better balance and has a clear directive, one that is more aligned with her spirit and reflective of the path she's taken to get to this point. That gives Karen time to concentrate on filling her own cup in a way that was sometimes lacking in her previous work life. "The thing I've had to carve out is a sense of self, remembering that as I fuel my own needs I can bring more to the other areas, like work, mothering, and partnering."

It also gives her time to build on the relationship she has with Sophia, now thirteen. "Having the chance to teach, raise, guide, and be with a young woman in the making has been a privilege for me," Karen says. "I view my relationship to work and my career as one of the ways I can model my version of myself to her. I hope she will see this either subconsciously or directly, and it will allow her to follow her true self and do her thing fullheartedly. Having a daughter and the opportunity to mother her has been the greatest gift of my being."

Advice from Karen Mordechai

BE MINDFUL OF YOUR FINANCIAL FREEDOM. "Sunday Suppers was always self-funded—and always profitable. This felt like a blessing and a curse. I enjoyed the thrill and satisfaction of keeping us going doing the things we loved. But our overhead was gigantic when we were running the space in Brooklyn and doing many things in different directions. Looking back, this pressure sometimes splintered my attention. Freedom is the double-edged sword here. Learning how to harness freedom to your advantage and making sure you don't overdo the work scale is a challenge."

FOLLOW YOUR OWN SCHEDULE. "I thrive from disciplined structure, sprinkled with a bit of freedom and spontaneity. My mornings are sacred, for yoga, walking, stretching, meditating. I love a slow start. Then I work from 11:00 a.m. to 4:00 p.m., and I try to have one to two days out in the world for meetings and appointments. I am pretty diligent about shutting off in the evenings, but I work on the weekends. I like the quiet and find I can really focus on tasks that need more attention."

TAKE THE SHORTCUTS THAT WORK FOR YOU. "I love a shortcut, and I love support when it is possible. I definitely do the typical: order groceries, subscribe to toilet paper, et cetera. But I never had a nanny. I tend to wear lots of hats in both my work and personal life. I cook almost all of our dinners—if you can imagine, I do not know how to shortcut in the kitchen. (My fast meal go-to is a mushroom risotto.) I could flex this muscle a little more, and when I do I'm surprised at the level of relief that comes with it."

the kidswear couturier

It was 9:00 a.m. Shanghai time when Tia Cibani found herself holding the attention of a crowded train full of quizzical Chinese commuters. Back in New York, it was 9:00 p.m., and her nearly two-year-old son was inconsolable, so her husband made a call with the hope that Tia could conjure some of what her children call "mommy magic."

"He was missing me so terribly and wouldn't go to sleep until he heard me sing the lullaby we always sang at bedtime," says the kidswear designer (and former creative director at Ports 1961). "So there I was on the train, singing 'Powder Blue' by Renee & Jeremy, and everyone was staring at me like, 'Who is this crazy lady singing into her phone?' And he fell asleep! I was on my way to a textile show of hundreds of exhibitors showing their fabrics and buttons and ribbons, but sometimes you have to just put on your mommy hat for those few minutes."

When she started her children's clothing line in 2004, Tia didn't have to contend with bedtimes and school schedules. "It was breezy and manageable when I was single," she says. "I could grow my business at my will. I never had to limit myself." She began designing for kids as a hobby while she was still on staff at Ports 1961, when her cousin, who worked in retail at Giorgio Armani, lamented that she couldn't find stylish baby clothes for her daughter and suggested they start the brand together. But about two years in, her cousin felt overwhelmed after having her second child, and Tia took full ownership.

"The business had quite a few years to marinate without the pressure of it needing to be paying me a salary," she says, adding that it was profitable enough to cover its operating expenses and some employee salaries. Yet she continued to think of it as a hobby, investing as much as $40,000 into it each year because sales continued to double—and sometimes triple. It wasn't until six years later that she left her job at Ports and turned the business into her full-time gig and main source of income.

"And then I had my first kid," she says. "And it got harder, and then my second kid came, and it started to get even harder, but it was still very manageable because my au pair was keeping them occupied so I could do my work."

She insists that regular trips like the Shanghai visit were possible because having an au pair made her little ones feel like they weren't missing a beat, whether she was working from home during the pandemic or away sourcing materials, courting buyers, or walking trade shows halfway across the world. "My husband did some of the housework, but it was my au pair who was my real co-parent," says Tia. "She made it possible for me to get my work done and have some time for myself and not feel as stretched. I didn't have to juggle as much."

But a year and a half ago, Tia decided to make some big changes, parting ways with both her husband and her au pair. "I just needed to take charge of my life," she admits. "I wanted to have my autonomy without having to answer to anyone about anything—what I feed my kids in

> "There were so many times I wanted to throw in the towel, but I had to keep going."

"We didn't have a very clear plan. Because I thought of it as my hobby, I felt like we were okay as long as I didn't go broke doing it."

the morning, when I put them to bed at night. But then everything in my life was all on me: the groceries, making dinner, the school runs."

For two years, she and her kids, now ages eleven and eight, adjusted to the new routine, but there were always trying times. One night, after a trip to the movies, Tia directed her children to shower and go to bed because she had a Zoom meeting with her team in China. "Well, I was downstairs and I could hear them talking, singing, yelling. It was 10:30 p.m., and they were still up. And I felt this *stress*. If they were at their dad's place, I wouldn't feel that. So I did my work whenever I could, however I could."

Tia acknowledges the inherent difficulty of trying to do two things at once—mother fully while being the lifeblood of her business. "Of course it was challenging; of course I was tired. And, of course, I would pause and have the family time that I wanted to have and the work would suffer, but I accepted it," she says. "It gave me a better sense of self. I can do a job; I can be financially autonomous; I can be the mother I want to be. It's the best of all the worlds."

But ultimately she had to recognize that her mental health was suffering and she needed help: Another au pair joined her family in January 2024. "I tried to go the part-time nanny route, and it was not working," she says of juggling schedules and taking an à la carte approach to her family life. "I am happiest when I have an au pair, so I opted to go back to it," she says. "Good childcare is everything."

Tia's Schedule

5:30–6:00 A.M.	Light incense and do a meditation, then enjoy my cappuccino while checking for any time-sensitive questions from my team or clients.
6:00–9:00 A.M.	"The Astounding Eyes of Rita" by Anouar Brahem is the kids' wake-up call. While my au pair, Angie, prepares breakfast, I get the kids dressed. Angie packs the kids' gear and snacks for the day, then drives them to school while I finish getting ready and then head to the office.
9:00 A.M.–3:00 P.M.	Attend marketing and sales meetings, work on mood boards, and prepare design materials; sketch and develop styles for the newest collection.
3:00–6:00 P.M.	Check in with Angie. If the kids' activities are not in sync (this happens once or twice per week), we divide and conquer. Angie makes sure that the kids are showered and in their PJs before I get home.
6:00–8:30 P.M.	I leave my office—luckily, I am fifteen minutes from home—and get dinner started. We eat by 7:00, and then watch a show or play a game together. Both of my kids play musical instruments, so sometimes they perform for me.
8:30–11:00 P.M.	I read to Archie while Castine snuggles with us, reading to herself. We cuddle until bedtime at 9:00 p.m. Then I have late-night meetings with my team in China and, finally, head to bed.

JEANINE VALRIE LOGAN

the natal expert

Jeanine Valrie Logan has always had big plans, and for the last decade and counting she's announced them around town by way of introduction: "I would say, 'Hi, I'm Jeanine, I'm going to be a midwife, and I'm going to open a birth center.' So everyone knew that's what I wanted to do," says the Evanston, Illinois, native and mother of three. Over the years, that simple declaration has not only held her accountable, it has telegraphed the conviction of purpose that has guided her throughout her adult life.

Though she graduated from Fisk University in Nashville, Tennessee, with a degree in biology and the goal of becoming an obstetrician-gynecologist, Jeanine's path changed after acting as an unofficial doula for her roommate while in grad school at George Washington University in Washington, DC, attending all of her doctor's appointments, and providing support at a local birth center that she says felt like a maternal utopia. "That was the moment," she remembers. "There were a lot of women of color, especially Black women, on staff, providers who were from the community and understood the health disparities. It was such a beautiful place and

> "Many of us have dreams that seem insurmountable. Sometimes they are, but one step at a time gets you closer to the finish line."

experience, and I remember asking a lot of questions and learning that they had a volunteer doula program. And that was it."

Before volunteering at the birth center, she spent a year and a half in South Africa doing HIV work, with a focus on maternal-child transmission, then another ten months in Cuba studying medicine, all the while meeting providers and midwives and learning as much as she could about their effect on maternal health outcomes. But in 2004, midwifery education wasn't a particularly accessible specialty in the US. "You had to be a nurse," says Jeanine, "and I was like, 'I am not doing this whole undergraduate thing again.'" So she ended up studying public health, with a focus on global reproductive health policy, as a graduate student at George Washington.

Yet her interests kept returning to the efforts being made in Africa with traditional birth workers in postwar nations. She had been volunteering with the White Ribbon Alliance, providing resources to midwives globally and advocating around issues like preeclampsia and bleeding disorders—conditions that are only now coming into the spotlight in the United States. So when she moved back to Chicago in 2009, where certified professional midwives were not yet recognized by the state, she thought she could do the most good for women in her community as a doula. But when a friend introduced her to a new accelerated degree through her nursing school, suddenly midwifery was back on the table. "Too many bills," she laughs, recalling the stress of paying for four degrees.

Back at school, Jeanine and her husband welcomed their first daughter, at home,

midwife /
mother of
three

in 2010. Jeanine had her second daughter four years later, while she was in nursing school. The birth at home was an amazing experience, but the support postpartum was predictably chaotic. "When we had exams, I would get to class early to sit with her," she says. "My friends would do a test out, and then they'd rotate watching her while I did my test out, or she'd come to the library while I studied. I'd rent a private room and bring all her toys and snacks and have her just play in the room, and I would study. She was a real nursing school baby." Most times, her husband watched the kids (at this time he was a full-time caretaker for his aunt who had dementia), or she drove forty-five minutes in traffic to drop the kids off with her in-laws. Sometimes neither scenario was an option. "I have pictures of myself presenting a group project when my daughter was two weeks old. It was terribly hard, but it was all-hands-on-deck because of my dream. When I look at it now, I have no idea how we made it work, but we just did."

Jeanine worked throughout school to make ends meet, supplementing her income with a few scholarships—"That was food, lights, gas," she says. She also breastfed her girls for three years or so each. "There was no sleep," she recalls with a laugh. Yet her dream of starting a birth center was a constant thought. When she graduated from midwifery school in 2018, she landed a job at the organization where she had been doing her clinicals, and also began her campaign to open the birth center in earnest. "It was me working on everything in between shifts or at night on the labor and delivery unit; I was doing all of our legislative work, testifying in the break room in my scrubs on how to change the law to expand birth centers in Illinois," she recalls.

Her hard work paid off at the end of 2021, when she was contacted by funders at Chicago Beyond, an impact investor that heard about Jeanine through members of the community and were interested in

partnering with her for their three-year leader-in-residence program. They gave her an office, a salary with benefits, and access to a network of potential partners and resources for professional development. "It's been so life-changing and amazing because it's given me the space to dream, to rest, to put my kids first," she says, noting that for the first time she was able to acknowledge just how burnt out she was and take a step back from midwifery to get momentum going for the center. "I'm just focusing on my kids. And I'm just trying to be normal to start this birth center so that I'm alive to enjoy it."

Since 2020, she's raised over $1 million for the center, with more donations on the way and a contract signed for a potential site. She's become its de facto birth justice movement advocate, writing and booking speaking engagements, and meeting with local officials to keep things running smoothly. And she's doing more than ever with her kids. "I feel like I'm making up for lost time," she says. "I spent so much time having to study, having to go to births, getting up in the middle of the night, being away for hours and hours, and definitely feel like that was a sacrifice. Now, I go to work at nine, I come home at five, and I have time to go to my daughter's basketball game at eight at night."

It's a pace she hopes to keep up going forward—even if it's still likely that she's sending an email at midnight or 5:00 a.m. "One of the best things about building the center from the ground up is that we determine the culture," she says. "Balance is something I try to stress because I'm not going back to the way it was before. We will have a space for families at the center because our children might need to be there, and we're also looking at what it means for everyone—not just leadership and the board but workers—to decide how and when we work. Because I really believe that our work has to be woven through our whole selves and our families."

Advice from Jeanine Valrie Logan

CONQUER YOUR FEARS. "Talking with government officials is very intimidating, but this phase is so necessary. I try to keep top of mind how much people deserve this kind of care. If I don't step out there, if I'm not brave, if I don't help people understand why this is needed, then we'll never open."

REMEMBER THAT YOU'RE NOT ALONE. "In the beginning, the idea of opening the birth center seemed very scary and like something no one would get behind. But I've been surprised to see how much support and encouragement we have received. Including the community in the celebration of each step is so important, as it is because of them that we have been able to get this far."

SEE YOURSELF IN THE VISION. "One of the folks at Chicago Beyond was like, 'Jeanine, where are you in the vision? I haven't heard you talk about what your role will be at the birth center.' I realized that I didn't know where I was going to put myself in the picture, but over the last year I've been doing more writing, more speaking engagements. Someone has to raise the money, someone has to do the birth justice movement work, so that's where I've landed."

the apron lady

Becoming a parent is a lot like starting a business, at least according to Ellen Bennett. "I equate a lot of the growth of parenthood to entrepreneurship because a big part of both is change management and adapting to new situations," says the mom to Nico, age three, and the woman behind Hedley & Bennett, the Los Angeles apron company turned lifestyle brand. "It's also about being vulnerable and having to say, 'I don't know how to do this.'"

Ellen was a line cook at Michelin-starred restaurants, stuck in an unstylish, ill-performing kitchen uniform, when she had the idea for Hedley & Bennett. With just $300 in her bank account, a "doing business as" trade name for her nascent apron idea, and a small window of opportunity—the chef at one of the restaurants she was working at wanted to replace the staff aprons, and Ellen volunteered to make new ones—she had to be resourceful. She bartered her cooking services to a friend in exchange for a pattern, then pounded the pavement to find seamstresses and manufacturers to turn her dream into a reality. That she didn't have a business plan or any experience in fashion or entrepreneurship wasn't a concern. "It's in my nature to go to the extreme," she says.

Yet for all of the hoops she had to jump through to turn her one-woman business into a multimillion-dollar empire, Ellen says the

> "If you don't want to grow, then just get a dog. If you want to grow, have a child."

early days of her maturescence were even harder. "Having a baby knocked me off my feet for two and a half months," says Ellen, referring to the latch issues that made Nico's nourishment a constant worry. "I think the transition was pretty stark for me. When you don't have kids, you're selfish. You don't even mean to be, but you are because you're not having to worry about anything but yourself and your dreams and your goals and your world. Having a kid is like somebody bulldozing through the side of your world. It felt like a cartoon busting through the wall."

Ellen says the timing of her pregnancy was serendipitous in that Covid-19 had already coaxed her into letting go of old habits, including a demanding entertaining schedule that included dinners and events, both personal and on behalf of Hedley & Bennett, six nights a week. "I think there was some mourning in the FOMO of everything else that's happening in the world that you're not present for. The dark side of Instagram came to light for me during those times because I've always been at a lot of events or created them." But with her son now born, she had to rethink the way she worked, so she stepped down and let go of the day-to-day details of the company, hiring a president to handle the operations of Hedley & Bennett so she could focus on more strategic branding partnerships and big-picture items. "I realized that I was going to prioritize these outside factors more than my own family, so I started limiting what I did and choosing more wisely," she says.

She also had to readjust her schedule. "My husband and I used to stay at the office until 8:30 p.m.," Ellen says. (Her husband is now the company's chief creative officer.) "Now

kitchen gear
retailer /
mother
of two

one of us is home by 4:00 or 5:00 p.m., and the other one is home by 6:00 p.m. at the latest. It's crazy that that's the new standard. And we maybe do one or two work dinners a week instead of five or six because we are trying to be present for this human that we made. I'll have meetings at my house so I can be around Nico. And when I go to the factory or office, it's calculated. I know that when I'm gone, that's time I'm not spending with my kid. It better be worth it."

Motherhood has also made Ellen relive some of the community building of her early entrepreneurial days. "I had to start building a tribe around me that I didn't have before," she says of surrounding herself with friends who already had kids and could help her through that first year. "I needed a different perspective. I couldn't call my friends who didn't have kids 'cause they didn't get it. They didn't know what I was going through. And I had to admit that I didn't know how to do stuff—a lot." She credits her nanny with picking up the pieces when things got particularly overwhelming. "A lot of times she would come over, and the house had exploded, I'm crying, Nico's crying. You just feel so fragile and think, *Can I glue this glass vase of myself back together?* But it's never going to look the same."

As much as she was evolving personally, those experiences also made her a more compassionate employer. "I was the first person in the office to have a kid, and it changed my perspective. I'm more helpful to other people who are parents. I give people a lot of grace." Part of that grace included official company policies to improve people's quality of life. "When I came back from maternity leave, I changed our policy to three months paid parental leave. We only had maternal before. The whole process was so brutal and so hard, and I couldn't have done it without my husband being present, so I wanted to give that to other people."

"When you take on investors, it's not like the money comes with answers. The money comes with an opportunity to figure out the answers, but you still have to get resourceful and continue to be creative."

Mothering Nico for the last three years has coincided with another big change for Ellen: Her self-funded company now has some financial capital from outside investors to help fuel its growth into the lifestyle sector. And she has welcomed another son, Bodie. Being able to take a step back has given Ellen something approaching an idea of balance. For now, she is embracing her evolution. "There is so much that is no longer a priority since the boys were born," she says. "Previously, I didn't have to worry about anybody but myself. I was very free. Now that I have them, it's such a contrast. I'm on another chapter of this older, wiser Ellen."

Advice from Ellen Bennett

HAVE WEEKLY FAMILY MEETINGS.
"Every Sunday night, we have a family work session where we just go through bills and schedules and Nico's classes. We're always asking, 'What are the things you want to do to fill your cup?' We're trying not to lose our humanity and become martyrs to parenthood or work or everyone else's needs."

WHEN FUNDS ARE LOW, BARTER.
"Everything became this puzzle-piecing game of getting the most you can out of every opportunity. La Colombe set up a coffee shop in our factory, and it became this really nice perk for our staff, and then La Colombe got the benefit of a space they didn't have to pay for. If we threw an event, I'd say, 'Let's find a company that doesn't know how to build a community, so they get ours, but they're going to pay for food or drinks.'"

REINVEST YOUR EARNINGS. "We were slowly but surely building this thing profitably by self-funding for nine years. My main rules were to never spend more than you make, and to put every penny you can back into the company. When you make a bunch of money, don't go on a crazy vacation. Reinvest it into the thing that made you get that success in the first place. If we used a type of fabric, I'd say, 'Let's buy more of that fabric.' That perspective helped us through some hard times when we didn't have cash."

You're Never Too Old to Be an Intern

I *love* being an intern. I have no shame admitting that I've interned four times—including when I was freelancing full-time from home—at firms that ranged from a letterpress studio to design firms. The knowledge I gained from those experiences—especially at the firms run by self-employed mothers doing what they loved—was priceless. Nothing gives you training like real-world training. My most rewarding internship was with Suann Song (page 80), a single mom running her own graphic design and stationery studio while her son was in school. She was so patient with me as I was learning, answering all of my questions and sharing tricks of the trade that I still use today, like how to present your work and files to clients. She was so confident and capable—and doing it all on her own. I remember leaving that summer, empowered to follow my dream. She has continued to be a mentor and friend all these years later.

If you're thinking, *I'm a mom! I need to make money! I can't be an intern!* I get it. Instead, think about smaller apprenticeships. I've helped friends pitch themselves to like-minded business owners, explaining why they'd be an amazing apprentice for one day a week. You'd be surprised how many people gladly accept an extra pair of hands around the workplace.

I've also been bold enough to invite a woman I admire for lunch, or ask how much she'd charge for an hour of her time to answer questions. People love to share what they've learned and give advice—pretty much to anyone who will listen.

There are also wonderful resources online that you can use to your benefit from the comfort of your own home. Joy Cho (page 28) offers business consulting online with other entrepreneurs. Jessica Hische offers similar courses that you can download and view on your own time. For the creatives out there, I'm also a huge fan of Skillshare. I've taken so many classes online after my kids go to bed, in an attempt to keep up with the ever-changing technology needed to run a business today. We're never too old, or too *late*, to learn.

WHAT'S THE BEST ADVICE YOU'VE EVER BEEN GIVEN?

"Be so good that they can't ignore you, especially when you're starting out. I still live by that one."

SARAH SHERMAN SAMUEL,
INTERIOR DESIGNER (PAGE 114)

"Tomorrow is a new day. No matter how much life falls apart today, take a deep breath and you will get through it. Also, no matter how bleak things seem, turn it into a positive."

LEONOR PERRETTA, LAWYER
(PAGE 148)

"A therapist once said, 'Never miss an opportunity to say nothing.' It became a mantra because at a certain point you have to back off. And the more you allow a person to feel respected and admired and loved—and the more you make yourself a little bit in the background—the better off everybody is."

MAIRA KALMAN, ARTIST
(PAGE 38)

"My dear mother-in-law told me, 'Be kind to yourself and to your partner. Life is a journey, and you will both need each other.' You give what you can. Some days you can give 40 percent while other days it's 70 percent, and that's okay."

NINA BARNIEH-BLAIR, INTERIOR
DESIGNER (PAGE 50)

"One of my favorite pieces of advice is to change your mind frame from thinking that you have to do something to you *get* to do something. Once you shift this perspective on whatever work that's required, even when it's something hard, it will change the way you approach your goals and the inevitable hustle."

ELLEN BENNETT, KITCHEN GEAR
RETAILER (PAGE 256)

"Don't let perfect be the enemy of good. I resented that advice when I was younger and had all the time in the world to make something better. Now that my attention is more fractured, that simple statement reminds me to just get going and worry about refinements later."

JENNIFER FERNANDEZ, WRITER

"My parents instilled a belief in me that I could do anything. I thought, *If I can think it, I can build it.* What I didn't realize at the time is that I was manifesting."

BETSY FORE, VENTURE
CAPITALIST (PAGE 264)

"It really does take a village. It is so important to be a part of a community you can trust your children with, as well as to surround yourself with positive, like-minded people who can also serve as role models."

PRISCILLA GRAGG,
PHOTOGRAPHER (PAGE 274)

the serial entrepreneur

Sometimes running a business means doing a lot of the heavy lifting—quite literally in Betsy Fore's case. When the eight-months-pregnant founder, inventor, and investor found herself lugging a cooler filled with baby food containers through Brooklyn's Prospect Park, it was all in a day's work.

"We built the company around one hundred founding families who would meet us every week and tasted all of our first twelve recipes for a year before we ever went live," says Betsy, who started the vegetable-based frozen baby-food brand Tiny Organics after researching the market and being disappointed with the lack of healthy, textured meal options (read: real food) for infants approaching the weaning stage. "These parents were taking food that was unmarked—we didn't have the branding built out yet—from strangers and feeding it to their infants in front of us. It was incredible."

In reality, those parents had nothing to fear. After he was born, Betsy's own son Sebastian was part of the testing pool. And going above and beyond the usual due diligence, Betsy and her cofounder, Sofia Laurell, partnered with the Friedman School of Nutrition Science and Policy at Tufts University to ensure that their idea for combining whole vegetables with gourmet seasonings was rooted in science and efficacy. "We know that if we can introduce a child to vegetables early, they come to love and prefer vegetables later on," says Betsy, who went vegan eighteen years ago and knew firsthand the benefits of a plant-based diet. "If I could give that love of vegetables to my son, that would change the health outcomes of his life. That was so much of the heartbeat of where Tiny was born."

This wasn't Betsy's first start-up. Before having children, she bootstrapped to launch a Fitbit-style pet activity monitor called WonderWoof that landed on Oprah's Favorite Things list, with a $50,000 grant from a nonprofit in St. Louis as funding. As a mom with limited time to give, she vowed to do it the opposite way with Tiny Organics: She courted investors early on (she's led the company through post–Series A funding to the tune of almost $20 million). A key to her funding success, she believes, is that she came to the table with a proven demand for her product out of the gate. "The way I coach all of the founders I invest in and mentor now is to have these one hundred founding customers that come along the pike with you," she says. "That is the affirmation that you need to have that lightbulb moment."

Betsy aligned with her cofounder to help carry the load when she was on maternity leave, but as the company grew, Betsy continued to stack her days. "It was prepandemic so things were a little different, and I immediately went back into the office," she says, ruefully, of being the only mom on the team and pumping in the bathroom at her funder's office at just three weeks postpartum. "I distinctly remember going to one of my first investor meetings with Gary Vee [Gary Vaynerchuk] at his offices, having forgotten my pumping supplies and feeling like I could burst. I would do it so differently now."

> "I've led with my heart through every one of my companies."

venture
capitalist /
mother
of two

Nearly four years later—after three years and multiple rounds of IVF and IUI, a life change she says she didn't feel like she could talk about with investors—she had her second son, Azi, which gave her a new perspective on work and motherhood. "He was like a miracle baby," she says, admitting that, ironically, he was conceived as soon as they had quit medical intervention. She exited Tiny Organics and took what she calls a "full, glorious, six-month maternity leave" just before launching her nonprofit, Natives Rising, a career accelerator offering grants to Indigenous founders. "I realized that these moments are fleeting, so I let the work stuff fall off so I could always be at everything," she says. "It's been a luxury because I've been running my own show, so I've been able to work my meetings around when his things are so that I can be present. It's clearer to me that the work will always be there."

Even with that realization—and a move to Chicago to be closer to her husband's family—it remains difficult for Betsy to reserve time for her own spiritual nourishment. "You wind up letting go of so much of yourself; you think, *I have to be selfless so they can thrive*," she says. "I wasn't exercising or putting focus on my breathing techniques or things that make me centered. What I realized in the long run is that that's what makes everyone else around me feel better, too, so that's probably the worst thing to let go. I shift that thinking now so I can pour more energy into myself, but I'm still not quite there yet."

She's found another way to fill her proverbial cup: by mentoring female founders through her nonprofit and two investment funds, XFactor Ventures and Velveteen Ventures. Betsy is credited with being the first Indigenous woman in the country to raise Series A funding, and she feels compelled to pay it forward. "It is my mission to help raise up founders who are then able to create generational wealth for their families. It feels like I've come full circle."

Advice from Betsy Fore

IDENTIFY A PAIN POINT. "Having to make my own baby food for Sebbi, I realized it was taking me hours to be able to freeze it, to try and get everything ready for daycare, and then get him on his way before I commuted into Manhattan. It was so much work, so we thought, *Can we provide this really easy, convenient solution for parents?*"

MAKE STRATEGIC PARTNERSHIPS FROM THE START. "The partnerships that you forge in the earliest days speak volumes in terms of what your values are. I believe in having strong advisory boards and advisory members from the beginning. I like to break it out in categories: I want someone in marketing, in product development, in fundraising. And then you can seek out and make a wish list of who those folks would be—almost like your dream team."

BE OKAY WITH FEELING UNCOMFORTABLE. "During a hackathon one weekend, a coder friend and I built the first Fitbit for dogs. For me to be in that setting, I was not in my element. But putting yourself out there is when those connections can be made. That got me thinking I could build this into something. That's when I took the leap."

the waiting-room artist

When her first son was just a toddler, Los Angeles artist Carolyn Suzuki made the biggest gamble of her life. Using a small loan she secured from her father and armed with an arsenal of original greeting cards embellished with her illustrations, she hopped on a plane to attend the annual stationery and gift show in New York. "It was the first time I had ever really been away from him, so there was a lot at stake for me," says the mom of two of parting with her older son for that fateful trip. "Even though it was only ten days, it seemed like an eternity. It felt like I was sacrificing a ton to leave my baby for that long, so I had better make it count. I remember I had this vague notion of *Okay, if this works I'm going to go for it, and if not I've got to figure out how to pay my dad back.*"

Thankfully, the trip worked out in her favor. She met an art director at *Martha Stewart Living* who loved her designs and later featured them in an issue, made meaningful connections with buyers from several retailers, and landed an East Coast agent. "And then I took orders at the show, which gave me a real-life gauge for demand. All of these wonderful things happened in that first showing, and I would have never done any of it had I not physically taken myself over there."

> "Only create space for what matters to you because you are sacrificing a lot of your precious time."

She kept up the momentum, drawing here and there while her son slept or played, but it wasn't until three years into the business that Carolyn felt she was earning enough that she could step away from her day job as a consultant and producer in the animation industry. "It wasn't a ton, but it was just enough," she remembers, noting that her oldest was in daycare so she had time to devote to figuring out how to scale her work. That was especially true while she was sick during the first and second trimesters of her second pregnancy. "Have you ever seen that photo of Frida Kahlo painting in bed? That was my setup," she says. "My business is my third baby." She recalls an instance when her work was top of mind as she was rushed to the hospital after giving birth to her second son. "My father-in-law was the one who drove me, and he said they were putting this IV in me and I was almost unconscious but I told him to call my husband and tell him to take this box to DHL because we had this big order that had to go out. I mean, I was about to die," she says. "I am my own business's ride or die, and the day it becomes not that, I will stop."

She credits not personally being on social media, though her team runs her business's Instagram account, with giving her a lot of time in her day to get work done but also spend with her children. "That frees up a ton of space in my mind and soul, so I don't feel so overwhelmed," she says. "I don't feel like I'm lacking balance." But she's also always been good at being creative on demand. "A very close friend who's in a similar line of work but doesn't have kids is always saying, 'I cannot believe you're able to draw in your car or in the waiting room at the doctor's

illustrator /
mother
of two

CAROLYN
SUZUKI
GOODS

office,' and I do that because I have no choice," Carolyn says. "I have to make space, especially if I'm against a deadline. I had this luxury before where everything had to be clean and I had to have my desk and my coffee. And I still wish for that sometimes, but I just don't have that luxury with kids, so I learned to drown out the exterior noise and focus when I need to be creative. I'm able to fluidly move in and out. For people who are in my line of work, where you make the thing that you sell, there is no separation between work and life 'cause I'm constantly working, in terms of thinking and being inspired. It's so nuanced."

She does, however, have the luxury of an engaged partner who takes on childcare and housework. "I don't think it's possible to be even," she says of maintaining their home life. "I had him read that article about emotional labor that came out a few years ago, and it really shifted his thinking. He's stepped up over the last four years, and it's given me more space to work and take care of my own needs." Carolyn also has a studio team of four who can take over when she is particularly busy at home. "You can do a lot, but you can't do it all at once," she explains. "It's like the flow of life. If you have a partner, sometimes you're in sync and sometimes you're like roommates. The same with your kids: Sometimes you're a superinvolved parent, but sometimes you're in work mode."

It's for that reason that Carolyn has a problem with a certain buzzword of productivity. "I never like to say that I'm the queen of multitasking because it's not real; it doesn't exist," she admits. "To even put that out there is such a disservice to our community because I see so many moms struggling with that. Whatever you're focused on, that other thing has to take a back seat."

One thing Carolyn vows never to cut back on is dedicated time away from home, when she can connect with friends and reinforce her identity outside of motherhood. "I've always been very focused on not losing myself," she says. "That comes with having a varied life where you maintain friendships and you're doing things outside of the home without your kid. Those are things I've always kept up with because I want my kids to see that I'm a full person; I'm not just here on earth to serve them. It's important for them to see that because it affects their worldview, especially because they're both boys. I want them to have an understanding of women and who we are and how powerful we are."

"You cannot manufacture desire. It has to come from within. And then, if you have desire, you can make a goal. If you set a goal, then you can make a plan."

Advice from Carolyn Suzuki

JUST GET STARTED. "I meet a lot of people who want the magic password to get from zero to a hundred fast, and it just doesn't exist. Everything takes a long time, but unless you start it's never going to happen. For something as life-changing as becoming an entrepreneur, you have to break it down in chunks. You should at least commit to a small incremental step. Write down what some of those steps are when your kids are napping, when your kids are in daycare. You have to chip away at it."

PAY IT FORWARD. "I started my business by asking questions, asking my friends who were already doing it. These were all women who shared their resources: how it's done, how much things cost. There was no gatekeeping whatsoever. So I always try to do the same for other people, because without that I would not be here."

BREAK OUT OF YOUR MOLD. "I had another business before I started my own, where I partnered with two men who came from the same commercial animation background I did. Because of who I was, a woman who had experience producing, I just went right back into that same role that I wanted so desperately to leave. I didn't want to be the caretaker, I didn't want to be the organizer but pretty immediately I became that, even though we were three partners. I was just like, 'Wow, I can do this for myself and grow my own business and make my own designs.'"

the shutterbug

If there's one thing Priscilla Gragg wishes she could have told herself early on, it would be this: "Becoming a mom won't ruin your career."

In fact, the complete opposite was true for this third-generation photographer. After spending three years trying to make it in the overly saturated fashion and lifestyle industries, Priscilla decided to rebrand when her firstborn was just four months old, changing her focus to commercial children's photography. "It was the best decision I could ever have made for my business," she says. "Once I found my niche, everything started to fall into place."

The funny thing is, photography was the last thing she expected to pursue. Born and raised in Brazil, Priscilla took on her first job as a teacher's aide at the age of fourteen. The pay? The equivalent of $20 *a month*. But she put 40 percent of that income toward private English lessons, taking on a second job at sixteen and opting to finish high school via night classes so she could work and save to put herself through college. Yet even after earning her Portuguese and English teaching degrees, she still felt like she couldn't conduct a proper conversation in English. So she applied to an au pair program to get some real-life exposure to English and was matched with a family in Vail, Colorado, where she met her now husband and also, unfortunately, discovered that her Brazilian degree had no validity in the United States.

Discouraged but determined, she became a concierge at the Apple Store and moonlit as a photographer, following in the footsteps of her father and grandfather. "I would approach people on the streets," she remembers, "explain what I was working on, and take their photos." She also shot family and friends to build up her portfolio. "I shot weddings for free until I felt confident enough to charge."

But for all of her determination, there was real fear that once she became a mother, she wouldn't get to put her newfound photography skills to work. "Both times I was pregnant, I was hesitant to share about it," she says. "I had this feeling that if my clients knew that I was pregnant, they would feel that I wasn't capable of delivering the job and wouldn't hire me."

Once her children arrived, she had to figure out how to ease back into her professional life. "I didn't work for about three months," she says of her self-imposed maternity leave. Her mother flew in from Brazil both times to give her family the support they needed for those first three months. "When I started [again] with small jobs, I would work with my baby in the carrier, attached to my body, until I felt confident enough to take on bigger jobs." A nanny helped smooth the transition a few days a week, a point Priscilla makes sure to tell new moms when doling out advice.

> "Running a business and parenting is all trial and error. As long as you follow your heart and do the best thing you can for both your family and your career, you'll be okay."

photographer /
mother
of two

As her children grew and went to school, things began to get easier. Then Covid-19 hit. Out of necessity, she and her investment advisory–professional husband homeschooled and juggled work and family more equally, transforming their garage into a studio space where Priscilla shot for brands like Apple (no longer the concierge!), Old Navy, Converse, FabKids, and *Parents* magazine. "The studio is like a blank canvas," she says. "I had two backdrops built that we can paint and do fun things with. My kids love the space, and sometimes they are my assistants." Despite all of the upheaval, Covid forced the family to make changes in their home that still work for them and their efforts to create balance in their lives.

Meanwhile, Priscilla continues to teach her daughters about the joy of work. "I never tell them I must work for money—not ever, not once," she says. "I tell them I do what I do because I absolutely love being a photographer and working on set." She says to her kids, "Mommy's work is fun. How do you feel when you play? Do you feel happy? So do I!" Now when she leaves for a work trip, her oldest says, "Mommy, good luck on your job. I hope you have a lot of fun!" The idea that work can be fulfilling is an important one for Priscilla to pass along to her children, one that already seems to be catching on.

Advice from Priscilla Gragg

SPLURGE FOR A LITTLE CHILDCARE— IF YOU CAN MANAGE IT. "If you can, arrange childcare for once or twice a week so you can focus on building your business. This leaves five other days for you to be fully present with your kids. You are showing your kids just how strong you are and how happy you can be when you go after your dreams. I cherish every single minute with the kids after coming home from a long trip. It's okay for them to miss you and for you to miss them."

GIVE BACK. "When your business is stable, don't forget to pay it forward. In 2016, I founded the Portrait Project, in which I offer personal photography sessions once a year and donate 100 percent of the profits to organizations that support children in need. So far the project has contributed 1,500 toys and over $50,000."

LEARN FROM YOUR MISTAKES. "I once sent an estimate for a job and forgot to account for the digital tech fees and equipment rentals. (These are some of the highest costs for a photo crew.) I only noticed after the client had approved and signed the budget. I didn't have the guts to go back and ask for more money, so I paid out of pocket. I will never forget that mistake!"

the sugar sculptor

On weekday mornings, the multidisciplinary artist Maayan Zilberman walks in a neat triangle from her Brooklyn apartment to her daughter's elementary school, and then over to her studio. That each location is only a few blocks from the last is by design—a simple calculation that keeps Maayan close to both her work and her child at all times.

"I'm with her a lot, and I love being with her," says Maayan, who has never hired a nanny or babysitter to help with her four-year-old daughter, Freddie. "A lot of my projects tend to ebb and flow, so I make it work. But I've always felt that I needed to make my art. My work and my child are equally important, and it's essential that she *sees* that my work is important." By all accounts she does. Freddie often spends time in the studio after school while her mom is on a deadline or under pressure to figure out a project. "She loves to tell people that I'm an artist," Maayan says. "She's really proud of it."

The former lingerie designer and fashion consultant didn't always have the freedom to engineer her days around the kinds of practices that would fulfill her both personally and professionally. "I missed doing things that had an immediate product," she says of shutting down her intimates brand, the Lake & Stars, and taking a break from consulting more than a decade ago.

"The way that I was working over the years became much more distant from any of the handmade pieces that I loved doing because the more successful you get, the further you are from making them. You're managing people or managing a factory. So I just stopped doing it."

To get back to her creative roots, she started making things at home for fun—anything that imbued her time with meaning. She quickly gravitated toward sugar as a medium. "I always loved sweets and have always been really curious about how candy is made, so I just started making it," she says, emphasizing that none of the experimenting that she began doing nearly twelve years ago was intended to be legwork for forming a business. "And I loved the idea that the work is ephemeral." She began to study YouTube videos and test recipes, carving her own molds from clay and silicone to make one-of-a-kind shapes: geometric sculptures, floral cocktail rings, translucent butterflies—all cast in welded sugar.

But as Maayan says, personal projects can often turn into market research, and when word spread of her candy creations among friends and other people in the fashion industry, she got an opportunity to show her work in the form of a fake candy shop that garnered press and, to her surprise, more than a few order inquiries. "When I realized that the jobs were quite lucrative, I thought, *Wow, there's a business here*," she says. "I didn't have any kind of business plan. I just continued to do what I was doing but scaled it. I got a studio and assistants, and then I was able, bit by bit, to build it into something that could sustain my life, which in the end became a lot more lucrative than working in fashion."

> "I started making things at home without the intention of it being a company."

fine artist /
mother
of one

The beauty of the business—called Sweet Saba, after her confection-loving grandfather—is that it doesn't require a lot of overhead. "I didn't take out any loans," she says. "I had some savings from having worked for a long time, and when I did my first show, I needed to build the shop and invest in materials and pay some assistants, so I probably spent about $10,000 for the initial launch. Then I invested a little bit of money, like hundreds here and there for packaging and branding. Not a lot."

Now that she's a mom, Maayan has purposely kept her business small as much to preserve her personal life as to maintain her sense of self-sufficiency and creative independence. "I don't want to be tied to whatever it is that I need to make for my bottom line," she says. But staying true to her creative vision has its trade-offs. "I knew that that was not going to be a supercommercial or scalable way of working, and I'm okay with it. I've never been driven by that endgame. Over the years, I've met with investors that wanted to put money into the business, or strategic partners that had the infrastructure to do stores internationally and maybe water down the art of my work and make it more commercial. To other business owners that might be really appealing, but it's not why I make the work."

Though Sweet Saba always keeps her days busy, prioritizing creative fulfillment extends beyond the business. Maayan makes watercolor pieces for gallery shows, sews all of Freddie's clothes (often using fabric from dresses in her own closet), and does makeup tutorials on her Instagram feed. And she continues to foster a spirit of creativity and open-mindedness for her daughter. "It's all very organic, as they say," she says of her willingness to adapt her schedule to Freddie's needs and whims. "We take each year at a time. I don't like to think too far ahead because I don't know where she'll be developmentally. She may surprise me, or she may need some extra help. I kind of just go with the flow."

Advice from Maayan Zilberman

DON'T STRESS ABOUT YOUR WEBSITE. "People don't care that much about your website being the best thing ever. It's not 2002. People just want to be able to find you easily and get the information and buy something if there's something to buy. Everything else is smoke and mirrors. I check my analytics, and no one even looks at my website, no one cares. All of my clients find me through Instagram."

REFINE YOUR MESSAGE. "When I talk to people about starting businesses, so much of what they're afraid of isn't real, it's aesthetics. What you need to focus on is what you are actually communicating: What's your story? What's different about it?"

DO WHAT WORKS FOR YOU. "My least favorite thing about being a business owner is managing people. I don't like having a ton of employees. In different chapters of my career, I've had a bigger staff, and I didn't enjoy it. I like to zone out and make my art and sometimes labor day and night to finish things, and I do it all myself. It just makes me feel really good about the work I'm doing."

the adventure maker

Slim Pickins Outfitters isn't just a retail store to Heather Dawes and her husband, Jahmicah. Though the first Black-owned outdoor shop in the United States began on a whim, it has become a bastion of inclusivity for the husband-and-wife owners' small Texas community, a symbol of hope for Black recreation enthusiasts across the country, and a labor of love for the couple and their extended families, who continue to scrap to keep alive their dream of outdoor adventures for all.

"A big thing for us is safety in the outdoors," says Heather, who learned that she was pregnant with their first son, Silas, six days before they opened Slim Pickins nearly eight years ago, with a $50,000 investment that included money from friends and community members. "There are so many stories of Black men being attacked in the outdoors or feeling unwelcome, and the main sticking point for me was Ahmaud Arbery. I want to be part of creating a more diverse outdoors so my boys can run or go wherever they want and be safe. A lot of it has been me being in the background to give my husband a platform as a Black male to share things that he's experienced."

> "I've had a full-time job while pursuing the shop. Is that ideal? No, but having that to fall back on gives us some peace."

For Heather, that meant working a full-time job at a nonprofit to pay for their living expenses while Jahmicah worked at the store during the day; afterward, she'd take over the shop floor while he worked on back-office items. Though family members pitched in pulling shifts, there was only so much he could do on his own, so Heather quit her nonprofit job in 2022 to see if the extra help she provided—taking on the bookkeeping and social media duties—could grow the business faster. Unfortunately, she had to take on a part-time role as an office manager to make up for the income gap, as well as a few other odd jobs: She helps out on her parents' farm and sells vegetables at weekend farmers' markets; operates a small cottage bakery out of her kitchen; and has begun writing for outdoor brands, with a self-published children's book in the works. "We had to take the risk, but that resulted in me being entrepreneurial in other aspects," she says.

Keeping busy is something that comes naturally to Heather. "I will work from the second I wake up to the second I go to bed if I'm left to my own devices," she says. But she recognizes that isn't always an option as a mother of two kids under ten. "There may be times when it's required, but it's not something that can become a regular part of my life. I have become a lot more balanced because I've had to."

Sometimes that balance is hard-won. Because the store's staff has been primarily made up of friends and relatives, family celebrations have often caused Heather and Jahmicah to close shop, even on their most profitable days. "Just a few weeks ago, my husband's brother's partner was having her baby shower, and I had to go to the farmers'

outdoor
gear retailer /
mother
of two

"We've had to work hard and give clear expectations of what we need from one another. It's both of us trying to give 100 percent, knowing that when the other is struggling we'll pick up the slack."

market, and the person who was supposed to fill in for us got sick and couldn't come in, so we had to close down on a Saturday, which is our biggest day of the week," she says. "We did miss out on business, and we needed the money. But that's part of being more balanced."

But other times, the couple shifts into work mode, with Jahmicah traveling as part of his marketing efforts and Heather picking up the slack at the store. He was recently featured in *Blackwaters,* an indie documentary film on Black outdoorsmen, and is frequently booked as a speaker and panelist at events across the country. That has brought more visibility to the shop but has also introduced more strain as Heather juggles her many tasks. Usually, she relies on her mother and teenage sister to help out with her kids during those busier times. "It is the most stressful part of my life right now," she says. But she knows that it's all part of the journey.

Heather and Jahmicah have recently moved the store into a location closer to home and her boys' school to cut down on their commute and the need to close down the shop for family events. "The hope is that this is a move for us in all ways: physically, financially, spiritually, mentally, emotionally," she says. "We hope this means more traffic, less scrapping, and increased health for the business." But in the meantime, she knows that success isn't guaranteed. "For us, ultimate success would be that someone else handles the nitty-gritty of the shop, that we are able to compensate someone and step back and enjoy what we've built," she says. "For right now, success is making it till the end of the week. And our kids seeing Black men and women on the water fly-fishing and hiking and skiing. It feels good to know that we've been able to do that and take our kids along for those things."

Advice from Heather Dawes

ACKNOWLEDGE YOUR LIMITATIONS. "I've told Jahmicah when I don't think I'm doing well emotionally and mentally. In the past, I've taken two weeks off from everything. Sharing those decisions at our team meetings is always hard for me. But if I don't set the example, then when somebody else feels this way, they won't do it. I don't want to be part of a culture that makes somebody feel like they have to push until they're burnt out."

DON'T EQUATE SUCCESS WITH WORTH. "My paternal grandmother had a candle shop, wrote books, and had a successful magazine about our little community. Watching her, I learned that you can try something, and if it doesn't work, you can go try something else. And also that you can be really good at something and maybe it doesn't work out. It doesn't mean that you're not gifted."

DO RIGHT BY MOTHERS. "When I worked at the nonprofit, I had twelve weeks off but it was unpaid, so I saved up all of my vacation and sick days so that I could use those on the front end of my maternity leave. We decided we would never do that to an employee. Even though we have struggled, we offer twelve weeks fully paid. And then kids can come with our employees whenever and however long they need them to. That started because when I worked full-time, Jahmicah had to bring Silas with him to work."

Boundaries

The term *self-employed* often registers in people's minds as "very flexible schedule." In some cases, that's true. As a people pleaser, I've found this to be a hindrance in my career. I've had a hard time saying no, both in my personal and professional life, which has negatively impacted my mental health. The key (for me, at least) has been to establish limits, the first being around work hours. In her book *Set Boundaries, Find Peace,* Nedra Glover Tawwab says that "clarity saves relationships." I think we can say that clarity saves our *business* relationships, too. It's essential to communicate and not assume that people are aware of our expectations.

I learned very early on that if *you* don't set your hours, others will set them for you. Now, when someone asks me to help watch their kids while they run to the dentist or to meet up for a playdate or to grab lunch to catch up, I firmly say, "I have work from 9:00 a.m. to 1:00 p.m. today, but I'm free afterward." Kid-free work time is precious, and if you constantly give it up, you'll absolutely *never* achieve your goals. You wouldn't ask your dentist to watch your kids during her work hours, would you? (Note: I'm all for volunteering and helping—I actually do it quite a bit. But *not* during my work hours. I often include my family in ways that fit into our schedule.)

To set my clients' expectations, I micromanage the ways they can get ahold of me and provide clear communication about the times when I will be available. Almost none of them have my phone number, and that is by design. I don't text with clients, and if we have a call, it's online. I do most of my communication via email, which I check only during *my* office hours. Other boundaries I've set include no work on the weekends (unless it's absolutely necessary), and no work calls when my kids are home. This is what makes sense for me, but there is no one way to do this. Find what's best for you.

I should note that sometimes this is all easier said than done, and might ruffle feathers—it's hard for those who have never been self-employed to understand.

Saying yes when I feel like saying no sets off a feeling of overwhelm in me. You don't need to say yes to everyone. If they think you're worth it, they'll wait.

Create Your Own Community

In 2020, our family moved to Utah for my husband's work. Coming from Chicago, which is so rich with culture and history and art, I spent the first year, admittedly, depressed. I was missing my community, especially my artistic/entrepreneurial one. Then my illustrator friend Mika Rane invited me to join a self-employed artist group where we meet and create and share ideas. It was just what I needed. It provides the support I suspect I'm missing from not being in a studio or office environment. I've also found kinship through volunteering and fundraising. Serving your community is one of the fastest ways to find a network of friends and maybe even colleagues. It's made me feel connected on a whole different level.

But gaining support from others starts with you. Share—on social media or in your everyday conversations—when your peers are doing something you think others should know about, whether that's a new product they're selling or service they're offering or shop or restaurant they've opened. Support your neighbor's Kickstarter campaign if you can. When you're self-employed, the community in many ways becomes the backbone of your company. Most of my work comes through word of mouth, so if I burn a bridge, I'm really the one who gets burned. (I'm not proud to say I've burned a few during my decade as a freelancer. It's usually when I overbook myself, or when I don't set or take responsibility for proper boundaries. I've always regretted a terse email, but I've never regretted being kind. Kindness *always* wins.)

Another great way to expand your community is to collaborate. It's a fun way to introduce your name to a new audience and also a great means of diversifying your offerings. I've worked with many brands—Schoolhouse Electric, Artifact Uprising, Solly Baby, Revival, Opinel—and you know what? Those opportunities didn't magically appear. Many times, I design something that I love and wish were on the market, create a PDF showcasing my ideas, and find someone's email and pitch them. A lot of companies say no, but you only need one person to get on board. One collaboration leads to another, and then you're on your way. (Also, don't forget to shore up your contract—see page 96. It's important to establish what royalties you plan to take, how long the company is able to use your design and for how many products, and how each of you will promote and photograph the product. The details matter!)

the side-hustler

You could say retail is in Caroline Rodrigues's blood. Her grandfather owned a children's clothing store in the 1980s and '90s, and her father still has his own shop at the tender age of seventy-three. She even remembers perfecting her nascent marketing skills in the back office there as a five-year-old.

"I pretty much lived and worked in my parents' store, where I would frequently sketch out merchandising plans and help my mother stock her store," recalls Caroline. "It was my favorite thing ever. I think that's where my passion for design really grew—that was all I knew."

So it was perhaps inevitable that she would follow in the family's footsteps and open a shop of her own—even after earning a business degree and working at marketing and branding jobs in New York City for more than a decade. (She still has a full-time job at Letter A, a mother-run creative agency specializing in mother-founded brands.) At Merci Milo, which comprises two shops in Portland, Oregon, and Los Angeles and is named for her youngest daughter, Caroline and her husband stock one-of-a-kind handmade children's toys and accessories that put big-box plastic playthings to shame. Curating the selection is one of Caroline's greatest joys, but getting there hasn't been all fun and games.

"Stay focused, keep doing what you do, and never give up on your dreams."

"When we started, we invested our entire life savings into the company, so we weren't in a great place financially," says Caroline, who also has two teenage kids. "We couldn't afford proper daycare and often had to bring Milo, who was four when we opened, to work. After a lot of searching, we were so blessed to find a small home daycare by our shop that was affordable."

But that's just one piece of the small-business puzzle for Caroline. She and her husband usually find themselves wrapped up in some work commitment, whether it's for their day jobs or the store. "Monday through Saturdays is pretty much nonstop," says Caroline. "We hardly ever cook dinner because we simply do not have the time. It's a whirlwind of getting work done and juggling homework with the kids, then at around 10:00 p.m. we have some downtime—unless we're working until midnight."

Weekends are often spent ordering inventory, packing and shipping orders, and attending to customer service emails. But Sundays are sacred. "We make sure we keep a no-work policy," she says, noting that their freedom hinges on employees who keep the shops running while they're with family. "We shut off our phones so there's no email checking, no texting. Learning to keep those boundaries is so important because burnout is very real within this household."

Like many working moms, Caroline often feels like she's floundering. "Today, I felt like giving up," she admits. "The journey of being a parent and a small-business owner is a roller-coaster ride. The emotions are so intense—there are so many highs and lows, days I want to scream, days I want to cry, days

toy store owner / mother of three

No Cash Accepted

of joy. You just have to be flexible and ride through these waves."

She also frequently navigates the waters of self-doubt. "I'm often told I'm a workaholic—my mom guilt is always kicking in," she says. "My older kids understand the demands, but Milo is still young. She often complains that both my husband and I are working all the time. Every weekend, we end up working at our shop or warehouse, and I can see Milo completely upset because she wants to be elsewhere." But her daughter isn't all mad. "Milo is probably the number-one salesperson in the shop—she is so persistent." Caroline laughs about Milo's tendency to push bath crayons. "I love how passionate she is about all of the products and is particular about where everything goes."

Despite the constant hustle, Caroline insists that the life that she's made for herself makes her feel whole. "Growing up in a Korean household, I always thought that success meant you were either a doctor or a lawyer, or made tons of money. After starting my own business, I realized that success for me meant that I was happy. I truly want happiness and time with my family. And I hope Milo gets inspired by our work ethic," she says, as Caroline was by her own father. "My hard work and dedication come from his many lessons while growing up."

Advice from Caroline Rodrigues

COMMUNICATION IS KEY TO MARRIED OWNERSHIP. "My husband and I have different perspectives on how to run the shop. There are many disagreements, but in the end we realize that we have the same goal in mind. We've learned to be patient with ourselves and come back at a later time to discuss instead of getting heated in the moment."

MAKE WORK FUN FOR YOUR KIDS. "Milo is such a trooper. Coming to work has always been fun for her, but long evenings, especially during the holidays, sometimes became unbearable. We would take turns reading her books while one of us worked, or we would build forts from leftover cardboard boxes. She had the best time. Of course, we would also bargain for special toys she had been eyeing in the warehouse."

PAY A LIVING WAGE. "I started this business not wanting to be like the corporations I used to work for. I give my almost full-time employees a full paid week of vacation. We also give raises twice a year; end-of-year bonuses are pretty generous for a retail shop. I am currently trying to pay my staff a living wage depending on their household. I want to break that barrier of having a constricted retail wage. We don't want to work within the confines of corporate management. We consider everyone in our company like family."

the dance partners

Marilyn Sheperd likes to joke that she is long on resolve but short on resources. That was especially true thirty years ago, when the then forty-seven-year-old college recruiter—having no background in education, corporate finance, or community organizing—had the somewhat audacious notion to start a ballet school after learning that the one her daughters attended had abruptly closed. "Looking back now, I would say I was crazy," she laughs of the Hyde Park School of Dance's unlikely beginnings. "It boggles my mind. Who does this? I had some money—not nearly what we would need to start a school; we're talking four or five thousand dollars, not a lot—but I figured there were enough people in this world with business sense who would help me."

She enlisted her daughters' teacher, then twenty-four-year-old August Tye, to be the school's founding artistic director, leased a space in the basement of Hyde Park's Unitarian church, of which she was a member, and opened the school's doors with a five-kid class (it grew to thirty by the end of the year) and a staff of three. "When we started, August was teaching, maybe her sister, too, and we had a pianist because we always wanted live music. And I said, 'Okay, now who really doesn't need to get paid this week? Be honest: Who can go without getting paid?' And we'd go around the circle. Peter, the pianist, was the first one who said, 'Okay, I don't need to get paid. I can go another week.' That's how we were."

Wanting to establish the school as a nonprofit and knowing she was out of her league, Marilyn moved to create a board, seeking out like-minded individuals who loved dance as much as she and August did. But she quickly learned that the best board members are the ones with resources. "I used to say, 'Do not kid yourselves. The fact that you love dance is great, but at the end of the day, you've got to have money,'" she explains. "We've gotten much better at finding people who love dance but also have the resources that we need to fund it." To raise money to keep the school running, she tried every trick in the book: She sought donations from parents (she famously went around classes with a shoebox collecting funds) and people in the Hyde Park community, and she applied for grants, including a timely one from Oprah Winfrey through a tenuous connection.

"The biggest part of fundraising is asking, and it's generally the hardest part for most people," Marilyn says. "Most people say, 'I would do anything before I ask for money,' and I never really felt that way about it. The fact that the school started doing so well so quickly gave me the momentum to go on."

Her next hire was a treasurer who knew how to handle the business—the city, state, and federal taxes but also the finances and payroll. "Frankly, I thought, *We've got to get the business part up and running and*

> "No matter what the business is, it has to be mission driven. Even the most businesslike business has a reason for being." —MARILYN SHEPERD

dance
educators /
mothers of
two & three

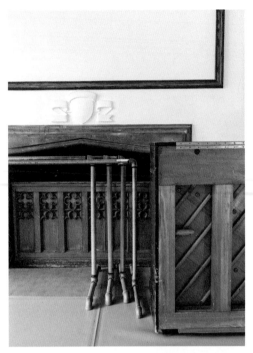

get money into the right checking account," Marilyn recalls.

Meanwhile, August managed the class schedule and the hiring of teachers, coordinating guest dancers and programmatic offerings around town to help build word of mouth. She also taught, in a studio that Marilyn herself painted, eventually bringing her newborn daughter to watch lessons because she didn't have the money for a babysitter (her husband, an opera singer, would often travel abroad, performing for months at a time). "I would plop her in this beanbag we had, and she was quite entertained watching the dancers and listening to the music and kicking her little feet," August recalls. "Board members would stop by and take her outside for some air. It was a great environment of nurturing women running the school together and caring for one another, and it was because of that that I could survive."

That compassionate atmosphere was by design. "As I thought about what I wanted the school to be, I envisioned that it would be a family," says Marilyn. "We weren't creating just a school."

But despite the spirit of camaraderie and support, August says that when her second daughter joined the family, the juggle became much harder. She often felt like she was working to pay for childcare, and the guilt of missing bedtime stories and goodnight snuggles—dance classes are usually held after school into the evening—was overwhelming at times. "I tried to scale back to have a few days off a week to be with my kids, but I needed to keep my job. And I loved the school. I wanted it to keep going." In 2009, August had her third child, a son. By that point, her husband was traveling less and could take up more of the child-rearing and home-keeping tasks, allowing August to continue to do her life's work.

"I don't think I could have ever been a successful stay-at-home mom," August says.

"Don't let a job flush a dream that you have. Figure out how to make it so." —MARILYN SHEPERD

"Teaching is in my soul. It's beyond making sure people are good dancers; it's shaping kids' lives. Dance was always something I wanted to give back."

Though the school has been a labor of love for both women, it has evolved over the last thirty years, becoming more established and less scrappy in its fundraising efforts and embracing a diversity of dance forms to better serve the community. Having retired, Marilyn no longer works at the school but returns frequently to see its progress, especially since her daughter Allyson, one of the school's first pupils, became an instructor and the director of community engagement. But their commitment to creating a safe, inclusive environment for the community at large endures.

"Hyde Park is a kaleidoscope," Marilyn marvels. "It's a quilt; it's every kind of culture you can find there. And I thought, as an African American woman, if I can contribute something to that artistic fabric—that was irresistible to me. But I never saw the school as mine. I wanted this to be a gift to the community and to be the property of the community. Giving this kind of experience to your daughters, having them see you work so hard for something you care so deeply for, it's a blessing."

Advice from Marilyn Sheperd

FIND YOUR MONEYMAKERS. "We believed in this school and knew the power of performance, so we said, 'We need to do *The Nutcracker*.' We didn't have enough people to perform the whole thing that first year, so we did excerpts from it to see who would come. The first *Nutcracker*, we had ten or twelve students. We said, 'Okay, realistically, how much money do we have to get out of this performance for us to continue,' 'cause we were really up against a wall. And I had no more money to put into the school without getting a divorce from my husband, who thought that I was nuts to do this. We figured out a magic number, and it was something like $500—we're not talking about a lot of money. It turned out that we ended up making more than that, and we said, 'Okay, we're on our way.'"

KEEP YOUR OWN MONEY. "My mother was one of three sisters, and they were all very strong professional women. They all said, 'Marilyn, always have a chunk of resources that you can use so you don't have to answer to anyone but yourself.' I used my own discretionary money to start the school, and for things like rent or to pay the teachers."

MAKE YOUR HOUSE THE MEETINGHOUSE. "When my kids were teenagers, ours was the house everyone came to. This way, I didn't have to worry about where they were. Board meetings, too, especially at the beginning, were always at my house. I wanted people to feel that this was where we met, where we came up with crazy ideas. And I could be closer to my girls."

> "My ability to dance for myself ended when I had kids—it was all just the work, the teaching, and the choreographing. I would say there was some resentment about that when the kids were little. But I don't regret it. It's the life path I took." —AUGUST TYE

the night writer

For many parents, there is nothing more tedious than reading the same mediocre stories at bedtime every night—or, worse, reciting them two, three, even four times in a row. Mississippi-born Freda Narh and her Ghanaian husband, Samuel, had a particularly low threshold for less-than-entertaining children's books, but compounding their mild annoyance was the simple fact that no one in the books they read to their then three-year-old daughter, Merrit, looked remotely like themselves. "We live in the library," says Freda, a former preschool teacher. "We've checked out close to six hundred books this year alone, so we've read a lot."

Samuel, a work-from-home engineer by day and author by night, addressed the need by writing and selling two books, one based on his family, to small publishers. But in between all the couple's late-night discussions about the stories' characters and themes, they realized they had enough ideas for scores more. To tell them the way they wanted to, the couple decided to start an independent publishing house, Chasing A Spider, from their Sacramento living room before moving into a small office space nearby. Neither of them had any experience on the production side of book publishing, so they relied on Google to find a designer

and editor to help them refine their ideas and hooked up with the printer of Samuel's first book. Freda and Samuel have written and published two books under the Chasing A Spider imprimatur, but they have plans for many more. "We want to cover hard topics like death or missing mom, things you don't hear a lot about. And we want to write books for Merrit and all kids, so that they can see themselves in those stories and be able to apply them to something later in their lives." The only question for them is how to figure out the timing on a tight budget.

While Samuel works from home full-time, Freda homeschools their now eight-year-old daughter, so evenings set the stage for busy work hours, with Merrit doing her schoolwork or reading next to them. "We're night owls," says Freda, who stays up until the wee hours on a regular basis and insists that, thanks to "tons of green tea," she can function well with as little as three hours of sleep. "I'm pumping out the work and doing the best I can, and it's good for Merrit to see. I want her to feel inspired. She's the motivation behind all of this." Sometimes, quite literally. "She's always saying, 'Mom, when is the next book coming? We can't stop now.'"

When she's not homeschooling, Freda is networking and taking interviews, essentially being a one-woman marketing machine. She says Merrit's support pushes her when the days feel too full, but staying busy is also in her nature. "We're at coffee shops. We go to the library. We go to classrooms and read our stories to kids, and sometimes she comes along," Freda says. "Then we have our quiet times when she's writing, and I'm writing." At home, Freda often finds herself down Instagram wormholes looking for illustrators

> "I love my life. I love that I can do something independently that I'm very passionate about."

publisher /
mother
of one

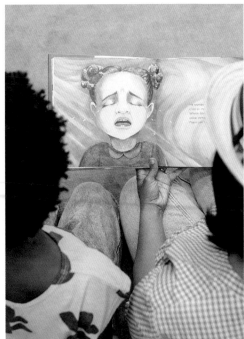

across the world and scouting new talent and ideas for the next book. "I can't tell you how many emails I've sent," she laughs.

For now, she and Samuel are Chasing A Spider's only authors, but she's confident that will change as the publishing house establishes itself and generates more press. Part of the couple's plan involves Samuel pitching books to larger publishing houses as both a means of income and a marketing strategy. "All of that helps network for the next book," she says. "It's kind of like you're piggybacking off the success of those previous books." In the meantime, she's content to keep the growth slow and steady. "We're not really looking for profit right now," she says, "just to sustain and make money for the next work. Everything we make goes right back into the business, so it's a slow process. But after working for others, I'm finally happy about being able to pour my energy into our family and our family business. It's very rewarding."

Advice from Freda Narh

GET CREATIVE WITHIN YOUR BUDGET. "Established illustrators are extremely expensive, and we know they deserve every dime. Unfortunately, we only have a budget of $10,000 to $15,000 for each of these stories, so there's a lot of combing through social media, LinkedIn, and Instagram to find artists who can capture our characters for a reasonable price. Some of them have never done book work before, so it's attractive [for them] to add that to their portfolio."

FIND A WAY INTO THE CONVERSATION. "We knew how important reviews are for networking and social media. So we paid for lots of ads and sent books to friends on LinkedIn and Instagram—we couldn't afford the real influencers—and paid for a submission in *Kirkus Reviews*.

After that, there was a lot of word of mouth, and there were a lot of unpaid reviews online through social media. That goes so far, because when you have a network of children's book writers, we help each other. That's how *A Kite for Melia* became our breakthrough book. It won independent book awards and recognition without us applying for anything."

NORMALIZE SAVING. "We're always saving for the next book. We live very frugally in general and pay for everything out of pocket, with no loans. We do a vacation once a year; the rest of the time we have a lot of picnics together. If there's a work trip, we're bumming a ride with Dad. We only have one car. We're just really good savers."

the free spirit

When Beatrice Valenzuela's children were very small, she carried them on her all the time: while working on her phone, strolling through the park, soaking in a bath, simmering food for dinner. "Once, I was getting one of my favorite clients ready for an event while my son, Dimitri, was nursing," says the Los Angeles–based hair and fashion stylist turned designer, whose eponymous line of shoes and accessories is a favorite among West Coast creatives. "He was so loud. He sounded like a suckling piglet. At first I thought, *Oh no, is this embarrassing?* Then I decided it wasn't. We all giggled about it."

More of that intimacy with her children was what Beatrice was after when she decided to pivot her career into designing. "I made my living with the work I did in person," she says. "The idea that I could be generating an income without being present at all times was appealing. I wanted to create a new way of life for myself so that I could be more present as a mother and a better partner to my love."

She had already begun to experiment with making her own clothing and art four years earlier, after the birth of her daughter. Drawing on her eclectic life experiences—growing up in Mexico City, attending school in Paris, and collecting art pieces from her global travels—she began weaving and sewing items that she felt weren't represented in the

> ## "Being a mother is my favorite thing about myself and my life. I find immense joy in it."

market. "I was a new mother, and with that came so much inspiration and opportunity," she says. But it also came with expenses and limitations on her time, and she felt that items she had previously been drawn to were suddenly out of her reach. The circumstances led her to design shoes, jewelry, and clothing that were made locally and therefore were more accessible. "And there was a moment when I realized, 'If I want this, then there are others who want it too.'" She reached out to fashion-industry friends who were generous with their advice and contacts in the manufacturing space and started producing pieces with just $800 capital in reserve, maintaining her styling jobs until Beatrice Valenzuela, the brand, became profitable six years later.

She attributes much of her success to the conscious choice not to scale the company too quickly in the beginning. "We didn't try to go too large or make too much from the start," she says. "The stakes were low, and there was no big risk." Having childcare when her children were small gave her the freedom to work out the logistics and figure out the manufacturing side of the business. But her homegrown approach to marketing was another important factor. In 2009, she cofounded the Echo Park Craft Fair with another creative friend, reaching out to local artisans with unique wares, many of whom were friends, and hosting its first event in her front yard. "The fair was great for getting your name and work known and sharing information," Beatrice says. "The face-to-face contact provided such an amazing opportunity to birth something and grow it slowly."

Fifteen years later, Beatrice does most of her work from home and has a full-time

fashion
designer /
mother
of two

team of two, with three or four more people contributing on a project basis. Outsourcing the administrative work has given her the time and flexibility to embrace her autonomy at home and at work. Every other day, she and her kids "sing all the way to school once the caffeine kicks in," she says of the morning drop-off (her partner, who also works from home, takes the off days). Once a week, they all take a flamenco class. And when she stops into the studio a few times a week, she loves to "order lunch and catch up outside on the patio" with her team. "That's when I usually download any new ideas to them, and we come up with a plan on how it will all play out. It's all very organic and lovely. It's such an honor to watch my team learn and evolve. I feel incredibly grateful."

The reason it all works is that Beatrice maintains a fluid sense of equilibrium, which starts and ends with her. "I think the idea of finding a balance needs to change because it means totally different things to people," she explains. "It also feels unattainable, and people can be very hard on themselves when they aren't finding it. I work when I have to and when I want to. Whenever I'm doing what brings me joy, be it designing a new collection or cooking a meal for my children, that's when I'm the best version of myself. I can be a better everything. That includes being a better mother, which means not being resentful because I feel that I haven't given to myself or my creativity."

Her children also benefit from that outlook. "Sometimes I choose work over family moments, because the idea of sacrifice is not in my vocabulary," she says. "I see it as a choice, and there's pleasure in choosing. I try and have a very open conversation about it with my family. They understand that work brings me joy and are happy for me. The best part about this is that my children can see me as a fully independent person and also as their mama. They can see that one can do both work and nurture. My children have already

designed things for profit. They are already little entrepreneurs. They have learned from us that you can make money from your ideas and creations and that you can be your own boss and create your dream life."

"I realized that there is not only one way of parenting, and that I could create my own path in it just as I have in my business."

Advice from Beatrice Valenzuela

LEARN FROM YOUR TEAM. "My nurturing instincts do not end at parenting. You must also nurture the people who work and collaborate with you. It is a different era. Young people want and ask for so much more, which is a great thing. Old concepts need to be left in the past and new ideas need to be cultivated."

COMMUNICATE YOUR FEELINGS OPENLY. "When there are hard times, I love to talk to my partner about it. He brings great perspective to the situation. It is not always easy because I don't take criticism well, but it is incredibly helpful once I can get past my own insecurities. I also have therapy once a week, and that is another fantastic way for me to sort things out and give myself the opportunity to expand."

SHARE THE HOUSEHOLD RESPONSIBILITIES. "For the first five years, my partner worked as a clay modeler for Tesla and was gone all the time. It was very difficult for me, and I had very tiring moments. Once he began working for himself from home, our life drastically changed. We found a great way to split school pickup and drop-off, for example. I do most of the cooking because I love it. My partner goes to all of the sports games, which I detest. Everyone does their own laundry except for Dimitri, who has just started to learn. I've felt liberated in a way. We are so much happier, and that has made everything better."

HOW DO YOU HANDLE MOM GUILT?

"All of my kids are adults now and I promise you they don't remember which soccer games or plays I didn't attend. They remember me being there when they needed me but focused on my own fulfillment, too."

SHANNON WATTS, ACTIVIST (PAGE 60)

"Whether I'm missing something because I'm on set, or I have to respond to an urgent email during our after-school time, communication with my kids has helped a ton. We always take time to make sure everyone feels heard and is open about feelings. This helps them; it also helps me. Having a partner with a flexible schedule and a strong sense of community has helped us as well."

HEATHER MOORE, PHOTOGRAPHER (PAGE 202)

"I feel a little bit of mom guilt on occasion, but it's not a big factor in my life. I like to think giving my kids the example of a mom who is working hard to accomplish her goals is invaluable."

AMANDA STEWART, KIDSWEAR DESIGNER (PAGE 130)

"When I miss something big, I tell myself it's okay, that it's a bigger deal in my head. My child's going to have my dad, my nanny, my parents there. I also think about all the other special times that we have, or will have. I'll tell them that we're gonna go on a nice solo date and get tea, and they're usually pretty happy."

SARAH PAIJI YOO, ECO GOODS PURVEYOR (PAGE 44)

"I don't believe in the guilt thing. You could always feel guilty about something. I always tell myself I'm in the right place and made the right decision."

MICHELLE RANAVAT, BEAUTY AMBASSADOR (PAGE 86)

"There have definitely been things along the way that I have missed. Recently, I was at a conference and had my husband FaceTime me in for Aana's recital. Mom guilt is so real. I have to keep reminding myself that we're doing this for them and so as long as there's that balance and it's not constant, we're spending time with our kids in other ways."

SUNEERA MADHANI, FINTECH FOUNDER (PAGE 316)

Let's Talk Taxes

My first year as a freelancer, I forgot to set aside anything for taxes. Big whoops. I'd taken a "business practices" class in college—and not so sneakily read paperback novels under the desk. I naively said to myself, "I'm never going to need this class. I'm an artist." Dumbest thing that's ever come out of my mouth.

It was a painful tax season. Lots of tears. Since then, I've learned to set aside about 30 percent of each paycheck for my estimated quarterly taxes and accounting (you may need to set aside more depending on your tax bracket and location) using a monthly service called Gusto. (This saves me the headaches from having to calculate all of my taxes at the end of the year.) I've also since hired an accountant. It saves time and money and gives us tremendous amounts of peace of mind. I feel so much better knowing a trained professional is looking over the details. Here are a few other tips I've learned since that first fateful tax season.

- To make my accountant's job faster and easier—and save myself some money on the hourly rate—I track all my income and expenses with spreadsheets: bank charges, dues and subscriptions, office expenses, postage, supplies, travel. Everything goes onto the spreadsheet.
- If you work from home, you can figure out what portion of your home is used for your business, and it can be tax deductible.
- Incorporate your business. This can save you so much in taxes, and it's a smart way to set up a salary for yourself as you budget.
- Set up a separate business bank account with a checking and attached savings account. I put all my tax money in a business savings account so that it's out of sight, out of mind. (Even better if it's a high-yield savings account.) Keeping your business transactions separate from your personal ones makes it easier to save for taxes and track your deductibles.
- Did you know that you can pay your children when they help at work? The payment is tax-deductible for your business and tax-free for your child up to the standard deduction, which in 2023 was $13,850.00. So if your kids help you pack orders or model, pay them! We've set up accounts for my kids in Gusto, and they get a small monthly stipend that goes straight into their own personal savings accounts.

the accidental baker

Before the sun casts its earliest rays over the Brooklyn townhouse she calls home, Alex LaRosa feels her way through the darkness, first navigating the creaking floorboards and heavy doorknobs of her top-floor prewar apartment, then the hollow chinks of measuring cups and aluminum baking pans on her kitchen's marble countertop. Sometimes, her only companion is the flashlight on her phone. "My friend says I should wear a headlamp," she says with a laugh, immediately dismissing the idea. "I'm like a crazy person—I can't do anything that's going to wake him up."

She's referring to her five-year-old son, Stellan, who usually sleeps until 7:00 a.m., giving her two hours to prep and bake the confections that have transformed her from a nine-to-five intimate apparel designer into an early-morning cake-decorating guru for the Instagram age. But it wasn't all sugar sprinkles and rainbows that led her there.

Like many, Alex came to her newfound profession after a moment of deep uncertainty, having lost her job during the Covid-19 pandemic. "I watched my then nearly-two-year-old son full-time, but I felt pretty scared, mentally, to have nothing

"I miss the steady paycheck and holiday pay of my fashion work. This is definitely more of a hustle, but I truly am happier than I've ever been."

creative to focus on," she says, having enjoyed the artistry and imagination that her twelve-year fashion career had brought her.

So the lifelong food lover turned to what she knew best. She began cooking meals and photographing them, figuring she could leverage her shots into a food-styling gig once the pandemic receded. But when she offered to make cupcakes for a friend's birthday party—it was, after all, another chance for a photo op—her plans were derailed in the best way. That friend asked her to make cupcakes for her sister's birthday, then some friends did the same after Alex posted a casual Instagram update, and before she knew it, she was operating the unlikeliest of off-hours bakeries out of her small kitchen. "I was not a baker," she says, admitting that she was able to embrace buttercream as a creative medium only after studying cookbooks and watching countless hours of YouTube and Pinterest videos. "I had never made a cake and very rarely made cupcakes. I started my business truly by accident."

Still, she relied on more than luck to get her business off the ground. Each of her cakes is a one-of-a-kind creation that she spends days, sometimes weeks, thinking about. After creating mood boards filled with inspiration images to give customers an idea of the vision, she designs each cake virtually in Adobe Illustrator, the same program she used to design lingerie. "It helps me see the whole picture so there are no surprises," she says. She also follows a meticulously organized weekly schedule (see the sidebar) and maintains spreadsheets for monthly costs and invoices. "Baking is all about precision, so it's definitely taught me to be more precise in other areas of my life as well."

baker /
mother
of one

"When you are a one-woman team, there's always some task to do since you are in charge of them all."

Some lessons came harder than others. Alex stopped showing clients progress shots after a particularly demanding customer pressured her into pulling an all-nighter to "fix" a cake design she didn't like. Exercising restraint was another learning curve. "In the early days of my business, I said yes to every order," she recalls, adding that she used to bake every day before learning to cherish her weekends. "I was so hungry for work and so excited to bake for new people. I've realized that I will burn out and have to be more thoughtful about how many orders to accept."

Now, she's adjusted her schedule so that she makes only about six cakes and ten dozen cupcakes a week, plus a monthly cupcake giveaway to brighten neighbors' days. "I don't go beyond that, as I'm still trying to be here for my son," she says. And when she's not in her kitchen, she's teaching baking and decorating classes for neurodivergent kids, a cause that's close to her heart given that her son was recently diagnosed with combined-type ADHD.

She's even figured out how to get her family in on the baking action. Her husband has become her chief recipe taste tester, and she keeps extra cupcakes and piping bags filled with colorful buttercream in reserve for Stellan to mess around with in order to buy herself more time in the kitchen. "He also has his own sprinkle drawer and gets to add sprinkles and food dye to his pancakes in the morning," she laughs, proving that the way to success is surely through the stomach.

WHAT I'VE LEARNED
Advice from Alex LaRosa

VALUE YOUR DOWNTIME. "I definitely turn down work when we have family obligations or birthday parties. I used to feel bad, but now I stand firm, as my family is my priority."

DO IT FOR YOURSELF. "For me, starting a business even during the pandemic has made me a better and more present parent. After losing my job, I needed something that wasn't child-related during the day, even though that meant waking up before my son woke up and working during his nap and after he went to bed. It felt really good to do something creative for me."

BE METICULOUS ABOUT PLANNING. "My biggest secret to success is organization. On Mondays, I bake all cake layers for that week and carefully wrap and freeze them. Tuesdays and Wednesdays are dedicated to making all the cake fillings, buttercreams, and decor (like meringues, homemade candies, and wafer-paper leaves). On Fridays, I put together and decorate all of the cakes and bake any cupcakes, and then on Saturday mornings most orders are picked up for the weekend."

the unicorn mom

At seven months pregnant and deep in a funding round for the booming billing and payments platform she started with her brother, Stax Payments founder Suneera Madhani stood in front of a panel of fintech venture capitalists addressing the very obvious elephant in the room—with a slide deck. Though the company's male chief technology officer was also expecting a baby in the coming months, she was the only one fielding questions about her family choices.

"There was a lot of sexism for sure," says the now mother of two, noting that less than 3 percent of venture capital goes to women founders and less than 1 percent overall goes to minorities. "Here I am, a woman of color and seven months pregnant, raising $20 million in venture capital. It's extremely difficult to make this choice to say, 'I am going to succeed as a CEO and a mother.' I'm so proud that I did it, but it's definitely not easy."

Given her ambition and very real fiduciary responsibility to a number of external actors and her forty-plus employees, she says there was no way she wasn't going to succeed in her professional life. But Suneera and her husband, also an entrepreneur, had vowed to not only start a family but also be very active parents, complicating—at least for the skeptics—what to this point had been nothing but forward momentum.

"I look back at the time that I had before I had kids, and I probably could have started two companies," Suneera says. "My first baby was the company. I dedicated everything to make it successful." Once Stax took off, she felt like taking a pause would hinder its growth. "We had so much momentum. I remember saying that I wanted to start a family, but I was in a lot of fear of how we were going to figure it out because both of us had these large, exciting careers."

Much of that fear stemmed from the fact that Suneera didn't have a road map on which to model her life path. "I never saw women that were successful at the level I wanted to be successful at balancing motherhood and their work," she says. "I felt like we had to choose between being successful at work or at home, and I wasn't willing to sacrifice either. It's crazy hard and really lonely and scary, and you have sleepless nights—you go through a lot as a parent and as a CEO."

Overwhelming as it was at times, Suneera was accustomed to the rhythms of a busy existence and somehow became even more productive. "I've been a multipassionate individual for quite some time," she says. "Productivity has never been an issue for me. I always had multiple internships while I was in school, and I started the company while I was working full-time. I had always been doing a million things all at once and was used to making them work in the time I had. I've always been part of this organized chaos."

Though she's lucky to have hired help and family who can step in when she's speaking

> "Being a leader and having a kid in the office is so vulnerable and real and relatable. Seeing that allows your team to be their full, authentic selves."

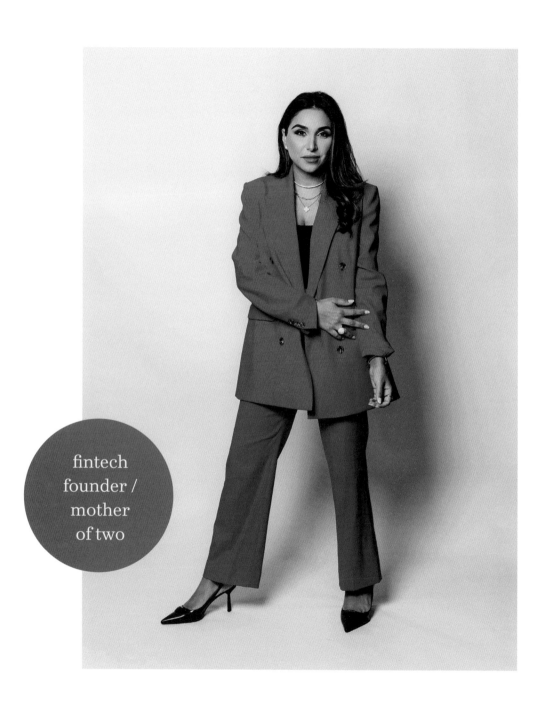

fintech
founder /
mother
of two

"To my kids, I'm the world's greatest mom, and even in those moments that are really hard, you just have to keep reminding yourself of that. There's no such thing as a perfect mom."

at a conference or her husband is traveling, much of her success is a result of her exacting time-management skills and adherence to the family calendar. Every Sunday, she and her husband sit down to hash out the week's plans—everything from school pickups and drop-offs to when she's going to exercise. "We just have a conversation and communicate what the most important pieces of each of our weeks are to make a game plan," she says. "That has been such a huge part of how we succeed as parents and entrepreneurs. We were always able to divide and conquer."

That's still the case, two years after exiting Stax (it's currently valued at over $1 billion) and starting CEO School, a podcast and platform to help female entrepreneurs build and grow their businesses. But Suneera continues to apply important lessons from her former gig into her current life. "There is just a different way that women do business," she says. "I was always trying to fit this mold of the pale, stale, male CEO," she says. "When my second daughter, Aana, was born, I felt like I had had enough of trying to fit everyone else's idea of what a CEO should be. Mom guilt is so real, and there were definitely things along the way that I missed. Now, I'm building the business around the life that I want." These days, that includes chaperoning a field trip or two.

Advice from Suneera Madhani

TAKE MATERNITY LEAVE. "When I was scaling the company, I had all this pressure on me but also a lot of pressure that I created for myself because I was trying to prove myself to my investors and to my board. It was so difficult. When you're at the top, no one is saying, 'Hey, Suneera, you should take maternity leave.' I remember thinking, *I'm going to take the time that I need and be in and out of work*, but I gave birth and the first day I came home I was in bed taking the company all-hands meeting and sharing my baby with my entire team. That's the moment where I should have led by example. After I experienced that, it was so important for me to ensure that the women at our organization had three months of maternity leave and the healthcare and benefits to take the time they needed."

SHOW PEOPLE THE WAY. "When I became a mom with my daughter Mila, I was sharing my journey on social. It was my way of inspiring in other women the idea that they could have a career and a child. That community started to form, and that is now my platform at CEO School, where I'm sharing experiences as a mother and as a CEO. It takes a village. The community is the most important part of motherhood and entrepreneurship."

DELEGATE LIKE A PRO. "Even when we didn't have huge budgets to do it, my husband and I were automating and delegating things in our daily life. I call them $10 tasks and $1,000 tasks. I would always try to do the $1,000 tasks and outsource the $10 tasks. For example, laundry is a chore that's very time-consuming and not something that we enjoy doing, so early on we decided we were going to delegate it. The quality time I have with my children is a $1,000 task. Cooking with our kids, when I'm not distracted by a million things I have to do at home and am fully present—that's a $1,000 task for *both* of us. Although we can delegate that with takeout or meal prep boxes, that's not something we want to outsource because that's something that brings us home as a family around the dinner table."

RANDI BROOKMAN HARRIS

the visual curator

LOS ANGELES,
CALIFORNIA

When she was living in Brooklyn, prop stylist Randi Brookman Harris rented a storage space across the street from her apartment packed to the rafters with her collections: bins of vintage toys and tools, antique instruments, and a mishmash of miscellaneous items that she calls "weird, funny stuff." In addition to housing many of the quirky things that have populated her meticulously curated still-life and interiors images for commercial clients like Target, Design Within Reach, and Google, and editorial fixtures like the *New York Times* and *Domino* magazine, the warehouse also became an appealing after-school diversion for her son, Marlowe.

"I always let him take something home to explore every time we went to drop something off or pick something up," she says. "He sees artistically in similar ways to how I did growing up."

It was her eye that led her to study graphic design at the School of Visual Arts in New York, but her preference for working with objects—"creating compositionally for a photo, with texture, color, scale, and tension," she says—made her better suited for prop styling. After graduating, Randi enjoyed a

fruitful styling career at Martha Stewart Living Omnimedia, then made the jump to working full-time in merchandising at Kate Spade. But even though it seemed like the two paths would have significant creative overlap, she found that merchandising didn't satisfy her passion for visual storytelling.

Randi quit her fashion job and went freelance full-time, working with her now former employers and calling every magazine editor and acquaintance she had ever worked with, many scattered anew. But confident as she was in her ability to find meaningful work, she was also very aware of the risk she was taking: The financial collapse was still fresh (it was 2009), her husband, Jacob, was enrolled in business school, and they had been talking about starting a family in the next couple of years. "It did not feel smart to leave a company that is paying me a salary and just go off on my own," she remembers.

But projects started to roll in, and she was quickly inundated with more work than she had ever imagined possible. Eventually, she settled into a rhythm and found the freedom to choose projects at her discretion liberating. "I keep my projects to pace one at a time, with time in between them for my brain to function optimally," she says, noting that she was diagnosed with ADHD at almost forty and now realizes how much her neurodivergence influences how she runs her business, from the way she processes expenses to her methods for sourcing props.

When Marlowe arrived two years later, she had busy and quiet times after taking a ten-month maternity leave, but always had a nanny to give her the option of taking on styling jobs as they came, whether spur-of-the-moment or with advance notice. Being

"I believe in abundance— that there is enough work to go around because we all have different offerings and ways of connecting."

a stylist requires running around the city gathering props in the days before a shoot, which can last for a day, a week, or more, then managing returns in the days following. "I had someone picking up my child at school every single day," she says. "It's the cost of doing business for me: paying for childcare just to give me the flexibility of working. But whenever Marlowe got sick when I was on a job, Jacob had to be the flexible parent."

They joke that Jacob is essentially her chief operating officer (even though he very much works full-time). "I'm efficient and smart and great at the creative parts of my job, but I'm not a serious person with an enthusiasm for business tedium," Randi quips. Outsourcing some help from Jacob with the financial aspects of her business without having to hire a bookkeeper or manager eases her workload and stress so she can be more present for aspects of their family life.

Now that Marlowe is a teenager and the family has relocated to the West Coast, Randi has become even choosier about the shoots she accepts. "Time is the currency at this point," she says. "For as much as me and menial tasks aren't BFFs, there is something very connective about running our life. I don't want to outsource it all." She also wants to be a solid presence in her son's life. "The time in my career during motherhood when I hustled most was when Marlowe was between two and eight. I felt like I could work a lot but still be around." That's not an easy feat in a city as sprawling as Los Angeles, so Randi finds herself working at home a lot more. "Now, I want to be there even if he doesn't want to hang out. Because you don't always get the time with them at the time you designate. You have to let older kids come to you—you have to be available."

"It felt risky to go out on my own at the time, but when I think about the whims of the economy and volatility of our capitalist structures now, it feels riskier to believe that a corporation will take care of you."

Advice from Randi Brookman Harris

As someone with a late diagnosis of ADHD, Randi wants people to know that being neurodivergent isn't a stumbling block to being an entrepreneur. Here are four ways she makes it work for her on the job and at home.

MAINTAIN EXACTING ORGANIZATIONAL SYSTEMS. "Keeping repetitive tasks running on autopilot helps not interrupt my flow for creativity, ideating, and problem solving. I have the same organizational systems for managing client work, maintaining my prop studio, and tackling day-to-day business functions but also for structuring tasks related to my home, my car, my tote, subscription ordering—even how I unpack my gym bag into a locker every day. My client projects tend to unfold as hyperwork, meaning lots of small things packed into a short timeframe, which can be overstimulating for me. I know that I need to recharge between totally immersive gigs, like a collaborative catalog or hotel shoot on location, to reconnect with myself, my family, and my friends, and leave room for serendipity."

SLOW DOWN TO SPEED UP. "I am a terrible multitasker, but my superpower is being able to bop from thing to thing very quickly. Allowing myself to 'chase the dopamine' to get tasks done in an order that makes sense to my brain— rather than getting hung up on how others might do something or 'the right way' (for whom?!)—helps me to work quicker and smarter."

ASK FOR HELP. "This is the hardest for me. I'm really lucky that my husband has honed his understanding of my functionality over the last twenty years and has it almost down to a science. He supports me in ways I can't and often don't ask of him and he can anticipate where I might need support, both in my business and our home life. This is the secret sauce to my successes."

PRACTICE BODY DOUBLING. "Having another person physically present, working alongside me, helps me stay focused and reduces distractions. Frequently, that person is a freelance assistant, so I take the opportunity to try to cultivate understanding of project needs and big-picture thinking by mentoring them on the ins and outs of the industry. That way, we're helping each other."

the sustainable mom

When they grow up, designer Julie O'Rourke's three kids say they might want to be candlestick makers or bakers or boat builders, but they could just as easily follow in their mother's footsteps. They've spent their lives assuming the rhythms of the family's handspun creative pursuits, both domestic and professional, as Julie and her partner, architectural designer Anthony Esteves, carve out an appealingly unconventional life from scratch for themselves on a small island off the coast of Maine.

"They see so much value in creating things with their hands that it feels really exciting to watch as that grows and blossoms," says Julie, who started the much-loved plant-dyed, organic, and sustainable clothing brand Rudy Jude while she was pregnant with her first. That's because her sons have been along for every step of the way.

"I think because I started the brand while simultaneously becoming a mother for the first time, the two things are inextricably linked for me," she says. "My children have been with me on almost every trip to LA,

> "Making a lot of money is nice, but the thing I'm after is time. Having time to live and time to enjoy the world you've created for yourself is where I see the most success."

where we do our production and keep our store. They've been with me as I bought the first rolls of denim for the jeans. They were there when we built the store." (She means this literally, as Anthony framed out the building himself.) "They sleep next to me as I hand-sew details on samples. They've been held and taken care of by coworkers who have become like family."

Though bringing the boys on work trips has become harder as they age—"their routines are so important to them," she says—it's also become easier for Julie to manage the business from home. "I've stopped going to LA as often, but I think this coincides with the brand not needing as much of me as it once did," she says, acknowledging that her "small but mighty" team can handle much of the weekly flow. "I used to wear all the hats for the business, but over the years it's been amazing to pass things to others who really know what they're doing and do it well. I try my best to be on a computer as little as possible. Most of my daily business is done on Slack on my phone."

Still, her children maintain their mark on her work. "At home, I'm someone who has a lot of small projects going on all the time, so I have little spots throughout the house to work on those, and often they will involve the kids: large weavings for store displays, experimenting with dyes or painting fabrics, hand stitching, photo work. I do the first round of clothing samples in my studio here in Maine, which then get sent to LA, where we finalize sampling and sizing, and grade, sew, dye, and finish. We have been manufacturing this way since the inception of the brand."

In addition to being the brand's sole designer, Julie takes an active role in the

fashion designer / mother of three

company's sales and marketing efforts—as anyone who follows her on Instagram, where she models the store's wares while hand-stitching rosettes for her Christmas tree or rolling out dough for homemade ravioli, can tell you. "I like to joke that a lot of my job now is just to live a good life," she laughs. "Our clothes are made to fall into the backdrop of your life, to support you and make you feel good as you move about your daily tasks. So I'm the guinea pig for this. I've gotta live the life to know what clothes we need for it."

Ultimately, that means more time for her family and the creative endeavors that feel important to her. "I'm an 'it can wait' kind of person when it comes to business, sometimes to my own detriment and the annoyance of others. But I suppose I'd rather someone be frustrated that I didn't return an email than miss a good meal with my kids, or a funny joke they heard at school, or a nice meandering down a grocery store isle. School, music lessons, sports—it all becomes a lot, and I'll be damned if I miss out on any of it."

WHAT I'VE LEARNED

Advice from Julie O'Rourke

LET MOTHERHOOD EMBOLDEN YOU. "Postpregnancy, I developed this tenacity that I think only a mother can understand. I've always been bold in my decision-making, but motherhood took it to the next level. I now have a certain kind of confidence that allows me to just go for it, knowing that there are steps along the way that I can't anticipate but that I have the tools for when I get there."

EMBRACE THE DETOURS ON YOUR JOURNEY. "I've spent a lot of time looking back at all the small jobs I had before I started my own brand: artist's assistant, waitress, moccasin maker, event designer, high school art teacher. In the midst of those jobs, I often thought about how silly and pointless they were for where I wanted to be in the future, but in retrospect, they gave me the building blocks for being able to be so self-sufficient within my brand. Understanding sales, web design, graphic design, content creation, customer interface, small-batch manufacturing, event planning—there is so much value in having this array of skills. I don't think I could have learned all of them in school or in an internship or office environment."

ACCEPT THAT IT'S GOING TO BE RELENTLESS. "The hardest part of owning my own business is feeling like everything in my life depends on this business going great; if it falters, it can be incredibly consuming. I'd be lying if I didn't say that I haven't wanted to shut it all down on a few occasions. My sister and I call it 'having desk-job dreams,' when it feels so difficult that all you want to do is trade it all in for a nice job at the bank where you have your desk and your pens, and at night you go home and you don't even think about that job once when you're falling asleep. I only have these thoughts from time to time."

Embrace the Seasons of Motherhood

In a lot of my conversations with the inspiring women in these pages, variations on a similar phrase kept popping up. For instance, "I'm open to the ebb and flow of motherhood and the changing of seasons," said nonprofit founder Jaycina Almond (page 98). I don't know where or when this idea of seasons of motherhood started, but it's something I realized that I had been thinking about even before I began working on this book.

I suffer from intense fear of missing out. It was a big reason why I chose to become a freelance writer while raising my daughters: I didn't want to forgo bonding time. But FOMO is an especially terrible affliction for a stay-at-home mom because, by definition, you're always missing out. At least that's how I've felt in terms of my career. I've turned down press trips to Provence, Tokyo, Costa Rica, and more—plus the potential stories and bylines that could have come from them. I'm never available for the midweek press lunches and editor breakfasts that occur across New York City, and I rarely accept a happy-hour event invitation because it interferes with my kids' bedtime.

These are choices I've made with intention. But in some of those moments, I feel as though, in the immortal words of Weezer, "the world has turned and left me here," and I have to remind myself that, for this season of motherhood, I'm in a self-imposed holding pattern. My children are my priority, and in another season, it will be time to recenter. My younger daughter just started pre-kindergarten in September—that daily window of freedom holds so much promise, and may just give me enough mental space to figure out how to flex my entrepreneurial muscles in the years to come.

A lot of the women in this book have felt the same way. Clare Vivier (page 108) started sewing laptop bags before she got pregnant but didn't start her company in earnest until after her son went to pre-kindergarten. Carol Lim (page 210) went fast and furious for years at Opening Ceremony as the breadwinner of her family but is stepping back now to be there for her nearly teenage kids. For indie magazine publishers Melissa Goldstein and Natalia Rachlin (page 90) the early days of motherhood were too much to bear without a creative lifeline, and so they jumped into entrepreneurship headfirst. Along the way for each of these women, there have been periods of hustle and moments of calm; instances when their families needed them more than their businesses did, and times when their careers took focus. Despairing moods and joyful ones; challenge and triumph. It's all part of the ever-evolving cycle of motherhood.

All of this is to say that over the course of writing this book, I've taken great comfort in knowing that things change, children grow, and however you define your motherhood and your career—and whatever effort you want to put into those endeavors—can adjust as your desires change and your kids' needs evolve. The path is not linear; it's a sine wave with the highest peaks and lowest valleys, but you can ride them with grace if only you embrace them. So if you're ready to test the waters and find space to launch or grow your business, go ahead and dive in. Or if you have an idea you want to pursue but feel it's not your season right now, that's okay. It will be—soon.

Resources

The Principles of Uncertainty
by Maira Kalman
We come back to this for inspiration and comfort time and time again.

Set Boundaries, Find Peace: A Guide to Reclaiming Yourself
by Nedra Glover Tawwab
Adventures in learning how to set boundaries in approachable, digestible ways.

ONLINE RESOURCES

Aeolidia.com
Development and design experts to help get your website off the ground.

BrittanyRatelle.com
Legal advice from a small-business lawyer.

TheCEOSchool.com
Suneera Madhani's podcast and coaching platform for female entrepreneurs.

@femalefoundercollective
This Instagram account offers tried-and-true advice from entrepreneurial women.

TheFemaleQuotient.com
Inspirational and aspirational content for all women.

How I Built This
We love to hear about how some of our favorite businesses came to be on this popular podcast from NPR.

JessicaHische.shop
Her Dark Art series is an affordable PDF that outlines pricing and budget setting for freelancers.

LeanIn.org
Career advice from the pros.

MotherMag.com
A wonderful site for all things motherhood.

Oh Joy! Academy
OhJoy.com
Mentorships and classes from the original content creator.

Skillshare.com
Online classes for creatives.

TimCoulson.com
Online photography classes.

TOOLS

AirTable.com
An easy way to get your team on the same page and organize your workflow.

Calendly app
A calendar app that takes back-and-forth emailing out of the meeting-scheduling equation.

Dropbox.com
Our favorite way to share files.

Faire.com
A website that makes providing and acquiring goods via wholesale much easier.

Gusto.com
Automate payroll and taxes in a snap.

Inshot app
Create video and add text, effects, and voiceovers for reels and stories with ease.

LegalZoom.com
Everything you need to get incorporated.

QuickBooks
Bookkeeping and accounting software that tracks invoices and expenses and makes tax time a breeze.

ShopLTK.com
This website simplifies the process of getting commissions from recommended products.

Slack
The easiest way to chat with your remote team in real time.

Squarespace.com
A user-friendly platform to help you build your website, automate shipping, and keep inventory organized.

Unfold app
Their minimal templates and layouts help make producing beautiful Instagram stories easy and seamless.

Zelle
An online resource connected to your bank account that makes it easier to pay and be paid (with no fees!).

Acknowledgments

To our founding mothers! We did a happy dance every time one of you agreed to be in the book. Thank you for sharing the highs and lows of your personal and professional experiences. It's been an incredible honor to illuminate and amplify your stories. We've learned so much over the last two and a half years. I'm inspired by each and every one of you.

Jen, I'm forever grateful you said yes to this project. Your talent, expertise, eloquence, organization, and kindness were just what this project and I needed. It's been an honor to work alongside you these past couple of years and to call you a friend. I'm excited to see where this journey of empowerment takes us, and I'm so appreciative for the love and care you poured into this book. Let's hope we continue to flood each other's DMs with quotes we love for years to come.

To Momoko! No one else could have photographed this book with your generosity, kindness, artistry, and care—and let's not forget, three trips to Los Angeles. You went above and beyond to capture each of these mothers in the best light possible. I'm so grateful that our friendship has lasted all these years. You're a wonderful artist and mother. I'm so lucky to learn from you.

To Lia and Bridget at Artisan. Thank you for seeing our vision and guiding us as we brought *Mother / Founder* to life. And thank you for your trust in us and this project! It gave us the motivation to push for the best as we moved forward. You're so excellent at what you do. It's an honor to be added to the Artisan bookshelf, and we find it so perfect that you became a mother, Bridget, right in the middle of this whole process! To Suet and Nina, thank you for all of your thoughtful feedback and care. The design process went so smoothly because of your expert eyes and helpful hands. And a huge thanks to the rest of the Artisan and HBG team, without whom this book wouldn't have made it into our readers' hands.

To Kate, the best agent in the biz. Thank you for always fighting for what we're worth, for being patient and accommodating, for being in our corner, and for always making time.

To Rubi Jones. Thank you for all of those text exchanges and calls as the idea for this book came to fruition. I'm incredibly grateful for your guidance and advice and support. You're a mother founder I look up to in so many ways.

To Mom, for making my childhood a cozy one. I saw you. Your efforts to hustle on the side: doing market research, cleaning houses, organizing garage sales, studying photography. Your entrepreneurial spirit is no doubt what inspired mine. To Dad, for teaching me how to work hard and enjoy the mundane parts of life. To both of you for supporting me and my dreams, even when they involved unpaid internships in New York City. And to Samuel and Will for always being there! It's been so fun to watch you become such great dads.

To Gary, for teaching me that "you don't have control over what happens to you, but you have control over how you can react." And to Deb for accepting me as part of your family and teaching me that there are no strings attached to your generosity and love.

To Cree, for being the best husband I could ever ask for. I love the life we've built and the sweet family we've made. Fatherhood came so naturally to you. It's been an honor to learn to navigate motherhood by your side. You're my best friend. Thank you for your enthusiasm and support and steady presence along every step of the way. I love you with all my heart, for ever and ever. (Like a mountain.)

To Jane, Miles, and Wesley. I love you three so much it hurts. It's the honor of my life to be your mama, and to get your sweet cuddles every night and morning. I did this for you and for the futures you will create for yourselves. May you have more choices and the courage to follow your hearts! Hug, squeeze, kiss!

by Amanda Jane Jones

Emerging from the ashes of 2020, with a three-year-old and a three-month-old and the growing feeling that my career might never live up to my ambitions, I could never have imagined that I'd end up here, in this moment. What a funny thing life is.

I'm forever indebted to you, Amanda, for shaking things up, sharing your perspective, and setting me on this beautiful path. I have learned so much about advocating for myself and honoring my voice from your example, and I am so grateful for the opportunity you've given me to meet and be inspired by this incredible community of women. Thank you for your generosity and wisdom, and for putting up with all of my late-night texts. I can't wait to see where our friendship takes us next.

I also thank my lucky stars for you, Momoko. Few people understand the logistics that go into creating a book of this magnitude, and you handled it all with so much positivity and easygoing accommodation. That made so many aspects of my job easier, and I can't tell you enough how much I appreciate your spirit.

A big thank-you goes to our wonderful editor, Bridget, whose endless patience and guidance has left a lasting impact on me. I couldn't imagine *Mother / Founder* becoming the book it has without your insightful intervention. And to our publisher, Lia, who immediately understood and helped us hone our vision. What I would give to have your intuition! Your trust has meant so much to us. Artisan is lucky to have you both. And thanks, too, to the rest of the Artisan and HBG team who brought this project to fruition.

Thank you to Kate, our tireless agent, who asked all the right questions and was the best shepherd through this crazy bookmaking process. (Another thank-you to Amanda for introducing us!) I don't think anyone has ever fought so hard to make my unique set of skills known and valued. You are simply the best!

I'm equally grateful for all of the amazing magazine editors and teachers who have imparted their wisdom to me over the years. What a privilege it was to come up in the industry at a time when there was some real opportunity for mentorship and knowledge building on the art of fact.

And, lastly, I have to thank my family. To my husband, Rich, whose support—and field trips to the park with our girls in tow—made my long and always late hours possible over the last two and a half years. To my friends, whose encouragement kept me going through tough, often sleep-deprived times. To my parents, who taught me the value of striving for something great. And to my daughters, Sophie and Maren, who push me to be just a little bit better each day. I hope you always feel empowered to take ownership of your lives and seize every opportunity that comes to you.

by Jennifer Fernandez

About the Authors

Amanda Jane Jones was the co-creator and founding designer of *Kinfolk* and is now a freelance graphic designer, illustrator, and children's book author. She has been featured in *Architectural Digest*, the *New York Times*, and *Martha Stewart Living*, as well as online publications that include Mother Mag, Cup of Jo, Domino, Wit & Delight, Oh Joy!, VSCO, Gap, and Click Magazine. Her product collaborations include Opinel, Revival Rugs, Solly Baby, and Schoolhouse Electric. She is a recent transplant to the Wasatch Mountains of Utah, after having all of her children (Jane, Miles, and Wes) on the south side of Chicago, Illinois, with her husband, Cree. Her kids were the inspiration for her books *Yum Yummy Yuck*, *The Hair Book*, *Fuzzy Furry Ouch*, and *Decorate the Tree*. Find her at amandajanejones.com and @amandajanejones.

Jennifer Fernandez is a former magazine and digital editor who has written about design, travel, and food for nationwide publications that include the *Wall Street Journal*, *Architectural Digest*, *Travel + Leisure*, *Esquire*, *Departures*, *House Beautiful*, *Elle Decor*, *Martha Stewart Living*, *Better Homes & Gardens*, and *Domino*. She currently resides in Brooklyn, New York, with her husband and two young daughters, Sophie and Maren. Find her at jennifermfernandez.com and @jenfernand.

About the Photographer

Momoko Fritz is a lifestyle, portrait, and commercial photographer based in Chicago, Illinois. She has worked on projects with Guinness, Del Monte, Kashi, Pringles, Cheez It, Soho House, and Jayson Home and is inspired by things that make her laugh or cry, colors, cultures, design, and things that taste delicious (she also hosts a supper club called Cowgirl Banquet). She and her husband have three boys and a dog named Nacho. Find her at mo-fritz.com and @mo_fritz.